Pete Duel

Pete Duel

A Biography

PAUL GREEN

Foreword by Pamela Deuel Johnson

McFarland & Company, Inc., Publishers

Jefferson, North Carolina, and London

ALSO BY PAUL GREEN

A History of Television's The Virginian, *1962–1971*
(McFarland, 2006)

Peter Deuel, the subject of this book,
adopted the name Pete Duel late in his career

LIBRARY OF CONGRESS CATALOGUING-IN-PUBLICATION DATA

Green, Paul, 1955–
Pete Duel : a biography / Paul Green ;
foreword by Pamela Deuel Johnson.
p.   cm.
Includes bibliographical references and index.

ISBN-13: 978-0-7864-3062-8
(softcover : 50# alkaline paper)   ∞

1. Duel, Pete, 1940–1971.   2. Actors — United
States — Biography.   I. Title.
PN2287.D787G74   2007   791.4302'8092 — dc22 [B]   2007009949

British Library cataloguing data are available

Cover photograph: Peter Deuel as Hannibal Heyes in the 1971
Alias Smith and Jones (courtesy Kim Darby)

Manufactured in the United States of America

*McFarland & Company, Inc., Publishers
Box 611, Jefferson, North Carolina 28640
www.mcfarlandpub.com*

To my wife Bev
for her love and support
and to the memory of
my father (1928–2007)

ACKNOWLEDGMENTS

A biography demands intensive research and the cooperation of people who were close to the subject. Special thanks to Pamela Deuel Johnson for agreeing to help me with my project, for writing the foreword and for recommending me to many of Peter Deuel's close friends.

I would like to thank, in no particular order, the following contributors: Jill Andre, for her memories of Peter's early years in Hollywood and introducing me to David McHugh; Beth Griswold for her continued enthusiasm for my project throughout many months of interviews and for sharing her private collection of photographs; Kim Darby for her thoughtful insights into her relationship with Peter and the accuracy of her memories; Dianne Ray for agreeing to talk with me, after much consideration, for the first time since Peter's tragic death, and for introducing me to her best friend, Lynne Karroll.

Thanks to Peter's close circle of friends, Donald Fanning, C. Davey Utter, Jack Jobes, David McHugh and Connie Meng; Pamela Deuel's daughter Jennifer Seymour and husband Richard P. Johnson; Peter Collinge, Robert G. Steele and Matthew Fassett; actors and actresses James Drury, Sara Lane, Jared Martin, Leslie Parrish, Bridget Hanley, Juliet Mills, Mike Farrell, Jared Martin, Joan van Ark, Bill Anderson, Dan van Husen, Barbara Luna and Celeste Yarnall; *Love on a Rooftop* creator Bernard Slade; *The Psychiatrist* writer and director Jerrold Freedman; *Generation* assistant director Robert Koster; *Alias Smith and Jones* pilot executive producer Frank Price; *Alias Smith and Jones* creator, writer and producer Glen A. Larson; and *Alias Smith and Jones* producer Jo Swerling Jr.

Thanks also to Peter Deuel's stand-in and part-time chauffeur, Harold Frizzell, for agreeing to a rare interview; former Hollywood police lieutenant John Konstanturos for his recollection of his investigation following Peter Deuel's death; Nikki Laird for granting permission to publish her late father Monty Laird's comments; Wendy McNay for taking time to transcribe details of the 1970–1971 DUI court hearings; Phil Watson for his memories of working on the 1968 McCarthy campaign, and Daniel LaRue for granting permission to publish Jim Ludwig's comments; Des Martin for his episode guide research; Brannon Walker, Ana Soler and Bev LaRue for providing video recordings; Suzanne Seko for her additions to my filmography; and special thanks to Mila Blurton for her intensive research over many months.

Finally, thanks to my wife Beverly for taking over typing duties following an injury to my eye in the final months of completing my manuscript.

TABLE OF CONTENTS

FOREWORD

by Pamela Deuel Johnson

Thirty-six years have passed since the death of my brother Peter. Hero, champion, protector, and loving brother are only a few of the roles he played in my life. Peter was flawed, as we all are, but the true essence of him was evident in his acting. Perhaps that is one of the reasons he is remembered by so many today. Reckless yet compassionate, volatile but vulnerable. In certain areas insecure, yet resolute in his convictions. Irreverent, but steeped in and proud of traditions. Peter's tender heart was often his Achilles' heel.

This book captures the real Peter with Paul Green's honest and caring appraisal of Petey. Paul has become a good friend, and I trust what he has

written. It is fact and not fantasy. Many who knew Peter well, including close friends, speak transparently about him and their loss when he died.

For many years following his death I convinced myself that, regardless of anything I and others would have done, Peter still would have killed himself. It was my way of living though the pain and horror of losing him. Working with Paul has helped me to realize that that night was a terrible mistake due to the influence of alcohol.

We are all selfish beings, but Peter's selfishness would never have intentionally left so many of us with wounded hearts. Especially if he had had any idea of how vast and far-reaching the effect of his death would have been.

Peter was a beautiful man inside and out. His talent was enormous and would have catapulted him to the top. I would give the world to see Petey's smile again, to know he is here, and to have him grow old together with our family and loved ones.

PREFACE

This book attempts to paint a realistic portrait of Peter Deuel based on firsthand accounts from people who knew him during his brief life, to shed the two-dimensional image created by publicists and the media, and to reclaim Peter Deuel the man, away from his on-screen persona.

Peter Deuel was not an easy man to understand, and my task in writing this book was also far from easy. His tragic death only adds to his enigmatic quality, keeping him out of reach for many decades except for fan magazine articles and newspaper reports that were often a mixture of fact, fiction and studio hype.

After much thought Peter Deuel changed his name to Pete Duel in the latter part of his career. However, he never officially changed his birth name by law.

Let his family, close friends, girlfriends and working colleagues speak for him. Only they knew Pete with any intimacy. Their story is his story.

INTRODUCTION

Actors desire to make illusion become reality, to convince an audience the character they portray has a life beyond the written words they speak. The one-dimensional attempts to become three-dimensional. The good actor makes us care, makes us laugh or cry and experience anxiety, fear, happiness and love. We empathize with the fictional character to such a degree that we feel their emotions.

Having a role as a recurring character on a weekly television series can be both a blessing and a curse to actors. They crave success and recognition but fear being typecast. They also fear the attachment of the public to a popular character will ruin their subsequent career. Many television actors achieve recognition and fame in one hit show and never work again with any degree of success. But there are exceptions. Buddy Ebsen went from playing Jed Clampett for nine years on *The Beverly Hillbillies* to seven years as the title private eye on *Barnaby Jones*. Michael Landon starred in *Bonanza* for fourteen years and then starred in *Little House on the Prairie* for another ten and *Highway to Heaven* for another five. But success can be short-lived for many actors. A familiar household name today may become a dimly remembered face in ten years' time.

Peter Deuel was part of the celebrity industry. The positive aspects of celebrity, including wealth, status and fame, have to be balanced against the downside, which include lack of privacy, overwork, stress, insecurity and fanatical fans, even stalkers. The relationship between the celebrity and his or her audience is carefully orchestrated by public relations professionals who create an image that the audience can connect with. This may or may not involve truth. Truth becomes a relative concept in the promotion of the image. Image becomes all important.

While some celebrities thrive on their public image, many see it as disingenuous and increasingly alienating. Peter Deuel wanted an authenticity to his life that working on a weekly television show couldn't give him. The fact he was becoming internationally known for playing a character in a light-hearted comedy Western frustrated his ambitions for serious and socially relevant roles — roles he was playing before *Alias Smith and Jones* came along.

But to emphasize the pressure and frustration of working on *Alias Smith and Jones* as a decisive factor in his death is to trivialize the complexity of the man and to look for simple answers. There are no simple answers because Peter Deuel was not a simple man. It would be impossible to tell his story in simple terms. The chapters that follow make that abundantly clear.

☆ 1 ☆

ARRIVAL

"...for life is holy and every moment is precious."
— Jack Kerouac, *On the Road* (1957)

Lillian Marcella Deuel held her newborn son in her arms. The firstborn was always considered a special child. Peter Ellstrom Deuel would prove that claim to be true. But the proud new mother had little idea how bittersweet that experience would prove to be. Her son's natural talent and charisma would be part of a trade-off, and fate would tip the scales toward a darkness that would threaten to engulf the family. But as Lillian Deuel lay in bed in Genesee Hospital, Rochester, New York, her mind was only filled with the light of joy as she looked her son in the eyes for the first time and smiled.

The *Stockholm*'s long voyage from Gothenburg in Sweden was almost over. Ripples of warm summer heat floated above the calm waters of the Hudson River as Jan Josef Ellström and elder brother Carl Fredrik anticipated their return to their adopted homeland. The date was August 26, 1919. Naturalized American citizens, the Ellströms had made their first journey to America years earlier from Köping, a municipality in Västmanland County, central Sweden. Situated on the western tip of Lake Mälaren, Köping received its charter on January 19, 1474. Starting life as a merchant city, Köping had become industrialized by the 19th century, with a major fire in 1889 destroying parts of the city. The Ellströms decided it was time to journey east to Stockholm and the Baltic Sea where they could begin their long journey to their new home and country, America. Settling into American life at 2027, 19th Street, and 1926, 19th Street, Altoona, Pennsylvania, they found employment in Altoona on the Pennsylvania Railroad, where Jan Josef worked as a blacksmith. Altoona, located in Blair County at the approach to the Horseshoe Curve, owed its existence to the railroad, with the route through the Allegheny Mountains giving the location of the Pennsylvania Railroad added importance during the Industrial Revolution.

Jan Josef and Mary Augusta Johnson had given birth to a daughter, Lillian Marcella, on March 12, 1915, following their wedding at a Swedish Lutheran church in Altoona three years earlier. While Mary Johnson was a Swedish blue-eyed blond, her husband, coming from a line related to the Waloons from French speaking Belgium and Turkish ancestry, had dark brown eyes and hair, and a dark complexion to match.

Lillian Ellstrom would later have younger sister Naomi and brother Theodore for company. Mary Johnson, an even-tempered woman with a gentle nature, maintained a strong Christian household, raising her children as Swedish Lutherans. The young Lillian proved

Ellström family home, Köping, Sweden (courtesy Deuel Family Collection).

to be strong-willed and very directed, exhibiting a firstborn's leadership qualities. Academically bright, she skipped two grades in school.

The Deuels had originally traveled to America from France after being driven from their homeland by King Louis XIV (1643–1715) in a purge of Protestant groups during the latter half of the 17th century. The French Heugenots later became Quakers in America.

Ellsworth Shaut Deuel, the eldest of three children and brother to younger sisters Catherine and Constance, was a third generation doctor, born August 5, 1914, in Perryville, New York, where his father and uncle M. (Melvin) Edgerton had been doctors, and his grandfather practiced as a general practitioner.

"My great grandfather was a country doctor before there were automobiles," recalled Pamela Deuel. "He was so dedicated to his practice that when he heard that someone was ill, he saddled his horse, even though the weather was stormy, to tend them. As he dismounted, the horse fell on him and he sustained a permanent injury."

Ellsworth Deuel and Lillian Ellstrom first met in New York City. Lillian was in training to become a nurse at Flower & Fifth Avenue Hospital, which was affiliated with New York Medical College — where Ellsworth Deuel was studying medicine. Lillian's dark brown hair and dark complexion, together with a cute 5'1" figure, attracted the young Ellsworth. At 5'10", Ellsworth was considerably taller than Lillian, but his brown eyes, dark brown wavy hair and small mustache struck a chord with her in return, and they started dating.

Joseph J. Ellstrom (Jan Josef) and Mary Ellstrom with daughter Lillian, Altoona, Pennsylvania, 1918 (courtesy Deuel Family Collection).

Lillian Ellstrom on the grounds of Flower & Fifth Avenue Hospital (courtesy Deuel Family Collection).

"My parents' first date was on St. Patrick's Day, 1936," recalled Pamela, "A Sadie Hawkins dance where the girl asks the boy out. The dance on the top floor of the hospital started at 9 P.M. They were both on late shifts, which they didn't complete until 11 P.M. Their date didn't start until after 11 P.M. According to my mother they went to the dance and it was pretty much exclusive after that. She was attracted to his quiet and serious nature.

"Mother went to nursing school when she was 17. When she graduated, Mom went to work to support our father in that last year of his medical school."

Their marriage on November 24, 1938, took place in New York City, attended by a best man and maid of honor, a fellow doctor and nurse.

"After the marriage ceremony my parents had no money for a reception but went straight from the church back to their apartment that they would now be sharing," continued Pamela. "In those days even modest places had doormen. My father had given his doorman five dollars and

Ellsworth Deuel, 1947 (courtesy Deuel Family Collection).

said, 'When we get back from the wedding would you have some cheese and crackers and wine waiting for us.' When mother and Dad unlocked the door this gentleman doorman greeted them with, 'Good evening Dr. and Mrs. Deuel.' My mother told me that when she heard someone call her Mrs. Deuel for the first time it was so exciting and romantic."

After graduation Ellsworth Deuel and his younger sister Catherine worked for Deuel's father, Jacob Bettinger Deuel. Born 1887 in Pique, Ohio, Jacob became a pioneer in the development of radiology in the Rochester area, and worked as a radiologist for Kodak as well as running his own practice.

Ellsworth and Lillian Deuel relocated from New York and lived with Ellsworth Deuel's parents in the small town of Penfield, New York, on Five Mile Line Road, also referred to as South Road. The property would be affectionately named *Lazy Lands* by the elder Deuels.

"My father had started practicing medicine and my mother was pregnant. As far as I know they lived there for financial reasons," commented Pamela.

"The large old house had a parlor, swinging doors going in to the dining room, and a big wraparound porch. It was quite a grand place at the time, with three acres of sweeping lawn in the back. My grandparents called it *Lazy Lands* because they saw it as their haven. Grandfather (named 'Boppa' by Peter) loved working around in the back garden. He even had a kennel raising collies. I was only six when he died but I recall him being quite a dapper gentleman and a lovely man."

Located in Monroe County, Penfield was named after Daniel Penfield, who, after buying up land in 1795, was given clear title to the township of 25,000 acres in 1803. The 1880s saw an influx of immigrants from Germany and Switzerland. Early industries, including

Ellsworth Deuel with his mother and father, Norma and Jacob Deuel, Little Hawk Lake, summer 1949 (courtesy Deuel Family Collection).

distilling, milling, soap, potash and paper production, were supplemented by quarrying and nurseries by the 1930s and 1940s.

Nestled among roaming fields and forests, Penfield was a good place to raise children, with summer evenings spent lazing on porches or listening to the radio.

Born Saturday, February 24, 1940, at Genesee Hospital, Rochester, Peter Ellstrom Deuel spent his early years at Five Mile Line Road, living with his parents and grandparents, before moving in 1942 to Lockport, New York, where his father was offered employment at Harrison Radiator Corporation, a division of General Motors. In 1942 GM converted its entire production into providing vehicles for the Allied war effort, including airplane engines and parts, trucks, tanks, guns and shells. Ellsworth worked as the plant doctor after failing his medical when trying to enlist, and Lillian worked for the American Red Cross. It was during this period that Geoffrey Jacob Deuel was born, followed 17 months later by Pamela Jane Deuel.

"When I was only 2 months old we moved back to Penfield. My parents had bought their own home at the other end of Five Mile Line Road, across from the school," recalled Pamela.

Following their return to Penfield in 1944, and a short stay on the Five Mile Line property, 1790 Penfield Road became the permanent home for the Deuel family in 1947. The large, sprawling house was over 100 years old when the Deuels moved in and consisted of a three-door manual garage, living room, dining room, kitchen, laundry room, powder room and six upstairs rooms, later converted into bedrooms for the children and a sewing room for Lillian.

Dr. Deuel's professional duties often cut into the free time he could spend with his

Lillian Deuel and baby Peter, summer 1940 (courtesy Deuel Family Collection).

Peter Deuel, Altoona, Pennsylvania, June 1944 (courtesy Deuel Family Collection).

family. Being the only doctor in Penfield, pleasantries over the dinner table were often followed by time spent with his patients in his evening office hours.

"When my parents bought the house on Penfield Road they converted half of the downstairs for his medical office," said Pamela. "When seeing patients he didn't wear the typical white coats. He always wore a dress shirt and tie. It was an advantage in some ways to have him at home. Each day we'd always go into Dad's office and say hello after school, but for three active children we knew we couldn't get away with anything with Dad always there."

Vacationing in central Ontario with his family at his parent's cottage, 150 miles northeast of Toronto on Little Hawk Lake, prompted Peter Deuel's enjoyment of nature at an early age. That strong interest would stay with Deuel throughout his life and be a source of both future pleasure and discontent. Time spent in the woods was the motivation, not hunting. Although their father owned a rifle, it remained in the closet of his bedroom as protection against intruders, and was never used for hunting.

"The piece of property we owned in Penfield originally had four acres," recalled Pamela. "There was a woods behind our house. It was beautiful. And behind the woods and down the hill was a little creek. If you went up the hill you came to a very small residential street called Liberty Street. I remember Dad went out in the woods with the boys building forts."

The woods behind the family home would also serve as a venue for the young Deuel and his friends to get into mischief.

"Peter had an ability to make things swing his way. I adored him from the time I knew who he was and wanted to follow him around. He was really kind to me even though there were times when I'm sure he didn't want me around because I was a pesky younger sister.

"One time I was wandering around in the back yard and went out in the woods because

Oakview Lodge, Little Hawk Lake, Ontario, Canada (courtesy Deuel Family Collection).

I heard Pete and some kids talking. My brothers and their friends dug a six or seven foot trench in the ground and covered it with branches and pine bows. They thought it was pretty cool. It was their fort. To a little child it seemed massive. You could hide down there and play. And there by the fort were Peter and his buddies smoking cigars. I was eight or nine and was aghast when I saw them smoking smelly cigars.

"I said, 'I'm going to tell Mom and Dad. You're gonna get it.' As I turned to run, Petey said, 'Pammy, come over here a minute. Just sit down and talk with us. Why don't you just have one puff on this?' 'No, I'm not going to have any of this stinky thing,' I replied. 'C'mon. Just one,' insisted Peter. Sure enough, I was stupid enough to have one puff. I coughed and coughed. And as I got up Pete said, 'Where are you going?'

'I'm going to tell Mommy and Daddy,' I replied. 'Oh, you're going to tell them that you had some too?' responded Peter. That's how smart he was," concluded Pamela.

A modest log cabin, complete with stone fireplace, situated in the right rear of the back yard, provided a place of seclusion for the young Deuel — a den for private thoughts and plans, where he could ponder his future and where it might lead him. When the young Deuel wasn't deep in his own thoughts he would join in family gatherings and parties in the cabin.

"The log cabin was by the corral and pasture where we kept our horse 'Babe,'" recollected Pamela. "We started out with a pony that got very mean and nasty, so Dad got rid of that quickly and bought a brown and white paint horse we named Babe. He was a gelding and a good-sized horse. When we first got Babe I was fearless. I rode bareback and loved him. Geoffrey used to throw rocks at the horse's rear end, and he bucked me off twice. I became quite skittish with the horse after that, and it became Geoff's horse. The boys loved to pretend to be cowboys. They were both excellent bareback riders and rode Western, even though we had a beautiful English saddle from World War One that had belonged to grandfather Deuel."

Peter and Geoffrey Deuel would get to play real cowboys when Babe escaped from his electric-fenced corral and head toward Penfield High school.

"Babe could be fairly aggressive," recalled Pamela. "The boys would get called out of class because Dad or mother had called the school and told them Babe was heading in their direction. Because it was a small town and there wasn't horrible traffic he would be okay. Sometimes he'd go running across the road in front of a car, but he was determined to have his own way.

"I remember Babe running across the front lawn of the school. Of course the kids thought it was absolutely wonderful. They'd say, 'Oh, there goes the Deuels' horse.' The boys would round him up and take him home and place him in the barn stall near the corral."

Pets were a regular fixture in the Deuel household, with dogs and cats especially loved by the children.

"The first dogs that I remember as a young child were a black and white collie called Sagebaby and a beautiful copper colored mixed breed medium sized dog called Candy. Even though your parents buy a dog for the entire family it generally becomes one of the kids' dogs. Candy became Peter's dog. It followed him everywhere and even slept on his bed. He was so attached to him. Not that we all didn't love that dog, but Candy somehow belonged to Peter.

"Our first cat was a beautiful Siamese. My mother named it Anna after *Anna and the*

Pamela, Geoffrey and Peter, 1947 (courtesy Deuel Family Collection).

King of Siam. We had it for years, and it was followed by another Siamese cat named Jake — after our grandfather," reminisced Pamela.

Deuel also found pleasure in listening to the classical music records provided by the record club their mother and father were members of. Composers such as Mozart, Beethoven, Debussy, Liszt and Chopin provided Deuel with an appreciation of music that transcended the popular music of the day and nurtured in him a sensitivity to quality that came to the fore in later life.

"We were exposed to every kind of music," said Pamela. "Classical and jazz. When Elvis and Buddy Holly and American rock 'n' roll emerged our folks were great. They weren't stuffy about that. They loved early rock 'n' roll.

"We all took music lessons. Peter and Geoffrey had to take piano lessons for a little while but they didn't last too long. I took piano longer than any of them. Geoffrey continued with the trumpet. Peter took a tremendous liking to drums and set up a drum kit in the living room of our home. You can imagine the noise he made. All three of us sang through school in choruses. My parents had beautiful voices and we inherited that ability."

Favorite reading material for the young Peter Deuel included the classics *Treasure Island*, *Ivanhoe*, *Huckleberry Finn* and *Tom Sawyer*. *The Hardy Boys* series of books also fascinated him.

Peter Deuel's education started at the tender age of four-and-a-half in 1944. He entered Junior High in 1952 and graduated High School in 1957.

The cabin, January 1949 (courtesy Deuel Family Collection).

"My mother always said if she had the chance to do it over again she wouldn't have started Peter so young," commented Pamela. "The Central School was one big brick building on Five Mile Line Road. Almost across the road from our first little house. All the grades were there. When I was in 6th grade they built a few elementary schools scattered around the area and the old original school was just junior and senior high school. That's where Peter graduated from."

Young Peter Deuel with mother, father and Sagebaby, March 1943 (courtesy Deuel Family Collection).

Deuel's entry into Junior High in 1952 coincided with new beginnings for the Deuel family, with the addition of a new family member. A small upstairs bedroom had been transformed into a nursery, and everyone in the household was excited at the prospect of a new baby in the family.

On September 12, 1952, at 4 P.M., a baby girl was born to Lillian at Genesee Hospital, Rochester, New York.

Pamela Deuel recalled, "I remember the next morning I woke up so happy. It was very early on a Saturday morning. I went out and got my bicycle and started riding up the sidewalk. My father called to me and I thought I was in trouble because I'd left without eating my breakfast. Dad was a stickler for eating a full breakfast and I often attempted to get away with not eating. I went back in and I saw that he had been crying. We had a screened-in porch at the side of the house and Dad sat me on his lap and just started to sob. He told me that our little baby had died."

Peter Deuel, 1945 (courtesy Deuel
Family Collection).

The baby girl, named Jennifer, had passed away at 8 A.M. on September 13. She had survived for only four hours. Underdeveloped lungs had caused her premature death.

"It impacted us children," concluded Pamela. "I was eight years old. I remember crying and crying for hours. Then Dad said to me, 'I have to go into the hospital to see Mommy. Why don't you ride with me?' Pete and Geoff were probably still asleep. I don't recall seeing them.

"I rode with my father in his 1952 red Pontiac Convertible. He parked in the parking lot where we could see Mom's room. He went off to spend time with her and I waited for him in the car. I was sitting there sobbing. Though only eight years old I knew our baby was gone. I looked up and saw my Mom waving at me from the open window on the third floor. She, too, was crying and said, 'I love you.' Her heart was broken, yet she was concerned about me.

"It was an awful time for the family. We were such a mess. It was going to be such an exciting time because we were going to have a new baby. My mother went through a severe depression over that and it took a while before we could dismantle the nursery. Jennifer was never buried because in those days the hospital took care of the baby. It sounds very cold and unfeeling today. I named my daughter after baby Jennifer."

Despite their tragic loss life had to go on, and Christmas of 1952 brought a pleasant surprise for the young Deuels — a combined television, radio and 45 r.p.m. and 78 r.p.m. record player in one large RCA Victor console. *I Love Lucy*, *Jackie Gleason* and *Milton Berle* became early favorites, along with the popular TV Western stars of the day, *Roy Rogers*, *Gene Autry* and *The Lone Ranger*.

Peter Deuel continued to progress through school. Jim Ludwig, a friend of Peter's from Penfield High, commented, "Peter was a year ahead of me at Penfield High School.... In short, he was a 'cut up' and had an undue influence. This caused commotion in some classes and caused one substitute teacher, in French, to vow never to return to Penfield because of the things Peter and I did, interrupting the class — all in good fun, of course. One vivid memory was 'storming' into her class with the French flag and parading down the aisles singing the French national anthem. I believe she quit after that incident.

"I recall a dynamic and brilliant radio address Peter gave at an assembly when the *Junior Town Meeting of the Air* came to Penfield High. Another time, in gym class, I remember Peter jumping so high to catch a basketball with such physical grace and beauty. He had such 'charisma' that everyone knew he would be famous as an actor. Pete had qualities of both good and aspects of being a 'devil' too. He had an ego, but was not egocentric and self-centered, in my opinion."

Peter's Christmas surprise, 1952 (courtesy Deuel Family Collection).

Pamela recalled an infamous Halloween prank concocted by her brother at Penfield High. Mischief Night, on the eve of Halloween, was a traditional time for kids to play harmless pranks, such as throwing toilet paper over telephone wires and over the roads. Peter Deuel's ambitions went a little further.

"Peter was mischievous and sometimes went a little too far and got himself in big trouble. The principal warned Peter and classmate John Klinkert this one time. They were put on notice that they'd be watched and warned not to do anything stupid for Halloween pranks. Peter and John were about to graduate, so they were a little bored and just goofing around. I knew they were up to something, but I was considerably younger and they didn't tell me many things because I might go to my parents and tell them.

"This is the way it went down, according to Peter. He and John Klinkert got several of their buddies, ones that would be easily influenced by them, to go to all the school buses in the big parking lot. Once there they took every one of the rotors from the engines out and dumped them down the sewer. At that time we had about 25 school buses.

"Peter and John were up at the Four Corners at a store named McGowan's. It was owned by a man we called Grandpa Jim and his son Uncle Guy. They weren't related, but they were close. The store sold magazines and some gum, and had a soda fountain where you could get a Cherry Coke and chocolate cream sodas. Peter and John sat there from about 8 P.M. on Halloween night until it closed, and went home in order to have an alibi.

"Next morning when the drivers got on their buses they wouldn't start. We missed a whole day of school. You can imagine how the school system was so furious. And they couldn't prove that Peter and John did it. Can you imagine the expense? These kids would

Peter and Geoffrey, spring 1950 (courtesy Deuel Family Collection).

be prosecuted today for doing something like that. Peter wasn't a real bad boy. He gave his all to school activities he was involved in."

In 10th grade, a 14-year-old Peter Deuel made his first journey across country to Sausalito, California, to visit his best friend, Christopher Clarke. Financed by his mother and father and his own earnings picking beans for 60 cents an hour at Morts Farm, Deuel traveled by Greyhound to the West Coast. His first experience of California had widened his vision for future possibilities and sharpened his fashion sense. Prior to his journey to California Peter Deuel had favored the preppie look, but the new, trendy pegged pants fashion presented problems for his mother.

"Mom would peg them because she was good at sewing. This was when it had caught on with Geoff as well," said Pamela. "They would take a ruler and would not wear them wider than a certain width. Mom would narrow them as requested. They would take the waist band of the Levi's and turn over the front part slightly. Sometimes they would wear what we called in Rochester 'Engineer Boots.' Quirky black leather ugly boots with a strap on them."

Peter Deuel's forthright manner often resulted in conflict with his father. Both had strong personalities and could be opinionated at times.

"My father and Peter were very often at odds," observed Pamela. "They loved each other deeply. The men in my family greeted each other with a hug and a kiss. There was never any embarrassment about that. They were very affectionate with each other, but on the turn of a dime Pete and Dad could be very volatile. Many times it would accelerate into yelling and screaming. After, they would be so sad, and I can still see them hugging and making up. We all spent lots of time trying to figure out how we could please Dad more."

Lillian Deuel was a bright woman who wore jeans and t-shirts around the home during a time when dresses and high heels were the fashion. The parents decided to join the First Baptist Church of Penfield. Ellsworth came from a Unitarian background and was raised a Methodist. He attended the Baptist church out of a sense of duty to his wife and family rather than out of any strong faith. Ellsworth believed faith was best exhibited through works and serving the community.

"My mother and Peter had a very loving relationship. Peter was closer to my mother because my father was hard to be close too. But she could get exasperated with Peter too. He paid so much attention to her. She was such a slight lady at 110 pounds that Peter would just pick her up and swing her around. I do not remember them at odds with each other often. Peter and Geoffrey would kid her sometimes and mouth off. Mother started off by taking a yardstick and whacking them on the back, and the yardstick would break every time. She also kept a crock of wooden spoons by the stove, and she'd pick up one of those and give them a whack. They'd laugh at her to make it worse. Those were funny scenes. The more they laughed the madder she got."

Lillian Deuel was an accomplished seamstress, a fact that delighted her young daughter.

"I had the most amazing clothes because Mom would make these wonderful formal dresses which she and I designed," commented Pamela. "She went to the tailoring class and made a camel's hair sport coat and a pair of houndstooth checked wool slacks for my Dad. She sewed, she knit, she sang, she played piano. I think in retrospect that my father held her back. Not consciously, because she made a choice to stay at home. She had been a nurse to my father when he first started his practice, but later on she became a housewife and two ladies worked as nurses. Mother would fill in when they were on vacation or sick.

"She seemed ahead of her times in many ways. My father said she should have had the opportunity to do more because she had this amazing capacity to excel in just about any area. I think she did get bored. She was a very fair mother but she could get exasperated and she could put up with a bunch of nonsense, but she was also extremely gentle and loving."

Describing the relationship between Peter and Geoffrey, Pamela said, "Geoff and Peter were competitive. Geoffrey was academically brilliant and aced everything. Peter and I got good grades but we had to work a little harder at it. Peter did take the role of big brother seriously, and although he would gang up on us and tease us sometimes, he was a good big brother. Geoff wasn't as good to me because we were only 17 months apart. Peter was old enough to think, 'I'm the older brother. I need to take care of my younger sister.'"

In sophomore and junior year, Deuel was involved in J.V. soccer and W.H.E.C. Town

Geoffrey, Pamela and Peter, Christmas 1949 (courtesy Deuel Family Collection).

Meeting of the Air (junior year). He also belonged to the National Honor Society, the Advisory Council, was a R.A.U.N. delegate, a member of the Student Council during junior and senior years, a member of the National Thespians, literary editor of the Penfield High Yearbook and vice-president of the chorus in his senior year. The class prophecy predicted that Deuel "would become a brilliant lawyer-president of the international bar association."

Making his acting debut as the Easter Bunny in second grade, Deuel graduated to the Ugly Duckling in junior high before joining the high school's National Thespians Society, spending three years — from sophomore through senior — as a member. He knew he had talent ever since being accepted into the Penfield Central School Dramatics Club inner circle. The National Thespian Society demanded quality performers and set high criteria for membership.

"You became a member of that, the Thespian Society, if you performed in school and showed promise," remarked Pamela. "We had two major productions a year, one in the fall and one in the spring. One was always a musical. Peter, Geoffrey and I all acted in the Thespian Society musicals and could sing, so it presented no problems.

"One of Peter's earliest major performances was in 10th Grade when he was 15 years old. He played the hunter in *Snow White and the Seven Dwarfs.* The hunter was conflicted about killing Snow White and taking her heart back to the Witch. The part was a good match for Peter's intense personality and a great showcase for highlighting his acting talents. The kids in elementary school got the part of the Seven Dwarfs. Geoffrey played Grumpy and I was assigned Happy."

"We were in plays at high school together," recalled Jim Ludwig, "and I have fond memories of rehearsals and attempts to get our lines memorized. Just thinking back, Pete was so warm, understanding and genuinely concerned if you ever had a problem, and a true friend. At his Senior class assembly for our Junior class, he conferred his title of 'class clown' to me. I remember 'campaign' speeches we gave together at an assembly during student elections."

Fellow Thespian Society member Matthew Fassett recalled his time at Penfield High: "Pete and Geoff Deuel were among the most talented actors in the school. They had fine powers of recall, and always knew their lines with near perfection. They were frequently chosen for leading roles in high school plays and were very popular with all of us. I was between them at Penfield High, so I didn't have much contact with either of them apart from the Thespian Club."

Deuel was kept busy editing the Penfield High yearbook or campaigning for student election. He may not have been a model student and he may have voiced a dislike for studying, but he was no idler.

"We were both involved in the Boy Scouts of America," said Jim Ludwig. "I remember, with surprise, seeing him at the Scout camp, located in New York's beautiful Adirondack Mountains, a few days after his high school graduation, with a troop of senior scout leaders. I was there on the camp staff and we had a good visit. Pete was always willing to help others."

Deuel spent a few weeks of each summer between the ages of 11 and 15 at the Boy Scout summer camp at Massawepie, located between Cranberry Lake and Tupper Lake in

Peter Deuel stringing a bow for archery at Massawepie Scout Camp near Tupper Lake, New York, 1958, as two unidentified observers watch. From the 1958 joint capital campaign brochure for the Rochester, N.Y., area Boy Scouts and Girl Scouts (courtesy Otetiana Council Historical Society, Boy Scouts of America).

Monroe County, followed by service as a summer camp counselor for the Otetiana Council.

"If you are selected to be a counselor on the camp staff you have exhibited some leadership skill," described Pamela Deuel's husband, Richard P. Johnson, a long-time Scouter. "They don't let anybody on the staff because you're teaching and training young impressionable kids either a Scout craft or camp craft for a merit badge.

"Peter was the Summer Camp Archery counselor at the Massawepie Scout Reservation. The boys from the troops would come under instructional supervision and shoot at targets on the archery range. But first they would be taught about the dynamics of the bow, including the pull weight and distance and arrow. They would have fun shooting at bullseyes or cardboard animal targets, such as a bird or a groundhog or a wild turkey."

Pamela Deuel, commenting on the protective nature of her brother, said, "It was Halloween and Geoff and I were still very young. Pete was just at that age in our very innocent, safe little town where he could go out trick or treating with his friends. This time our mother and father told Peter to take us out after dark, trick or treating in the neighborhood. We went to a few houses close to the village with our brown bags of candy. Two or three bullies came up to us and said they wanted our candy.

"Peter shouted angrily, 'Just leave them alone. Get out of here.' The bullies went to grab our bags and Peter started fighting them. Geoff and I stood there scared and rooted to the spot because they were beating Peter up. Peter turned and yelled to us, 'Run! Go home. Go home.' He was afraid we were going to get beaten up. They beat Peter up pretty

Peter Deuel and his dog, Candy, 1956 (courtesy Deuel Family Collection).

badly. But it just showed Peter was protective and kind. I always knew he would take care of me."

Deuel's protective attitude toward sister Pamela extended to the junior-senior high school dances.

"In 7th grade I went through a chubby stage and was just as round as I was tall," recalled Pamela. "I was feeling very self-conscious, but Peter put me at ease when he walked over to me and said, 'C'mon, let's dance.' Peter flipped me up in the air and between his legs. We used to jitterbug at home so I was used to dancing with him. I remember thinking I was so fat and ugly but my brother still thinks I'm great. That showed his character and what a kind guy he was. A lot of older brothers would have told you to go home and stop embarrassing them."

Deuel experienced his first bittersweet taste of love as a senior in 1956. Deuel found in Melissa Boomer an attractive girl who was top of her class. But an ongoing long-distance relationship with a boyfriend in her home state of Indiana meant she had to choose. Peter Deuel found himself rejected for the first time.

As Deuel entered his teenage years, an increasing sense of independence resulted in a certain recklessness. Mixed with the immaturity of youth, Deuel's actions would lead to serious consequences for his long-term future.

★ 2 ★

RECKLESS REBEL

"I have always thought the actions of men the best interpreters of their thoughts."
— Jon Locke (1632–1704)

A prankster full of dynamism and charisma, Peter Deuel's teenage desire for new experiences often resulted in trouble. Pamela Deuel noted, "When my parents were away the boys would raise havoc. Peter started drinking very young. He got away with an awful lot because he lived in a small town and my father was the doctor. If Peter or Geoff were about to get busted the Monroe County sheriff would call Dad and tell him to come over and get them rather than take them to the sheriff's station. In retrospect Dad said he didn't do us any favors. He should have put their asses in jail. Peter knew he could get away with a lot. He wasn't as belligerent as Geoff because Peter had a charm about him."

Deuel needed direction if his talents weren't to be dissipated into a plethora of diverse paths. And he needed to quell his demons to ensure the path he chose was the correct one. Unfortunately, the path presented to him failed to ignite any passion.

Founded in 1856, St. Lawrence was a co-educational university situated in Canton, New York, between the Adirondack Mountains and the St. Lawrence River Valley. The university offered little interest for Deuel, who felt it would strangle his individuality and creative spirit. Peter Deuel was a troubled teenager lacking motivation as he enrolled at St. Lawrence University in 1957.

Donald Fanning first met Deuel at St. Lawrence, studying the same Liberal Arts course. "We were both in the class of '61," commented Fanning. "Peter intended to go into acting right from the start. Studying at St. Lawrence was not the direction he wanted to go, but it was convenient, being close to Penfield. Having little interest in studying, apart from the English class where he loved to read *King Lear* and other Shakespearean plays, Peter decided to rebel. He was always outspoken and at odds with the current thinking of the time. St. Lawrence was one of those colleges that insisted you had to put away any indication of your previous life at high school. You had to move on and become an adult and not wear any of your old high school clothes. The first thing Peter did was to wear his Hot Rod Club 'Stick Twisters' jacket all the time. The jacket had a logo of a transmission with a twisted gear stick. Peter loved defying authority."

Fellow student and close friend Jack Jobes, echoing Fanning's comment, stated, "Peter and I were different from the usual crowd. I played the system more than Peter did. I kept to the dress code. He took a lot of heat in his Freshman year for his 'Stick Twisters' jacket.

Peter Deuel and Christopher Clarke at Little Hawk Lake, September 1957 (courtesy Deuel Family Collection).

At St. Lawrence the two of us used to raise all kinds of trouble. We were both on Lee Hall at St. Lawrence. They were all single rooms, and I was one room apart from Peter. The 'L Club' would raid our dorm. It was constant. Peter and myself would just laugh hysterically as they chased us down the halls. They would haze the Freshmen by making us wear beanies and signs."

Fanning continued, "Peter was in a fraternity. He and I and Jack Jobes joined Phi Sigma Kappa. In those days fraternity life was very important on campus. College students in the late 50's were not aware of anything outside of their particular life. It was just frat parties and drinking. In the Eisenhower years we didn't care about anything worldwide. It was very insulated. Nobody cared about anything political."

"I had spent four years at prep school," said Jobes. "Most prep students for the first two years at college sleep through the lessons because you are using the same books you used in prep school. But students from high schools have got their noses in the books because everything is new to them. Meanwhile, the prep students get together and go downtown drinking. There's a dividing line. Peter got in with us because he was a rebel."

In the biting cold winter of 1958, Deuel plunged headfirst through a car windshield. Recalling the accident, Pamela said, "He had that accident during his Freshman year in college. He let someone else drive my parent's station wagon. Two cars hit each other head on. They didn't have seat belts in those days and Peter's head went through the windshield. He had a very serious gash on his head and almost bit off his tongue. It was horrible. They also did surgery on his face because he had a deep laceration on his cheek which required a couple of surgeries. As the years went on you could barely see any scarring. Fortunately the tongue healed and didn't affect his speech."

Deuel would spend four long, inactive weeks in hospital recovering from a broken pelvis, followed by forced bed rest in a hospital bed in his parent's living room. His injuries had placed his own upstairs bedroom out of bounds, but he had no shortage of company, as friends visited him every day to check on his recovery. Eight weeks on crutches made him realize he couldn't be so foolhardy again. But a young person's memory is short, and lessons are hard to learn the first time around.

Recalling her brother's reckless streak, Pamela remarked, "I was a senior in high school and we had Dad's car. We drove through an area called 'Panorama Trail.' Peter started going too fast. It was the only time I recall that he didn't care how I felt. I tend to be very cautious, and I was scared and begged him to stop or let me out of the car. He wouldn't listen. He hadn't been drinking. It was just this reckless part of his personality. It was awful because we went entirely too fast for this winding road."

Returning to St. Lawrence for his Sophomore year, Deuel met newcomer Connie Meng.

"I sat next to Peter in English classes," recalled Connie. "Peter and I were very similar in temperament and we became very close friends, but it wasn't a romantic relationship. St. Lawrence isn't very big on the arts, and there were five of us that eventually went into professional theater. I was one of the guys. It was our own Rat Pack. Peter, Don Fanning and I studied together, although we didn't end up doing much actual studying. We had a wonderful time.

"There was no specific dramatic class, but Peter featured in two plays, *A View from the Bridge* by Arthur Miller and *The Rose Tattoo* by Tennessee Williams. We had a one-woman drama department at St. Lawrence. Marguerite Holmes built the sets, directed the plays and taught the acting class."

Deuel found himself at odds with the Dean of Men throughout his stay at St. Lawrence and left after only two years of his four-year course.

"Peter was asked to leave St. Lawrence. He was constantly ending up in the Dean's office because he was bored to tears," declared Pamela Deuel. "According to my parents, the letter from the Dean of Men suggested strongly that he leave St. Lawrence and go seek what he really wanted. I know Dad also had that feeling about Peter, and maybe he suggested he leave before the letter came."

David McHugh recalled, "He got thrown out of college after punching the Dean. He was on a panty raid, climbing down the drainpipe of the girls' dorm. The Dean had been called and he tapped Peter when he jumped off the drainpipe. Peter didn't even turn around; he just swung around and knocked the guy out. Unfortunately, it happened to be the Dean. That was the end of St. Lawrence University for Peter."

Jack Jobes, describing the same event, recalled, "Somebody shouted, 'The Green Dean is coming!' Peter took a swing at the Dean and starting running with his head down and ran straight into an oak tree. The 'Green Dean,' as we called him, was only 26 years old. He wrote a letter to Peter describing how he was 'persona non gratis' on campus and never welcome back again. Peter left after our Sophomore year."

"Pete had a long-running feud with authority figures of any kind," commented Connie Meng. "He had a manic streak, but we all had some of that. We were all rebels at St. Lawrence. Don Fanning was quiet but impish. He had a sense of stability that we all lacked at the time."

Close friend C. Davey Utter recalled, "Peter came back to St. Lawrence for revenge for kicking him out. One of the pranks he pulled was rolling an empty beer can the length of the chapel under the pews during a choral concert."

"Peter never had plans to go into medicine," commented Pamela. "He made it clear to my father and mother that he wasn't interested. I was the one who grew up wanting to be the doctor. My father talked me out of it because he thought I wouldn't be treated fairly as a woman. To this day I wonder how different my life would have been."

In 1960 Deuel set up base camp at the 63rd Street Y.M.C.A. in New York City and proceeded to learn his craft. The American Theatre Wing had been established in 1939 by a group of theatrical women, including the playwright Rachel Crothers.

"Peter investigated all the available options, applied for the Theatre Wing and was accepted," declared Don Fanning.

"Acting, voice production, fencing and text study were among the courses at the Theatre Wing," commented Connie Meng. "Helen Menken was in charge. Gene Feist, who was later instrumental in founding the Roundabout Theatre Company, was the acting teacher. The fencing teacher was the actor Raymond St. Jacques. I was all set to go to graduate school and be an English professor, but Peter suggested I speak to the people at the Theatre Wing. It was due to Peter that I ended up in professional theater. Peter was gone by the time I started."

David McHugh recalled, "Peter swabbed the floors in the Y.M.C.A. in New York. He made a deal with the management that he would clean the toilets and hallways in return for lodging, as he had no money at the time. He rarely spoke about the Theatre Wing. He studied there so he could say he had some training."

"The first time I met Peter I went up to his room in the Y.M.C.A., and his roommate was having his hair bleached," described C. Davey Utter. "He was going underground from the IRS. He was a big band singer and had worked with the likes of Benny Goodman, but he was in arrears with the IRS."

It was during his stay at the Y.M.C.A. that Deuel experienced what would prove to be a source of anxiety in his future life and career. His roommate witnessed Deuel undergoing a grand mal seizure.

"That's when Peter called mother and Dad and said, 'Something's wrong,'" recalled Pamela. "That fear that he could have a seizure at any time and how to handle it, and the fact he didn't want anyone to know, preyed on his mind. We weren't going to tell anybody about this. Mother and Dad said that Peter never had a seizure until after the car accident in Penfield, and that often a head trauma will cause epilepsy. Peter hadn't had seizures from birth, only after the accident."

During his time in New York Deuel dated Pat Carroll. Four years younger than Deuel, the 17-year-old Carroll was one of Pamela Deuel's best friends.

"It was serious for a little while," described Pamela. "They dated for almost a year. I was delighted because I'd introduced her to him. But I became jealous because he took her away from me because Peter and Pat didn't pay any attention to me when they were together."

Deuel enjoyed an active social life in New York with a group of friends that included Don Fanning, C. Davey Utter, Jack Jobes and Connie Meng.

"The street was our theater in New York," described Utter. "We would go out and spot guys who were obviously out of town and walk by them and say, 'Want girls?' and continue walking. We'd have guys following us through the city all night long.

"We'd often go out for an evening and acquire a couple. Peter would push people to the absolute brink of violence and then he would hit them with his smile and turn on those dimples and they would fall in love with him. It was always good-natured.

"Our friend Connie had some drag queen dancer friends, and we were in a drag club this night. There was a cute little queen. Just my type, had he been a girl. Peter leaned over and whispered in my ear. 'Just remember pal, in the morning it has a beard.' That brought me back to earth.

"He was always pulling stunts on New Year's Eve. One time he arranged a big New Year's Eve party at the apartment he had moved to in Brooklyn. 150 people showed up expecting to see Peter. Peter called at midnight from Penfield to find out if everyone was having a good time."

"One Christmas in New York, Fanning, Jobes and I had a parade down a snow filled Park Avenue banging garbage can lids together and singing at the tops of our voices," described Connie. "Peter was always the ring leader and enjoyed a good time."

Following graduation from the American Theatre Wing, Deuel returned to St. Lawrence in the Spring of 1961 to appear in the Mummers production of Garson Kanin's comedy *Born Yesterday* as part of the 'Moving-Up Weekend' program.

"We hired Peter in my Senior year to play reporter Paul Verrall in *Born Yesterday*," commented Connie. "I played Billie Dawn, originally played by Judy Holliday in the stage and movie versions, and Jack Jobes made his award-winning stage debut as the attorney. Pete Gottlieb played Harry Brock. Bob Walker, Alva Hellstrom, John Blaha and Linda Beir also appeared in the play. Peter was paid for his work on the play, which ran to three perform-ances. Our audience consisted of students at the University."

Later that year Deuel returned to St. Lawrence to attend the graduation of C. Davey Utter, Connie Meng and Jack Jobes.

Pamela Deuel recalled yet another near-fatal accident involving her brother on the road to Watkins Glen, New York.

"The motorcycle accident happened on a Sunday afternoon. When Peter drove out of the driveway on his motorcycle my mother looked at me and said, 'I have a terrible feel-ing.' He was going along the road when a car started to make a turn. Peter didn't see him passing and swerved to avoid it. He was thrown from his motorcycle and landed head first onto a cement guard rail. His helmet saved his life.

"He had a horrible gash that was several inches long on the inside of his left thigh, going toward the knee, that needed hundreds of stitches. It had to be stitched on one layer inside the wound and one layer on top. Peter could be very reckless. And I don't mean just

St. Lawrence University class of '61 graduation. Left to right: C. Davey Utter, Connie Meng, Peter Deuel, Mrs. and Mr. A. Michael Meng (courtesy C. Davey Utter).

Left to right: John Blaha, Pete Gottlieb, Connie Meng and Peter Deuel in *Born Yesterday* (courtesy Connie Meng).

as a driver. Even though his personality for the people that he cared about was caring and compassionate, Peter often was not that way with himself."

Modest beginnings to his professional acting career saw Deuel perform at the Master Playhouse Summer Theatre at Standing Stone, Pennsylvania. Deuel spent the summer of 1961 performing at the Mateer Playhouse at Pennsylvania State University. Then he went on to Bohemian Greenwich Village and the Player's Theatre. The Shakespeare Wrights Repertory Company production of Jean Giraudoux's play *Electre* saw him doubling as assistant stage manager and actor, and gaining his Actor's Equity card. The Family Service Group, touring schools and P.I.A.s, followed, leading to a trip to the Philippines and a small role in a war movie, *W.I.A. Wounded in Action*, that would take five years to find a distributor.

"Peter enjoyed working on the movie and liked the Tagalog language he picked up in the Philippines," recalled Don Fanning.

Deuel's return to New York City resulted in an appearance on the television anthology show *Armstrong Circle Theatre*, followed that winter by his debut in the National Road Company's production of Phoebe and Henry Ephron's play *Take Her, She's Mine*.

Originally titled *Age of Consent*, the play had run for 404 performances on Broadway at the Biltmore Theatre between December 21, 1961, and December 8, 1962, with a cast that included Art Carney, Phyllis Thaxter and relative newcomers Elizabeth Ashley and Richard Jordan. With production by Harold Prince and direction by Broadway veteran George Abbott, the show received lackluster reviews but still managed to last one year before taking to the road, where Tom Ewell replaced Carney. Deuel would be cast as college student Donn Bowdry, playing opposite a young promising actress called Joanna Pettet, and understudying Fred Burrell for the character of Alex Loomis.

Peter Deuel as Orsino (third from left) in *Twelfth Night,* summer 1960. Other actors are unidentified (photograph by James French, courtesy Deuel Family Collection).

Opening night for Deuel was on December 10, 1962, at the Walnut Theatre, Philadelphia, Pennsylvania. The show was a light-hearted comedy centering on the character of lawyer and school board head Frank Michaelson, played by Ewell, and his adjustment to the sexual awakening of his college-bound daughter, Mollie, a free speech advocate and modernist painter, played by Pettet.

"Peter had been in Philadelphia for a week in *Take Her, She's Mine.* He knew this private club, The Variety Club, where everybody went after the show to socialize," recalled C. Davey Utter. "That's where he met Wilfred Brambell. He was an amazing old British theater queen. As funny as could be and a total madman. He was appearing in a play called *Foxy.* Peter and I spent a week drinking and carousing with him.

"Brambell would be constantly pursued by these packs of 13-year-old girls because he'd worked with the Beatles on *A Hard Day's Night.* Peter and I would meet him at the stage door and act as his bodyguards. Brambell would stick his head out of the stage door and shout, 'Lads, protect me. Here they come.'"

Connie Meng observed, "Peter accumulated odd and interesting people."

When *Take Her, She's Mine* closed in Washington D.C. in the summer of 1963 Deuel returned to Penfield and pondered his future: to pursue a career on Broadway or in the film industry of Hollywood. Deuel had been reintroduced to California when the play had

Peter Deuel, alias Clark Gable, April 1963 (courtesy Deuel Family Collection).

toured the region. New York City, although culturally vibrant, offered little for an actor interested in film. He had to make the move from coast to coast.

"For Peter it was all about going out to L.A.," commented David McHugh.

Pamela recalled her brother saying, "I'll go out there and become a respected actor and then I'll go back to New York, able to demand better roles."

He would give it a try. The idea of living in the center of the film industry excited him. Deuel was familiar with the streets of New York and the green wooded land of small-town Penfield. Southern California had grown out of the thirsty desert. It would be a challenge, adapting to a new environment, but he was prepared for change.

☆ 3 ☆

PROMISE OF THE FUTURE

"Hollywood is a place where they place you under contract instead of under observation."

— Walter Winchell (1897–1972)

Arriving in Hollywood in the summer of 1963, Deuel set up residence in a modest apartment on Franklin Avenue, situated on a busy main road within walking distance of Hollywood's Grauman's Chinese Theatre. A move to a small $65-a-month, garage-top apartment at 1158½ North Fuller in West Hollywood followed. The multi-ethnic, liberal environment suited Deuel's temperament and gave him the opportunity to express himself freely in an open, non-judgmental atmosphere of creativity.

"The North Fuller area at that time wouldn't be considered an upscale area," described Pamela Deuel. "But it wasn't seedy either. It was safe. There were some colorful folks around there."

"The Fuller neighborhood consisted of friendly retired Jewish couples from the film business," observed Jack Jobes. "All kinds of bands lived in the area, including the Association, who lived up the street. Being on the edge of West Hollywood, there were also many gays in the neighborhood, including Peter's neighbor. Peter and his friends were straight, but nobody could care less who was gay or not."

Deuel expressed his preference for a simple life, and an apartment and lifestyle that wouldn't stretch his finances as he treaded the waters of Hollywood.

"Peter's apartment was a dreadful place," commented Pamela. "It was just this tacky little garage apartment. You had to go up the side stairs and you walked into what they called a living room. And to the left was the bedroom. You could barely get two people in the kitchen. And I kept saying, 'Pete? Don't you want another house?' And he said, 'I don't have time. It doesn't matter.' He felt comfortable in that apartment. He really didn't see that he had any need for anything greater than that. And Peter did not give a rip what anybody thought."

Jack Jobes fondly recalled, "North Fuller consisted of little old houses from the 1920's with narrow driveways leading to garages. Peter's apartment had a four-car garage with two units. His neighbor, Bob, was always playing jazz day and night. Peter loved his Fuller apartment. One time Peter redid the floor with linseed oil and found out it wouldn't dry. It was always sticky. He wasn't a great handyman."

Ironically, Deuel's first role after arriving in Hollywood took him back east to New York, for the service film *The Man Nobody Liked* (1963).

"In 1963 I was transferred by the Air Force to Monterey, California, at the Defence Language Institute as Detachment Commander," said Donald Fanning.

"I was very surprised to see Peter in a Defence film. He was playing a hothead young military man selling guns to the enemy. The Defence films were produced to teach you how to behave in the military. They used young actors who they could hire inexpensively."

The military draft had separated Deuel from his close group of friends, who would eventually follow him to Los Angeles.

"Peter was 4-F," explained Jobes. "Because of his motorcycle accident he got the golden parachute. Peter was making a career for himself in Hollywood, and I was saving Boise, Idaho, from the 'Red Menace' for nearly three years.

"Don Fanning rented the bottom apartment of the building in front of Peter. It was a four-plex. I joined him in January 1966 and lived on the couch for six months. The apartment was about 50 feet from Peter's place on the east side of Plummer Park. Davey Utter and Dave McHugh joined us at the apartment a little later that year.

"Peter would join us all in eating breakfast at Mister D's, a coffee house that was open 24 hours a day across from Santa Monica Boulevard. Our favorite thing was to take a nap after breakfast and then get up again and start the day. We were like one extended family."

Thanks to his agent, Georgia Gilly, Deuel had been slowly building up his resume with spots on *Target, Channing, Combat, Twelve O'Clock High* and *Gomer Pyle, U.S.M.C.* These early roles offered very little in terms of showcasing his acting skills, often consisting of no more than a few lines, but they did give him valuable experience in the day-to-day realities of working in television.

"Georgia Gilly was Peter's first agent in Hollywood. I met her once. She was considerably older than Peter, and, frankly, I think she had a crush on him," said Pamela.

Mickey, created by Robert Fisher and Groucho Marx's son Arthur Marx, was a vehicle for Mickey Rooney's comedic talents. Originally set in an acting school, a switch to Marina Del Ray and a motel on the Newport Beach harbor front resulted in a successful pilot, directed by Richard Whorf, with ABC commissioning a series. Despite personal problems involving Rooney and his fifth wife Barbara, the show gained respectable ratings. Filmed at M-G-M's Culver City studios, Peter Deuel appeared in "Crazy Hips McNish" (1:13) as a top athlete wanting to star in a school play.

By the time the episode aired on December 16, 1964, the show had been cancelled. Although Mickey Rooney was the star of the show, Chinese actor Sammee Tong had won over audiences with his portrayal of Mickey Grady's handyman Sammy Ling, thanks in part to his loyal following of fans from his time on *Bachelor Father*. ABC was giving serious consideration to picking up the remaining six shows of the season when news came through on October 27, 1964, of Sammee Tong's suicide from an overdose. Heavy gambling debts and connections to the mob were cited as the cause. *Mickey* was axed. The official reason for the cancellation was Tong's suicide. ABC declared they would have picked up the show had he lived.

The Fugitive, starring David Janssen, was one of the first TV shows to highlight Deuel's acting skills and to give him higher visibility. Viewers had become engrossed by the tales of Dr. Richard Kimble and his pursuit of the one-armed man, Fred Johnson, played by Bill Raisch, who was seen running from the scene of the murder of Kimble's wife. The show had become a hit, thanks to quality production values and scripts, and David Janssen's fine acting, complete with his trademark furtive glance over the shoulder whenever he sensed trouble. It also marked Deuel's first association with producer Roy Huggins. In the January 1965 episode "Fun and Games and Party Favors" (2:19) Deuel (credited as Peter E. Deuel) portrayed a quick-tempered teenager called Buzzy who attempts to blackmail Kimble. This early glimpse into Deuel's on-screen acting offered some indication of his latent talent without being overly impressive.

Deuel's sister Pamela had enrolled at Baldwin Wallace College, located in Berea, Ohio. The musically inclined Pamela had chosen the college because of the excellent reputation of its music conservatory.

"When I was home from college in the summer I would work in my mother's store. In 1961 she had opened a women's casual sportswear shop called 'Country Casuals' next to the drugstore in Penfield. Mother did all the buying. Dad said the only reason she ever started that was so she could put me in wholesale clothes. When I went to college I had a tremendous wardrobe. The business probably stayed open for five years."

Peter Deuel paid a surprise visit to his sister's college during her freshman year, making a dramatic entrance.

"Peter arrived in his red sports car and came to my dorm. Some of the girls knew he was an actor, and he came sweeping in his full-length, black leather trench coat. These 18-year-old girlfriends of mine just stood there with their jaws dropping. And, of course, he just worked it. He loved the effect he had on these girls."

Pamela Deuel and fellow Baldwin Wallace College student Donald Seymour married in January 1964.

"My parents were wonderfully supportive of my marriage. One of my tendencies for many years was to try to please everybody. Donald was a good husband, but in my heart I knew the marriage probably wouldn't last. We eventually separated in May 1966 and were divorced in the fall of that year.

A year and a half after his initial visit, Deuel returned to Berea to greet his new niece Jennifer when she was six months old.

"I had a very small apartment on Bagley Road, and Peter slept on the sofa in the living room," recalled Pamela. "Early in the morning a sound awakened me in the next room. I jumped out of bed and ran into the living room. And that's when I saw Petey on the floor. He was seizing. He was turning his head as he was moving, and he got serious brush burns on his cheek and his temple from rubbing his face on the carpet. I was so afraid he was going to swallow his tongue. Just as I went to get a spoon he stopped. I don't know how long he had been in that seizure. He was terribly disorientated, of course, and I put him on our bed and he slept for several hours. He was very depressed after that.

"The only thing he ever said to me, and it was very important to him, was that he didn't want the press to know about it because it would probably keep him from getting jobs. It was also embarrassing to him. It was probably a result of the head trauma. Back then epilepsy was almost viewed like leprosy. It had a stigma attached to it."

Deuel's health problems, while worrying, had to be pushed to the back of his mind as he returned to Hollywood to star in his first regular role as uptight psychiatry student John Cooper on the sitcom *Gidget* (1965). Gidget Francine Lawrence was inspired by the fifteen-year-old daughter of author Frederick Kohner. Kathy Kohner, who was barely five feet tall and weighed only 95 pounds, was affectionately known to her surfer friends on Malibu beach as "the Gidget." Hollywood released the film version in 1959, with Sandra Dee in the title role. The movie was quickly followed by two sequels and would be partly responsible for initiating a new genre, the beach comedy, aimed specifically at an undemanding teenage drive-in audience.

A combination of factors had culminated in the latest craze. In the mid–1950s the surfboard was revolutionized. The heavy wooden boards became extinct overnight with the introduction of lightweight boards made of balsa wood, fiberglass and polyurethane. The surfing craze took off, and California and Hawaii became the places to be seen. Furthermore, the postwar baby boom ensured beaches were packed with affluent teenagers.

Amid all the beach frenzy the idea of bringing *Gidget* to the small screen was thrown around the offices of Columbia Pictures' TV subsidiary, Screen Gems. Harry Ackerman, vice-president of Screen Gems, with a pedigree stretching back to *I Love Lucy*, would serve as executive producer on the show, with William Asher handling directing assignments. Harry Ackerman was one of the key figures in the development of the "sitcom." In the mid–1950s live shows were recorded on a kinescope. Ackerman suggested a new technique which utilized three cameras locked into a fixed position that allowed larger angles of coverage. The new technique was a breakthrough in that live shows were recorded on film for the first time. After becoming vice-president of Screen Gems, Inc. in 1958, Ackerman served as executive producer for *Gidget*.

When plans for a TV series were announced in 1965, over 150 young actresses auditioned for the part of fifteen-and-a-half-year-old Francine "Gidget" Lawrence. Sally Field, an inexperienced eighteen-year-old actress from Pasadena, was finally cast, following a request by Screen Gems' casting director Eddie Foy III that she test for the part. Field's stepfather was actor Jock Mahoney, who had recently starred as Tarzan and who also happened to be a friend of Foy.

Peter Deuel in *Gidget* (courtesy Deuel Family Collection).

"*Gidget* was before the contract program started at Screen Gems," commented actress Bridget Hanley. "Initially working for Screen Gems wasn't a paid contract but just a 'Stay with our stable and we'll use you' approach."

Gidget would be Deuel's first experience of regular work on a television series. Although only a supporting player, he would appear in 22 out of 32 first-season episodes.

"Peter was absolutely thrilled with getting the role on *Gidget*," recalled Pamela. "We kidded him about the character he played. He loved working with Sally Field. Peter said Sally and I looked somewhat alike, except I was blonde and she had dark hair."

"Peter enjoyed working on *Gidget*," remembered Donald Fanning. "He had a good time and was pleased to be making money. I bought him a color TV so he could watch *Gidget* when it first aired. He eventually paid me back for the TV."

The half-hour sitcom premiered 15 September, 1965, on ABC.

The *TV Guide* Fall Preview Issue of 11 September, 1965, commented:

> Gidget ... has a square older sister who's married to a cubed psychiatrist, is mother-less but has the wisest, kindest, most understanding daddy in the whole worldsville. Sally Field is appropriately cutie-poo as Gidget...

Bridget Hanley appeared in "Love and the Single Gidget" (1:25) and recalled an amus-ing incident involving name confusion: "On the *Gidget* episode I never got to meet Pete. But it was so funny. My real name is Bridget and the character's name was Gidget, and her real name was Sally and my character's name was Sally, and the whole three or four days of filming we never knew who they were calling. Whether it was Bridget, Gidget, Sally or Sally."

Stories of Deuel and Sally Field dating each other were discounted by Bridget Han-ley, Jill Andre and Jack Jobes.

Bridget recalled, "I don't believe Peter and Sally were ever boyfriend and girlfriend because Sally's first husband was on the *Gidget* set when I did my episode. And they later got married and had a baby. I know Sally and Peter did like each other, but as far as I know there wasn't a romance there."

"People on shows often felt they had to be involved with each other," commented Jill. "That was the way of the world. But I never felt that with Sally Field and Peter. They had a better friendship later on. It was my take it was just a friendship. It was all publicity for the studios."

"Sally was just a little kid hanging around us," described Jobes. "She would have her mouth open with our antics. We really could party and raised hell together. It wasn't just a bunch of people sitting around having a chat. It was really lively."

Despite the failure of *Gidget* to gain enough viewers to justify a second season, Deuel's work on the show prompted Quigley Publications, publisher of *Motion Picture Almanac* and *Television Almanac*, to present him with the "Most Promising Male Star" award, based on a nationwide poll of television critics.

In retrospect, Deuel's acting on *Gidget* was often uneven, and the chemistry between himself and his on-screen wife, played by Betty Conner, lacked total conviction. But Deuel was still learning his trade and, more importantly, attracting attention. *Gidget* did manage to achieve better ratings in the summer rerun of the show, but by then it was too late.

During the filming of *Gidget* Deuel began his association with business manager John Napier, press agent Phil Paladino and personal manager Ray Powers. Meanwhile, Deuel had been cast in a new ABC sitcom, *Love on a Rooftop*, alongside British actress Judy Carne, who would later achieve fame as the "Sock It to Me" girl on *Rowan & Martin's Laugh In*. Agent Mike Gruskoff from ICM had seen Deuel in the pilot and told Ray Powers he wanted to sign him to the agency. Deuel was presented with a dilemma. His loyalty to agent Geor-gia Gilly had to be weighed against representation by a large, influential agency based in Los Angeles. Deuel, taking the advice of Powers, decided to join ICM.

In 1965 Geoffrey Deuel moved to Los Angeles and obtained his first acting role in a walk-on part on an afternoon soap opera, *The Young Marrieds*. His brother had introduced him to agents Marvin Paige and Jack Groce, and told Geoff to do his own thing.

"It annoyed the hell out of Pete that Geoff decided to follow him into acting," commented Jack Jobes. "Pete had paid his dues, and Geoff just came into town and decided to become an actor."

"Peter and Geoff's relationship was based on insane sibling rivalry," declared C. Davey Utter.

Love on a Rooftop centered on the trials and tribulations of newlyweds David and Julie Willis, played by Peter Deuel and Judy Carne, living in a tiny rooftop apartment in San Francisco. David, an apprentice architect, struggles to support his wife Julie, an art student and daughter of a wealthy car salesman, on a weekly income of $85.37. Stories revolved around David's attempts to prove to Julie's father that he was capable of providing a decent lifestyle for Julie and himself.

The premise of the show resembled Neil Simon's hit Broadway play *Barefoot in the Park*. Both concerned a newlywed couple struggling to survive in a rooftop apartment. *Love on a Rooftop* creator Bernard Slade denied any connection to the Neil Simon comedy: "As an actor I'd appeared in dozens of those romantic comedies. *Barefoot in the Park* really didn't have an influence at all. It was just a genre."

The two main characters were introduced in a narrated filmed sequence heavily influenced by the pilot of Screen Gems' hit series *Bewitched*. Bernard Slade recalled filming the opening rooftop title sequence.

"The opening shot was a helicopter shot, and I remember being on the roof when they were shooting that, and I was hiding so they wouldn't pick me up. We had a terrific stage manager, the late Marvin Miller, who arranged the locations."

Born May 2, 1930, in St. Catherines, Ontario, Canada, Slade spent the majority of his childhood in England.

"I lived in England from the time I was four

Peter Deuel and Judy Carne in *Love on a Rooftop* (courtesy Deuel Family Collection).

until the time I was 18," recalled Slade. "I mostly lived in Croydon, south London, with my English parents. It was war time and I was shifted around a lot because my father was a mechanic who built airplanes. Then I came to Canada in 1948 and was an actor for ten years. I then started writing for the Canadian Broadcasting Company — variety shows and television plays mainly. The television plays were picked up by the States, which resulted in me coming down to Hollywood."

Moving to Los Angeles in the early 1960s, Slade began writing for television and achieved almost instant success. One of Slade's first writing assignments was on the new hit show *Bewitched*, for which he eventually wrote seventeen segments.

"I was put under contract by Columbia to create three pilot shows a year, and I was there for ten years and wrote eight pilots," commented Slade. "*Love on a Rooftop* was the sort of thing I'd been doing, which was basically a romantic comedy. I shared creator credits with Harry Ackerman, but he had very little to do with *Love on a Rooftop*."

Judy Carne, born in Northampton, England, as Joyce Botterill, began her television career with the BBC as a regular on *Juke Box Jury*, in which a team of panelists decided each week if the latest pop music records were voted a "hit" or a "miss." She followed this with work on the popular BBC comedy show *The Rag Trade*. Deciding to further her career in Hollywood, Carne found regular work on the short-lived comedy shows *Fair Exchange* and *The Baileys of Balboa*, followed by episodic TV work on popular weekly shows, including *The Man from U.N.C.L.E.*, *I Dream of Jeannie* and the *Gidget* episode "Is It Love or Symbiosis?" (1:09).

Carne had been one of over twenty girls, including Nancy Sinatra, originally tested for the part of Julie Willis on *Love on a Rooftop*. The lengthy casting process eventually saw Carne being short-listed among a final group of four girls.

"I was involved in the casting," explained Bernard Slade. "We looked at a lot of girls and Judy just came up. Casting her was a group decision. You've got a lot of pretty girls who can say a line, but they aren't comediennes. Judy could play comedy. I'm sure that was the factor that got her the part.

"Peter Deuel was up against Tony Roberts, among others, for the part of Dave Willis. Roberts was in a show on Broadway and we brought him out to Hollywood. Peter was just a natural talent. He was an amazing actor. I'd known Rich Little in Canada since he was about seventeen. So we cast him. Herb Voland played the father, and Edith Atwater had been a big star on Broadway in a production of *The Man Who Came to Dinner*. Barbara Bostock, who played Rich Little's wife, was a dancer. We ended up living on the beach together and had adjoining houses."

Viewers were introduced to the show in an ABC Special hosted by Batman and Robin, alias Adam West and Burt Ward, to promote the 1966 fall schedule.

"In those days they used to test the pilot in front of an audience at a preview house," recalled Slade. "The pilot tested very well. As I recall we had a wonderful theme song, but for some reason they changed it."

Bridget Hanley starred in two episodes, "Homecoming" (1:07) and "Who Is Sylvia?" (1:10). Her future husband, E. W. Swackhamer, directed 12 episodes for the show.

"I had just come to town and was doing plays, and Screen Gems decided that they wanted to have a contract program," explained Bridget. "They had many auditions, and Eddie Foy put my name in to be brought in to test under contract. Through the audition process I met Swack because he was directing the tests. He coupled everyone else male and female. I was the only one who tested with another lady. A young voluptuous blond. And years later this young woman I tested with became my agent.

"I had told them when I went under contract at Screen Gems that I would not appear in a bathing suit. And the first thing they wanted me to do was to appear in a bathing suit. I had a conference with Swack and told him I really didn't feel comfortable in a bathing suit. And Swack said, 'Come on in and put on the bathing suit and let me make the decision.' So I came in with my little polka dot bathing suit and they gave me Judy Carne's dressing room to change in.

"Swack said, 'Okay, turn around.' I turned around and he said, 'Wear a beach robe too.' It was so hysterical. And I wore a beach robe and a tennis outfit for the 'Homecoming' episode. We read with all the actors on a Monday and filmed the rest of the week. I recall visiting the set, and Swack would always say, 'Gentleman, let's hear it.' And the assistant director would call, 'It's a wrap,' and they would have a little party on the set."

Deuel's perfectionism could make him difficult to work with at times, but director E.W. Swackhamer's equally high standards resulted in a mutual admiration that led to a lasting friendship.

It soon became apparent that Deuel's acting seemed best suited to scenes shared with neighbor Stan Parker, played by Rich Little. Their styles complemented each other and provided some of the funnier scenes of the series.

"I started writing scenes for Rich Little and Peter because they worked well together," commented Slade. "And I knew Rich was an impressionist so I tried to find opportunities where I could use that. He's one of the few impressionists that actually wanted to be an impressionist. Most impressionists I know wanted to be actors. Rich could have had a career as an actor. I later worked with Jack Lemmon, and Rich reminded me of him. He was funny and he had this vague quality that worked for that part. You write to people's strengths and you try to get a mix in there."

The on-screen relationship between David and Julie Willis wasn't as convincing, and Carne's wavering American accent and boyish charm didn't always make for compelling viewing.

"Judy's character was not as grounded as Dave. He was the grounded one that had to look after things. She was used to having some money in the background. What you're looking for all the way through to keep something going is conflict," described Slade. "Peter and Judy were fine together, but I think the chemistry could have been better with another girl.

"People ask me about motivations for various characters in *Bewitched* and *Love on a Rooftop*. These were more spur of the moment decisions. I wanted parents that didn't approve of the marriage, and it was better to make them rich than poor. It was simple as that. Those things sometimes come down to mathematics in a way. The frustrated husband really wasn't the thrust of the show because Julie Willis really didn't use her money at all.

"One of the funniest episodes is where they paint a window on the wall. Those things are more an instinct of what will work."

E. W. Swackhamer encouraged visits to the set with an open door policy.

"The contract players had classes in the morning," recalled Bridget Hanley, "but we were always invited by Swack to come in and observe them filming *Love on a Rooftop* at any

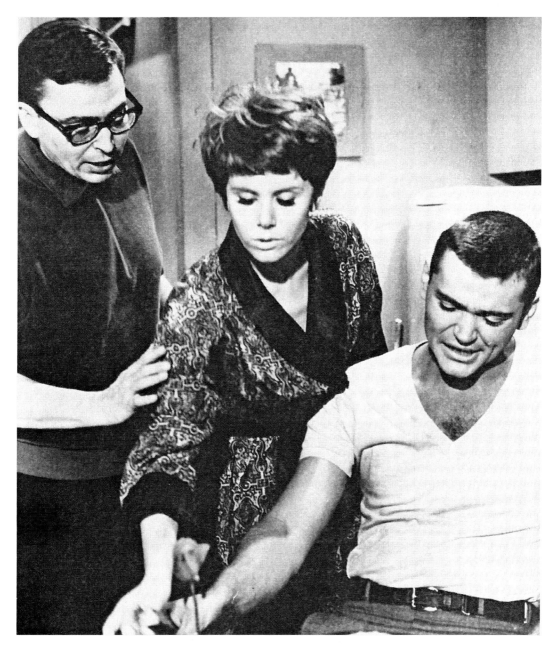

Peter Deuel and Judy Carne taking direction from E.W. Swackhamer in a breakfast scene involving an argument over finances (courtesy Bridget Hanley).

time. Whenever we would choose to be brave enough to take up Swack on his open door policy and visit the set the whole cast was so generous with their time. Peter was always there to greet us with a smile. So dear and sweet. And if we had questions he would answer them. But we didn't try to bother him with too many. Swack was a real lover of actors throughout his entire life, and Peter was at the top of his list. We could go there whenever we wished and learn more about film. And Swack would come and talk to us separately.

"I felt very relaxed at Screen Gems. I later went on to do *Here Come the Brides*, where we had the best time and still all see each other. The whole town at that time was like little families. Every studio had its own personality."

Although Slade's duties as story editor and writer on *Love on a Rooftop* kept him away from the set most of the time, he was present on the first day of filming.

"I do remember the first day of shooting in L.A. after we'd sold the pilot," recounted Slade. "Peter was late. And he came in and said, 'Well, I'm paid to act, not to be on time.' And I thought, 'This spells trouble.' Peter was an amazing actor, but I sensed he wasn't the most serene person in the world. As to why Peter wasn't happy, it was the clichéd young actor who wanted to do better things. Peter wanted to do *Long Day's Journey into Night* instead of *Love on a Rooftop*. But he had this tremendous comedic skill, which was very rare."

Exterior shots took Deuel and Carne to San Francisco every six weeks, and saw them housed in luxury hotels for the duration of the filming.

"The San Francisco locations were shot all at once when the scripts required it. It did help the look of the show," described Slade.

Burt Reynolds first met Carne in 1960 and described her as a "combination of Tinkerbell, Peter Pan and Sadie Thompson..." Marriage in 1963 was followed by separation in 1965 and divorce.

"Judy was a piece of work," declared Bridget. "She was such crazy fun. To me she was very British and hysterical. I found her delightful and witty and kind of smutty-mouthed. And I don't mean it in a bad way because on her it just seemed okay. They all worked as a team — the crew and the cast. It was the happiest place to be."

Carne's friendship with Deuel eventually resulted in a brief sexual relationship.

"Peter wasn't close to Judy but they were friends. They lived in separate worlds," declared Jack Jobes.

Bernard Slade admitted he didn't, at first, believe Carne's stories about her sexual preferences.

"I thought Judy was joking when she told us about her bisexuality. She would joke about it. We were very naive and young, and it wasn't as prevalent then. She told me a funny story that she was in a bathtub with a girl on her wedding day. They were just taking a bath and her mother walked in said, 'Oh Judy, not on your wedding day.'

"I knew that she was fairly active sexually, as I remember. She was kind of available. Judy was always kind of high strung in those days, partly because she'd just come out of a marriage with Burt Reynolds. I remember being in San Francisco, and Judy told me she'd only slept two hours the night before. But Judy was very accessible and friendly. I liked her."

Deuel was involved in a relationship with actress Jill Andre, a married woman with two young children, and Deuel's senior by five years.

"I first met Peter in 1964," recalled Jill. "He was dating this actress with reddish brown hair. Her name was called Constance, and she rented an extra room in my garage. It was a very short-lived relationship. And very soon, Pete and some of his friends from Ithaca College started hanging out at my house. My well-stocked fridge was always a big draw."

During this time, Jill's husband, Richard Franchot, was teaching at Columbia College of Television and Film.

"It was one of the only places, then, where one could learn the techniques of TV and film directing, editing, camera-operating, etc. And young unknowns like Greg Morris and Tom Skerritt volunteered their time and talent as actors to help the students learn their various crafts and develop their skills," recalled Jill.

Deuel and Andre appeared together in the Columbia College production of Tennessee William's *The Case of the Crushed Petunias.*

"They weren't theater productions as such, but scenes from plays that they would film and televise at the college facility," described Jill.

It soon became apparent to Deuel that Andre's marriage was in serious trouble. During this time of marital disintegration, Deuel sometimes served as a babysitter for the two children. Three-year-old Gabrielle and one-year-old Pascal were affectionately called Gaby and Packy around the Franchot household, and Deuel soon formed a close bond with them. It was during the separation proceedings that Deuel and Andre's relationship deepened.

"I had two terrific kids, and I married a sweet man, but it was a time when you were supposed to marry by a certain age," reflected Jill. "The whole 50's mentality was just ghastly. And I knew it wasn't healthy for him or myself to be trapped inside a marriage we both knew wasn't working.

"We were never engaged or had marriage plans. We just had a good time together. I still wear a very beautiful jade ring that Pete had made for me at an old jewelry store on Hollywood Boulevard. It's a tear-drop jade, on a delicate gold band. Peter loved my kids and they adored him. It was really good for me. There was something so fun and so silly about our time together. Peter always made me laugh. I learned to ski with him. It gave me a great sense of freedom to learn how to ski at age 30. You really have to stay in the moment and let yourself go, or you will land on your ass! A most important discovery for me at that time."

Jill recalled how Deuel's sense of fun often bordered on recklessness.

"Peter thought it was really funny to drive his car fast enough so that when he put the brakes on, and we were on a snowy road, it would go into a huge scary skid. He definitely was a daredevil. Some of this behavior was probably an unconscious response to his epilepsy. He seemed to be saying, 'That's not going to stop me. I can do anything. I'm a tough guy.'

"I remember when Peter bought his Toyota jeep. We decided to go for a ride in the hills, with my two kids and my friend Dom DeLuise. As usual, Peter was driving with wild abandon. Dom finally said, 'Oh, I can't stand it. I'm scared. Let me get out!' And we all did.

"Peter, in his motorcycle passion, bought a side car. I used to ride in it. One day we decided to take a trip up to Carmel, and we got less than halfway there when Peter said, 'Oh fuck this. This is too much work.' That was the end of the trip. Side cars really are very hard to maneuver, but it was a funny moment of reality."

Jill learned about Deuel's seizures from him, and though they posed no problem for her, his lack of regard for his own welfare did disturb her.

"He would do crazy stupid things like swimming by himself and drinking, which would exacerbate his epilepsy enormously. His drinking was a way to avoid dealing with some of the deeper issues that always hovered around him. And, of course, he smoked pot, another misused trend of the time. Maybe because I was a little older, and had two kids, I missed the heavy involvement in that phase. And I'm glad I did."

Peter Deuel and Jill Andre, back yard of Hacienda Place 1967 (courtesy Jill Andre).

Jill became familiar with Deuel's close circle of friends in his early years in Hollywood, with Jill's house becoming a major hangout for the group.

"Jill's husband, Peter, and I would often meet with other actors in their back yard on Friday evenings. It was very enjoyable," recalled Fanning.

"Don Fanning was a dear friend of Peter's when he was living at Fuller," said Jill. "In a time when they were drinking too much and acting crazy, Don was the level-headed one. He loved his music and was very close to Peter. Almost his silent other self."

"Don Fanning was Peter's closest friend. He was a reserved and likable man and always there for Peter," confirmed Jack Jobes.

"We drank an awful lot of beer, but it was just social drinking," declared David McHugh. "Just young guys hanging around bars. I saw no sign of alcoholism back then. It was just a way of life at that age. The biggest addiction he had at that time was four packs a day of Gaulois French unfiltered cigarettes. They had to shut down production one time because he lost his voice smoking those. That was the working class cigarette, and he always wanted to identify with the working class. He was rebelling against his middle class upbringing."

Jack Jobes recalled, "Peter and I got into heated arguments about politics. I would say, 'Peter, you're just full of shit. Your father's a doctor. You guys went to a country club with me. Remember?' Peter loved to think he was working class, but he came from the middle class."

David McHugh continued, "Peter was very observant and very sharp and intelligent. I never met another human being as sharp and charismatic and strong as Peter. He was the most disarming person ever. He was the ultimate man's man and the ultimate woman's man. The fierceness was combined with an underlying gentleness that he could turn off and on; but at the same time, just when you thought you were on intimate terms he could flip in a second. He could be kind of vicious at the same time. Peter was quite generous but aggressive with his friends. He was always pushing and challenging."

Jack Jobes, recalling an incident in 1966, said, "A group of us went down to a college hangout in Santa Monica called the 'Oar House.' We all got hammered. Peter cornered this black guy and asked him about what it was like to be black. He was always into it with some provocative discussion."

David McHugh said, "Peter's cynicism was overpowering. He was cynical about everything. But also fiercely courageous. One time he was driving down Santa Monica Boulevard with Jill, and a convertible passed him and a bunch of guys yelled out, 'Communist!' Peter chased these people down, cut them off, grabbed the guy out of the passenger seat, pulled him out of the car, punched him and threw him back in the car, and said, 'You fucking idiots, you better watch who you call Communist. You don't even know what the word means.' He wouldn't take any crap from anyone.

"What he lacked big time was his EQ — Emotional Quotient. How well we deal with our lives. How you interpret and process those experiences that are just natural to being alive, and how you handle the events that are inevitably going to happen in your life. Peter was so conflicted I don't know what he wanted."

Deuel confided much of his anxieties to Jill in a relationship of mutual trust.

"Peter was a really sensitive guy," observed Jill. "Enormously fragile to a dangerous degree. Emotionally he was terrified of confronting his family history. Peter felt he couldn't do anything to help his mother's alcoholism. It was very hard on him. His reaction was, 'What is my value if I can't help my family?' He felt isolated by the emotional distance. He couldn't make sense of the fact that his Dad, who was a small-town doctor, and worked very hard to make a good living, made so much less in a year than Peter would make in a week on a television show.

"Peter would say, 'I can't stand it that he struggles to help people with important things like their health, and I just come out to Hollywood and do this silly stuff and earn all this money.' Peter had an enormous sense of guilt about earning money, because the acting came easily to him. 'How do I deserve all this attention and earn all this money for this silly job?'

Deuel's need to please his parents was evident in a story he related to Jill.

"Peter told me once, 'You know, I have this fantasy sometimes that I've become a great pianist, concert quality, and my parents don't know. So when I go home to visit them, I sneak downstairs early one morning and play this brilliant music, and they are floored, and of course thrilled.' I think Peter loved music almost more than anything."

David McHugh, echoing Jill Andre's comments on Deuel's love of music, said, "I first met Peter at the Monterey Jazz Festival trip in September 1965. When we returned to Fuller everybody went to bed except Peter and I. He wanted me to listen to some of his classical records. Three violin concertos by Paganini. My older brother was a concert violinist and I knew all the repertoire. He was thrilled that he had a friend who knew more about classical music than he did.

Peter Deuel playing his guitar at his North Fuller apartment, June 1967 (courtesy Deuel Family Collection).

"I was a classical composer with a graduate degree and was studying in New York with a famous European pianist called Leopold Mittman. One time Peter was in town and wanted to meet him. So I introduced Peter to Mr. Mittman. He was an extraordinary artist. He gave his first concert at 12 with the Concertgebouw Orchestra in Amsterdam playing a Chopin piano concerto. Mittman had a nine-foot Steinway Grand in his living room, and Peter told him he would love to hear him play. Mittman replied, 'I really don't play anymore.'

"Peter said, 'Come on. You can see me on television. I want to see what you do. Play something.' And he played for half an hour. Peter had such a commanding voice and presence it was like he could hypnotize people. I saw it many times. Peter had never seen or heard an artist of this caliber before. He loved music."

Andre and Deuel drifted apart when Jill was hired to appear in a New York soap opera in 1967, and she decided to move with her two children.

"Peter was going through a lot of things and so was I with my two kids. He needed his space and he was so heavily involved in his film and TV career. I was wanting to live in New York again, and he wasn't. Another major issue was therapy. I had started working with a therapist, and he had no interest in doing that. I think he was frightened at the time. I had no idea who I was, and I did not value my sense of self or my talents. And I said I don't see how we can do anything to make this work if we both don't try to take care of ourselves. I was terribly scared to start therapy, but I knew I had to do it. I wanted to get my life squared away."

"I met Jill Andre at our home when she came to visit us from New York with Peter. She was a lovely lady," remarked Pamela Deuel. "She was quite a sophisticated girl, and Peter was taken with that. I think it was the first older woman he had dated. He knew the relationship would not last. But that's not to say he didn't care for her deeply."

Deuel's high profile on *Love on a Rooftop* caught the attention of Deuel's former college, St. Lawrence University.

"Pete received a letter from the Dean of Men inviting him to 'Come back and see us anytime,'" recalled Jack Jobes. "This after he had been told years earlier that he could never return to St. Lawrence again. We placed both letters side by side in a scrapbook and never had anything to do with St. Lawrence again. The hypocrisy of the situation was overwhelming."

When filming on the first season of *Love on a Rooftop* came to a close in the spring of 1967, hopes were high for its renewal. Reviews had been encouraging, if not spectacular. The series highlighted Deuel's skill with light comedy. In comparison with his often stumbling efforts on *Gidget*, Deuel's performance showed a certain maturity, with a fresh screen presence in evidence.

The *Hollywood Reporter* noted:

Miss Carne is not a beauty. Better than that, she is pert and pretty, a lively face gleaming with intelligence. Deuel is a nice-looking young man, adept in the romantic elements and with a surprising and refreshing knack for comedy.

TV Guide commented:

Along with its fine inventiveness, this show has splendid acting by the principals, Mr. Deuel and Miss Carne; as well as by its featured players....

"Peter was easy to write for because he was very skilled," described Bernard Slade. "And he could deliver. If you gave him a comedy line or a comedy attitude he would deliver it. He was comedic, and that's a very rare quality."

But ABC was stalling. The ratings were holding their own. Shows had been renewed with worse ratings. Finally news came through that ABC had made the decision to cancel. Desilu Studio's new comedy show, Marlo Thomas' *That Girl*, would be renewed, despite similar lukewarm ratings.

Creator Bernard Slade was dismayed at the news of early cancellation, having put his best efforts into *Love on a Rooftop*. Years later he would still consider his writing on the show to be among his best work in television.

"I came from Canada and I'd appeared in a lot of Noel Coward," said Slade. "And not to be snobbish about it, but my sights were a little higher than the average sitcom on U.S. TV. We just tried to do a sophisticated, for the time, show. We got knocked off the air by the Marlo Thomas show, even though it didn't have as good a rating as our show.

"We thought a lot of shows at that time were pretty stupid. The original *Dick Van Dyke Show* was the standard to aim for. I wanted to do something where the people were literate. We were sort of shocked when it wasn't picked up. It was one of my favorite shows, and I was rather unhappy it went off. I thought if it was picked up then it would go on for five or six years. You do all those situation comedy things. She would have had a baby and all that jazz. There were a lot of shows about the young marrieds, and I was pretty young at that point, although I had been married for a while. So you write from your own experiences.

"I never stayed with a show after *Love on a Rooftop*. I would get a show on the air and do three or four and then move on to the next one. I was at Columbia for around ten years, and then finally I wrote *Same Time Next Year* (1975), which was a big smash hit in the theater, and that liberated me from television. I didn't like dealing with network executives. I've been working in the theater ever since."

Peter Deuel and his father on Peter's 27th birthday, February 24, 1967 (courtesy Deuel Family Collection).

Official Nielsen ratings for October 1966 through April 1967 showed *Bonanza* as number one, followed by *The Red Skelton Show*, *The Andy Griffith Show*, *The Lucy Show*, *The Jackie Gleason Show*, *Green Acres*, *Daktari*, *Bewitched*, *The Beverly Hillbillies*, *The Virginian*, *The Lawrence Welk Show* and *Gomer Pyle U.M.S.C.* Comedy and light entertainment were popular with viewers, but the partnership of Deuel and Carne clearly didn't strike a strong enough chord with audiences of the day.

"Swack was very disappointed and very hurt," recalled Bridget Hanley. "He never quite recovered when *Love on a Rooftop* was cancelled. Everyone thought it would renew and go on. It was doing well in the numbers. It has nothing to do with personalities or quality, but numbers. And Peter's life would have been different if it had gone on.

"I remember at the end of a scene Swack always had this habit of pointing out an actor and saying, 'You were best!' And it got to be the joke, and everybody was working at the end of the scene to be the best. And I'm sure that Peter got that finger pointed at him many, many times."

Deuel had starred in two series that failed to progress beyond the first season, and needed time to reflect on where his career was heading.

✯ 4 ✯

NEW DIRECTIONS

"What is important is not what happens to us, but how we respond to what happens to us."

— Jean-Paul Sartre

In August 1966 Deuel paid a visit to ABC-TV's affiliate, WYNS Channel 9, in Syracuse, New York, appearing on *Charly's Place* and *The Baron and His Buddies*. He also took time out to visit nearby Hancock Air Force Base and be interviewed on WPAW and WFBL radio stations.

"I remember Peter visited Channel 9 in 1966 for publicity," recalled Pamela. "I was living with my parents in Penfield with Jennifer, and going through my divorce."

The Baron and His Buddies was hosted by John Michael Price as vampire alter ego Baron Daemon. A 1963 single by Price, *Transylvania Twist*, went to the top of the charts in Syracuse, selling 12,000 copies. The Baron originally introduced late night horror movies, before the show moved to a children's afternoon time slot and the Baron introduced cartoons, such as *Astro Boy*, and interacted with children from the audience. Deuel expressed his enjoyment at his time spent at the TV studios, when on his return to West Hollywood he wrote a letter of thanks to Carol Schell of WYNS-TV.

Dear Carol,
  Thank you for a gassey time—God we had fun huh? Even tho' that 100 yard dash for the big bird was a little wearing it sort of put a fun capper on my whirlwind day. Looking forward to next time. My best ball at the station.
  Sincerely,
  Peter Deuel

A fire at the Shoppingtown studios in 1967 destroyed the majority of the costumes, props and tapes at WYNS. Preservation of episodes wasn't a priority at the time, as all shows were wiped clean and the tapes used again to record the next show.

Between assignments, Deuel found time to visit old friends in Penfield.

"As fame took hold with Peter, he talked to my high school classes in 1964 and 1966," recalled Jim Ludwig. "My sister came to the class in 1966, and Peter drove her home to our mother's house in Penfield after his presentation. To this day, we still remember his charm and genuine warmth when he came back and talked with her for some time over coffee at the house.

"I recall a party we attended. I did a Ralph Edwards *This Is Your Life*–type radio interview with Peter that he really enjoyed and kept laughing about. Peter and I sat and sang together at a special high school Christmas evening presentation when former students returned and met on stage for Handel's *Messiah*."

Deuel's only previous venture into the movies had been in the war film *Wounded in Action*, a.k.a. *W.I.A.* (1966), shot on location in the Philippines, 40 miles outside of Colombo. Centering on an Army hospital in the Philippines in 1945, and based on the real-life experiences of producer-director Irving Sunasky, *Wounded in Action* featured Deuel in the very small role of wounded soldier Private Myers, with Steve Mario and Maura McGiveney in starring roles as romancing hospital technician and nurse.

Filmed in 1961 at a budget of under $100,000, the American-Filipino co-production lay on the shelf for five years until its U.S. release in March 1966 before becoming yet another discarded "B" movie hiding among rusting metal cans of long forgotten films.

Film Daily commented on 29 March, 1966:

> While footage devoted to actors ... is routine, due to their limited thespic ability and Sunasky's pedestrian direction and writing, there are some charming moments in scenes played by the Filipino cast members plus some shudderingly realistic ones of wounds being dressed and operations performed.

Daily Variety, 9 February, 1966, added:

> Mostly shot in local hospital wards, the film's plot involves the life against death struggle of the patients, with a tangential love affair between an officer nurse and an enlisted man.

Following the cancellation of *Love on a Rooftop*, Deuel appeared in an episode of Quinn Martin's *The F.B.I.* — "False Witness" (3:11), with Carol Lynley. With Deuel out of contract to Columbia and seeking work, Universal Studios bosses, seeing potential in the young actor, offered him a seven-year term contract in July 1967.

"We were the only studio to run a 'New Talent' program, where we'd take promising actors, put them under contract and try to develop them into series stars," stated former Universal president Frank Price. "We always watched promising actors under contract to other studios, and if they got dropped, we might go after the actor. We did that with Harrison Ford, who was dropped by Fox.

"Each actor's agent negotiated his or her deal. That deal depended on how promising we thought they were, and therefore the balance between how much we wanted them and how much they wanted a steady income. An actor's life can be lonely and economically insecure. The studio contract sounds good. Beginners, as I recall, probably got $300 to $400 a week, with a 40 week guarantee. Many actors paid attention to the amount they got per week and forgot that they might be on lay-off for the other 13 weeks.

"Once they were under contract, our New Talent Department, under a terrific woman named Monique James, read every script about to be produced at the studio in order to find potential roles for the contract players. The idea was to get these people some experience in the proper small roles so that they could grow into Stars. Someone like Harrison Ford we paid more, of course, but nothing astronomical. He was just another aspiring actor like Peter Deuel. Doug McClure, Katherine Ross and my wife Katherine Crawford were all contract players.

"They were guaranteed the amount in the contract. If they proved to be very popular and worked a lot, we would pay them more than the contract called for. That rarely happened. If

they were placed in a continuing series lead role, we then made a new contract with them
and they received considerably more money.

"In general, with most contract players it took a lot of diligent work for the New Talent people to find sufficient roles to cover the annual guarantees to these contract players.
Producers weren't that wild to hire young and inexperienced actors that might not perform
dependably in front of a camera. Generally, experienced pros that could deliver under pressure were preferred.

"I became disenchanted with the whole New Talent program. It had, in my opinion,
a serious flaw. Promising young actors, with fragile egos, were often not treated well by producers, directors and production people because they weren't important, and they sometimes caused problems because of their inexperience. By the time some of the most talented
of these actors became experienced and professional, they hated the studio for treating them
so badly. They forgot how hard everyone worked to get those jobs for them and paid them
while they were unemployable elsewhere. I came to believe that it was best to stay out of
that New Talent mess and hired those people we wanted when we wanted them, even if it
cost somewhat more."

Universal contract player Sara Lane recalled, "The most I made during my seven year
contract was $40,000 a year. I started at $650 a week on *The Virginian*. In our union contract there was a certain amount you could be paid a week. The long-term contract was a
lower rate, and during the hiatus between seasons you weren't paid. I was one of the few
actors who worked four years solid in a series. But working in a series meant there wasn't
any time for acting lessons, and you didn't get a chance to develop as an actor. Any young
actor was immediately put under contract because it was beneficial to Universal."

"When someone offers you the choice between a seven-year contract with guaranteed
raises or scuffling around and looking for work by yourself, it's always a difficult decision
for a young actor," declared Donald Fanning. "You achieve financial independence, but you
may later regret it because you are tied up for seven years."

"Peter sought my advice on his seven year contract," said Jack Jobes. "I said, 'Look, I
can't advise you about this, but there is a saying, "Bird in hand." But you'll get practice and
steady pay.' An actor needs an audience and steady work to progress."

Deuel celebrated the signing of his Universal contract with the purchase of a 1953 black
Cadillac from actress Bonnie Bedelia in Ontario, New York. The long journey to his home
in Hollywood was shared with his mother Lillian, despite her misgivings regarding the contract.

"It turned out to be a lovely trip for the two of them. That was the first time he went
across country with his mother, and she loved it," described Pamela.

The following month Deuel returned to the East Coast by plane for a one-day appearance at the Rotary Horse Show at Finger Lake Race Track on 13 August.

Following his stalled relationship with Jill Andre, Deuel started dating yet another
attractive blonde. San Francisco–born Beth Griswold lived with three of her four siblings
and her parents in their home in northern California.

"I first met Peter on a blind date, Friday the 13th in October of 1967," recollected Beth
Griswold. "Peter's childhood friend, Christopher Clarke, lived in Mountain View, just south
of my home town. Peter would fly up from Los Angeles now and again to see Chris and
his wife. She worked at a bank with Joan, a friend of mine from high school. Joan was

asked if she wanted to go out with Peter Deuel but declined, as she was already engaged to be married. So Joan suggested me for the date. When she called to ask me to go I was sure she was joking with me. Peter was pretty well known from *Love on a Rooftop* and had recently appeared on *The Dating Game*. My sisters and I had watched that show together, and I remember us fantasizing about being the girl that he chose. So I was sure my friend was playing a practical joke on me.

"When the door bell rang, my sister Mary, who was just 15, ran to be the one to open the door. She was flabbergasted! It was really him! In amazement, she started backing up from the door and didn't stop until she fell over my father's chair. Peter was so sweet to her and my 11-year-old sister Ann. They were both giggly, and Peter just giggled along with them and said how happy he was to meet them.

"At our first meeting I was all smiles too. Peter was so engaging in person. His presence literally lit up the room. His smile was spectacular, and he had the deepest dimples I had ever seen. When he arrived for our date he was dressed very casually in light colored cords and sandals. His hair was longer than he had worn it in *Love on a Rooftop*, and he had a trimmed beard. Peter was 27 and I had just turned 20.

"That night we went to a private party with Chris Clarke and some of his friends. I don't remember talking very much myself but just listening to and observing everyone, especially Peter. He had such an easy way about him in a crowd. He could tell an amusing story and then very easily segue into a serious subject. He was as comfortable speaking out against the war in Vietnam as he was speaking about the latest music or whatever.

"Peter picked up a book, looked though it, and when asked by someone who had read the book what he thought about its subject matter, began a dialogue that eventually drew the attention of most everyone at the party. I was amazed at how quickly his mind grasped the premise of the book with such a brief review and how well he expressed his perspective. That evening I told Peter, 'I like the way you think.' Months later, when we talked about what drew us to each other in the beginning, he mentioned that compliment and how pleased he was that I was equally as attracted by his mind as I was his physical presence.

"We must have gone out almost every night for the week he was visiting. I loved his enthusiasm. He loved that I was so 'down to earth' and treated him like a regular guy, not a celebrity. We both loved that we could comfortably communicate about anything and everything. By the time he left to return to L.A. we were deeply infatuated with each other. Our plan was to continue the relationship by phone and by one or the other of us flying south or north for the weekend. And so we did just that and our feelings for each other grew."

Within two months of their first blind date Deuel and Griswold were officially engaged, choosing matching wedding bands at Gleim's Jewelers in Palo Alto.

"They were green gold and in a pattern of interwoven leaves reflecting our love of nature," Beth recalled. "We set a tentative wedding date for June of 1968 and decided that I would move to L.A. after the first of the year. Because my parents were already upset that I was dating an older man (and a Democrat at that), I concocted a small white lie to tell them about where I'd be living in L.A. The girlfriend of a 'friend' of Peter's had a spare room, and I would be moving in with her, although I would be getting my mail at Peter's address. I'm sure they weren't fooled, but they preferred this story to admitting to themselves or anyone else that I was living in 'sin' in L.A."

Their long-distance relationship became more intimate in January 1968 when Beth moved into Peter's North Fuller apartment in West Hollywood.

Describing the apartment, Beth recalled, "The living room was a small rectangular room with a couch against the same wall as the entry stairs. The stairs up to the front door were painted dark green, as were the garage doors and the window trim. The bathroom was straight ahead as you walked in the front door, with its door opening out into the living room. The only closet was to the right of the bathroom, in the middle of that wall. On the outside of the closet door we hung a 'KEEP THE FAITH' poster. The door to the kitchen was at the far right end of the living room. It had one small counter with the sink, a very old refrigerator, 'antique' stove, and a window that looked out onto the driveway and the front building.

"The bedroom was just to the left as you entered the apartment. It was very small, an afterthought added onto the studio apartment at some time, with French doors. Peter had a double bed that was practically wall to wall, and a small dresser. I seem to remember a free standing coat rack opposite from the bed and a life-size cutout of Humphrey Bogart leaning in that corner.

"The apartment was above a garage where Peter kept his 1953 black Cadillac sedan. He would rarely take the car out because it barely fit through the driveway. It was so narrow there were only two or three inches on either side of the Cadillac. It was incredible that he could maneuver that great big automobile through that narrow space without ever damaging it. He loved driving the Cadillac. His other vehicle, the 'everyday' car, was a beige Toyota Land Cruiser with a canvas top.

The week before Christmas at Beth's parents' house, December 1967 (courtesy Beth Griswold).

"It was a magic time when we were first together. We were both very happy and enthusiastic about life and our future. I was very much in love with Peter. He was my first serious, committed relationship. The first man to ask me to marry him, and the first man with whom I was willing to share my deepest feelings. I allowed Peter into my heart as I had not done with any man before. In the beginning we preferred intimate conversation to going out, talking mostly about politics, the environment and whatever book(s) he was into at the time.

"He saw acting as his creative outlet and acting's celebrity as a platform. It was a lot of fun to watch him practice his craft. I had never seen or heard one line expressed in so many different ways. He wouldn't rehearse with me, but in my presence. I'd see him practicing his expressions in front of the long mirror on the hall tree and hear him while he was sitting on the bed, going over his lines — not only to memorize them but to find the best inflection and emphasis on each word. When I would visit him on the set and watch him work, his dedication to his acting was obvious, and at the same time he had so much fun doing it."

Deuel's enjoyment of music and his deeply resonant voice led to an assignment to promote the Moody Blues album *Days of Future Passed* (1967) for a local radio station.

Engagement photograph taken behind the stairs at the North Fuller apartment, January 1968 (photograph by Del Hayden, courtesy Beth Griswold).

"On a shelf behind the bed Peter had a KLH FM radio which was on much of the time we were in the apartment. We would listen for the intro cuts from "Nights in White Satin" or "Tuesday Afternoon" and wait for Peter's voice, 'This is Peter Deuel.'"

Often walking barefoot in his apartment, and sometimes in the streets surrounding the Fuller apartment, he told Beth, "It's good for you."

"He always spoke with authority," recalled Beth, "and I believed what he said. At that time I didn't feel he was controlling me so much as guiding me and sharing his experience and knowledge."

Beth abandoned her shoes and joined her boyfriend's barefoot treks. Eating out was a regular event, with Pinks a favorite place for enjoying chili dogs.

"There was a part of Peter that was really down to earth and so 'normal,'" said Beth. "I think I loved that part of him the best. We would take a walk to nearby Plummer Park, watch some of the locals play bocci ball, and then just sit and talk. We would walk down to the local laundromat, put a load or two in the machines, then go hang out at some little 'walk-up' burger joint while the clothes were drying. I remember on occasion when Peter was recognized in that laundromat and how he enjoyed his celebrity in that easy one-on-one situation where he could be himself naturally."

Peter and Beth in Plummer Park, a block from Deuel's apartment, mid–September 1968 (photograph by Curt Gunther, courtesy Beth Griswold).

Commenting on Peter's and Beth's relationship, Pamela Deuel said, "She was a darling and pretty girl. They told me they were 'in like.' Peter brought me out for a week in 1968 where I met Beth and went to a bar called 'Barney's Beanery.' I remember the place being crowded with people bumping into each other. I looked at Peter and said, 'Look to your left. That's the tallest woman I've ever seen.' And he said, 'Don't stare, that's a man.' I was so naive. I said, 'You're kidding? She's beautiful.' And Peter said, 'Yes he is.'"

Barney's Beanery dated back to 1920 in Berkeley, California, before relocating to Santa Monica Boulevard on the old Route 66 in 1927. A hangout of Hollywood writers, actors, musicians, Beatniks and rock 'n' roll performers, the diner attracted counterculture icons such as Jim Morrison and Janis Joplin in the 1960s.

"Peter liked Barney's a lot," exclaimed Beth. "We'd go there often. It was the whole atmosphere he liked, besides the good basic food. Among the many signs and paraphernalia hanging on the walls and from the ceiling was a sign that said 'Faggots Keep Out,' or something similar. I think that sign was hung as a statement that bigotry exists out there and not as a statement of the owner's personal beliefs. A few years later there was a big stink about the sign and it was removed. But when Peter and I were there the place was known for its tolerance and the diversity in the lifestyles of the clientele."

Commenting on meeting Pamela Deuel for the first time, Beth recalled, "I was very nervous because I knew Pamela would be 'reporting back' to her parents what she thought of her brother's new girlfriend. I remember a very pretty blond with blue eyes, coloring opposite of Pete's, but she had a similar shape to her face as Peter's. I know that by the time I met Pamela, Peter and I were past the initial explosive intensity of falling in love. We were asking ourselves those difficult relationship questions. Could we be as good a friend as a lover for each other? Could we maintain a mutual respect for each other even though we may be in disagreement? Outwardly we presented a very light and carefree façade, but neither of us revealed our core feelings to others."

The Hell with Heroes (1968), the first assignment under Deuel's new contract, would also star Rod Taylor, Claudia Cardinale, Harry Guardino and Kevin McCarthy. Set in 1946, Rod Taylor and Peter Deuel played Brynie MacKay and Mike Brewer, a pair of 8th Air Force pilots who have decided to stay in Algeria after World War Two in order to set up an air cargo business. Forced into black marketeering to raise cash to pay for their battered C-47 plane the pair use in their air cargo business, they become involved with Lee Harris (Harry Guardino), an American smuggler operating out of France.

John Mahoney, in his review of the film for *Hollywood Reporter*, 12 August, 1968, wrote:

> [*The Hell with Heroes*] is a trite and unpleasant tale.... You are aware that the director is trying to punch up deficient material.... Deuel scores best of all as the ingenious young writer whose zest for life is both believable and infectious.

The Motion Picture Herald, 21 August, 1968, stated:

> [T]he hero and the heroine reform at the end in a tradition of old fashioned melodrama, which is what this picture basically is.... Newcomer Deuel (of TV's *Love on a Rooftop*) is quite personable as Taylor's buddy.

Deuel failed to make any impact on reviewers from *Daily Variety* and *The New York Times*, who made no mention of him by name in their reviews of the movie. They both agreed the film was mediocre, with the *Daily Variety* review of 7 August, 1968, being particularly scathing:

> *The Hell with Heroes* is a tired programmer ... mired in talky, sermonizing exposition, fumbled pacing and formula production.... Overall result resembles a muffed attempt to make a switched-on pot boiler.

The Hell with Heroes marked an unremarkable beginning to Deuel's career as a Universal contract player.

Peter and Beth in another pose for an engagement photograph taken behind the stairs at the North Fuller apartment, January 1968 (photograph by Del Hayden, courtesy Beth Griswold).

Meanwhile, Beth Griswold proved to be a positive influence in his life at a time when he had been drinking heavily.

"I understand that Peter fought with his drinking constantly," said Beth. "But in the time we were together he gave up alcohol completely following a DUI incident. He was really happy with himself for quitting. And he was very open about his problem, admitting to friends that he considered himself an alcoholic. I would not have stayed with him had he continued to drink. He was a very different person when he had alcohol in his system — mean, intolerant and belligerent.

"He was verbally very talented. He would speak wonderfully when he wasn't drinking. But when he drank he became extremely verbally abusive and physically combative.

Alcohol ramped him up, much like the common reaction to cocaine, making him angrier and more contentious the more he drank — it intensified his own natural intensity!"

Pamela Deuel, echoing Beth's comments, noted, "Around me I didn't see Peter being negative but I do recall him yelling and being verbally abusive with other people. He could be mean with strangers. Especially if he was really drunk. Peter didn't take criticism well if he'd been drinking. He'd be out of control in the way he would talk, and I'd leave. There was no point in hanging around. He was usually contrite the next day because he didn't like acting that way."

Deuel's search for an answer to his alcoholism took him in diverse directions, including Scientology.

"An actor friend of Peter's was also a recovering alcoholic and into Scientology as a technique for healing his addiction," commented Beth. "He encouraged Peter to take some of their training to help him with his problem. Peter decided to give Scientology 'a try.' I felt encouraged by this because it seemed Peter wanted to discover what it was within him that made him drink. So he went through a few sessions but decided Scientology was like brainwashing, and to continue would mean giving up his own self-control, just as he did when he drank."

With Deuel's abstinence from alcohol his seizures became less of a problem. Beth declared, "Peter had told me of his epilepsy. He took medication for it which was, to me, like my diabetic brother's insulin shots. Something he had to do to have a normal life. I never saw any seizures, so it wasn't an intrusion at all in our life. He had it under control."

Deuel replaced alcohol with his drug of choice, marijuana. Experimentation with other drugs also occurred at this time. Mescaline, LSD, and other hallucinogens were popular and easy to obtain in 1968 L.A.

"I tried mescaline with Peter, but it was too much for me," admitted Beth. "Once was enough. I had to draw a line for myself, so I watched when Peter tried LSD and experimented with other drugs at some of the parties we went to. But they were purely a 'once-in-a-while' kind of thing. It was just marijuana when I was with Peter. We smoked a lot of pot, and he did stay stoned a lot of the time when he wasn't working. I guess that in itself is an indication of his addictive personality. The pot had a more positive effect on him though. He seemed to relax, to lighten up on himself, and he was much mellower. Things were funnier to him. He saw more humor in everything and laughed often."

Beth Griswold also discovered Peter Deuel could be confrontational and wasn't one to back down in any situation.

"During the spring of 1968," related Beth, "when Peter was doing some studio work and I was driving all over L.A. for McCarthy, I met another volunteer who was also working for McCarthy on the local college campuses. We really hit it off, becoming almost instant friends. He knew I was involved with Peter and committed to our relationship, so friends it was for us. We decided to combine our efforts, working to make each rally and appearance a success. When I introduced him to Peter at McCarthy headquarters, Peter confronted my friend with his jealousies, which, up to that moment, I didn't know existed. Peter and I tried to talk it over for the next few days, but Peter was convinced that I could not be friends with this man without getting involved with him. My choice, as Peter stated it, was to stay with Peter and give up this new friendship or leave. I gave up the friendship.

"Towards the end of our relationship, Peter became angry and jealous when I made a connection with his friend, C. Davey Utter. He was a talented guitarist and I was an aspiring amateur folk singer when we played together after Thanksgiving dinner. Peter did not like the attention Davey and I were getting. During a break in the music, he accused me of having feelings for Davey, and so I stopped playing and singing with his friend. After confronting me, Peter fell asleep in the bedroom."

Despite his faults, Deuel had a light side that delighted Beth.

"He could be explosively funny," she related. "He would he out in public and just start to dance, do a little jig, sing a little tune, or laugh out loud. We'd be outside a movie theater or a restaurant and the people around us would just start laughing with him. He would just crack me up, and occasionally I would try to join in. But most of the time I would be laughing, tears rolling down my cheeks and begging him to stop 'embarrassing me.' Peter would reply, 'What does it matter? It feels good! Go ahead and just do something because it *feels* good!'"

Pamela also recalled her brother's spontaneous behavior in public.

"After I was done with my show in Las Vegas, a couple of members of my band and Peter and I went over to Caesar's Palace. We walked up these four steps to the carpeted entrance and we were immediately into this huge gaming room. Peter stood at the top of the four steps, stretched his arms out to the side and said, 'I'm here!' Many people turned around, and some of them recognized him, and Peter took bows and laughed and talked to the people. I was a little embarrassed but I loved it too. I was laughing."

Deuel's public outbursts weren't limited to joking around. Sometimes it could verge on the offensive.

"One day we had just exited the grocery store," recounted Beth, "when Peter started yelling the 'F' word at full voice. He repeated it about 20 times in a row. People would pass by, looking at him sideways, and Peter would say, 'You just say it until it doesn't mean anything. It becomes nonsense like any other word repeated over and over again. You can do it anytime you want.' We would be leaving the apartment and he would be shouting the word as he descended the stairs.

"There was a three or four story apartment building next door where a lot of older folks lived. I would cringe when I saw their windows open and knew Peter's shouts were filling their kitchens with the 'F' word. He would use the word casually in his everyday speech. It would just come out naturally. I think it became a habit when he was working with Judy Carne in *Love on a Rooftop*. He told me when either of them had made a mistake with their lines that word came out in rapid fire more often than not.

"Peter was very bright and articulate, with a quick mind. When he was 'on' he was

Beth and Peter pet a stray cat at a walk-up hot dog stand on Santa Monica Boulevard, mid–September 1968 (photograph by Curt Gunther, courtesy Beth Griswold).

really on! It was fun living with Peter during those times ... never a dull moment. One of our favorite things to do if we were home on Friday night was to get stoned and watch *Star Trek*. We were real "Trekkies" and appreciated the show's political allegory. Afterwards we would discuss the plot's social commentary and relevance to current affairs or, if there was none, just laugh about its absurdity. We rarely went out to the movies, but the 'big' movie that year was *2001: A Space Odyssey*. We got stoned and went to see it in April of 1968. I'm sure the entire audience was high that night, and we were blown away by the movie's spectacular visual effects."

David McHugh, recalling another mind-altering cinematic experience, commented, "One time Peter visited me in my penthouse in New York and he brought two tabs of mescaline with him. We went to watch *The Charge of the Light Brigade* after taking the mescaline. With mescaline you reach this point of objectivity. You have no emotional response and just observe reality like a radar registering a plane. By the time we got to the climax of the movie Peter and I were peaking on the mescaline. It was like watching a cartoon. We had no emotional response to horses and people being blown apart on the screen. We cried with laughter and the people in the theater started yelling at us. So we left and got lost and couldn't find our way out of the theater. For looking at existence from a totally objective point of view it was an amazing experience. But I only took it that one time."

Deuel's Universal contract stipulated he attend certain promotional parties given by the studio.

"All the actors under contract with Universal would have to go to these publicity parties," said Beth. "When we arrived at a party he would typically have to pose for a series if publicity photographs. It was one of the studio contract requirements he disliked. He knew he had to 'network' and 'kiss ass,' but he hated being false. Sometimes he would mumble things through his wonderful smile as they were taking pictures, interjecting the 'F' word quite freely."

Jill Andre echoed Beth Griswold's comments regarding Deuel's dislike of studio parties.

"He'd just started having to do these publicity functions when I'd met him," recalled Jill. "I remember going to Palm Springs one weekend for some big event, and all he wanted to do was get into his Toyota and get out of there and ride into the desert. He didn't like the falsity of it at all. He was very turned off by the sycophantic behavior of most of the people involved. And everything having to be cheery and up, and obviously that wasn't the way he was feeling most of the time."

Deuel gave voice to his true, and often complex, personality away from the stifling atmosphere of the various studio functions.

"Away from studio parties, he was very animated when he spoke," declared Beth. "His voice would rise and fall with bursts of laughter, as well as blasts of shouting, depending on the point he was trying to make and the person he was speaking to. I was waiting for the day when Peter would allow that freedom of expression, verbally and physically, to enter his acting and see him achieve the level he aspired to."

"Peter was exuberant. He was always out there when he was feeling good," recalled Jill. "Sometimes he'd feel like he needed to prove himself so he'd get very vocal and find himself very humorous, and other times it would be a reaction to his own fears. And sometimes he would just shut down and not communicate at all. He was a very complex guy, to say the least."

Pamela Deuel remembered, "Peter told me that he wanted to be the first person to say the 'F' word on the *Johnny Carson Show*."

"Peter was crude at times and he would be purposely loud, but people took to him," recollected David McHugh. "He needed a lot of attention. The neglect of his parents created this need in Peter. But he wasn't comfortable confronting his own feelings."

Deuel was also becoming frustrated with the roles he was being offered at Universal. Beth Griswold understood that "success" and "meaning" were two words central to Deuel's self-image.

"I know Peter was always concerned about his success, or lack of success in regards to what his parents, especially his father, thought of it," explained Beth. "Because he didn't follow the family tradition and because both Geoff and Pamela followed him into show business, Peter felt exceptional pressure to become a successful actor. The fact that at 28 he had not yet achieved a level of success to match is expectations affected him deeply. Peter knew he was good at his craft, but it wasn't satisfying him on a life achievement scale. He longed for scripts with more depth and meaning in them. He had begun to regret signing the Universal contract."

Deuel's frustrations would be put on hold as a certain senator was attracting attention and causing quite a stir in the Democratic Party.

☆ 5 ☆

SAFE IN THE PARK

"As he gazed around him the youth felt a flash of astonishment at the blue, pure sky and the sun gleaming on the trees and fields. It was surprising that Nature had gone tranquilly on with her golden process in the midst of so much devilment."

— Stephen Crane, *The Red Badge of Courage* (1895)

"Peter was very political when I knew him, although I do not know who Peter supported or voted for before 1968," remembered Beth. "What I do know is that when I met Peter he was vehemently anti-war, but his concentration on his work and career had kept him actively protesting. He was inspired to get involved in politics in late 1967 when Senator Eugene McCarthy announced that he would be running for president. McCarthy was the first politician, the only one on the national level, to speak up and out about bringing an end to the Vietnam War."

January 1968 saw Peter Deuel and Beth Griswold working from a small office on Fairfax, the original Los Angeles Headquarters of the McCarthy Presidential campaign.

"The office was tiny," Beth recalled. "Only 15 feet wide by 30 to 40 feet deep. It had probably been a small cafe previously, as one side of the room still had booths along the wall. I remember walking in that first evening and Peter introducing himself to the six or so people there, although most of them recognized him. Peter sat down in a booth with two of them and began talking about the war and McCarthy's campaign. The rest of us sat nearby on a few scattered chairs listening to the discussion. His enthusiasm about McCarthy's campaign was obvious. The conversation went on for quite awhile, and in the end Peter asked them how he could help. By the time we left, Peter had volunteered to do whatever he could for the campaign. I followed Peter's lead and volunteered too.

"We were at the headquarters quite often over the next several weeks. Peter was between scripts and series, so he was able to get very involved spreading the 'word' for McCarthy and for peace. I was the typical McCarthy volunteer, collating materials for mailings, putting college presentation packages together and making signs for peace rallies. We would be there for long hours some days, so we'd hop across the street to a Jewish deli for the best sandwiches (pastrami or Reubens) we'd ever had. The campaign outgrew that small office some time in March, when the McCarthy L.A. Headquarters moved to Westwood.

"After the move to Westwood, Peter and I spent less time together in our volunteer duties. Peter would turn up at political functions as a celebrity for McCarthy, having his picture taken and speaking conversationally with the guests.

During those months he began to get a few scripts for TV and then a movie, so he had less time to spare for the campaign. I continued to collate publicity materials and make signs, as well as make phone calls and canvas neighborhoods, until I was designated L.A. Regional Campus Coordinator. I drove around Los Angeles in Peter's Toyota Land Cruiser, which we had covered in McCarthy daisies. Driving from campus to campus, I helped coordinate events and scheduling for McCarthy's college appearances.

"When Peter received acting assignments I would take time off from the campaign to visit him on the set or on location. Peter would just give me cash to cover my expenses, which were minimal. We had talked about me getting a job, but Peter thought it would interfere with

Beth at McCarthy headquarters, Westwood, California, late March 1968 (photograph by Bernard Nagler, courtesy Beth Griswold).

his schedule and come between us somehow. That was fine with me because I loved being a 'full-time' McCarthy volunteer.

"I became active politically because I was with Peter. Up until the time I met Peter I had been sitting on the sidelines, a closet Democrat. My parents were adamant Republicans, my father especially. Peter's politics were one of the reasons they didn't like him. When I met Peter, my parents had been on vacation in Hawaii. They came home to find me dating an older man, an actor, *and* a Democrat — all good reasons, in their opinion, to disapprove of our relationship.

"During one of my visits home that spring, I brought Peter to meet my sister Lee's husband, who had just returned from duty in Vietnam. He was an Air Force pilot who had flown the big transport planes, C-130s (I think), during his tour of duty and had taken many photos of his friends and the countryside when he was there. He started a slide show after dinner. As my brother-in-law was describing each scene, Peter started making antiwar comments, calling the men baby-killers, etc., and the military sadistic terrorists. The more slides that went by the louder and more confrontational Peter became. My parents were appalled, and my father-in-law withdrew, having just personally experienced anti-war rage for the first time since coming home. Peter and I left my parents' house, and he returned only once after that. Politics were never brought up as a subject of conversation in my parents' house again, and he'd wear sandals and cords and flowery shirts."

The counterculture attracted Deuel, like so many young people in 1960s America. Mind-altering hallucinogens created an interest in new ways of viewing 'reality,' and alternative religions and philosophies became the latest 'rage.' Writers such as Herman Hesse, Henry David Thoreau and Lewis Carroll became fashionable again. Eastern philosophies such as Yoga, I Ching and Buddhism, for centuries ignored by the West, were viewed in a new light borne out of the drug experience, whilst traditional church-based Christianity was seen as being out of touch with the needs of the young. The youth were increasingly disillusioned with, and alienated from, their own culture.

A "pop" culture was emerging in America and Britain, geared to the exclusive interests of a consumer-driven youth culture, and based in drug-influenced music and a communal hippie lifestyle. The drug scene in America centered on San Francisco, more particularly the Haight-Ashbury district, and the "Californian Sound" was captured in the music of groups such as the Beach Boys and Jefferson Airplane.

The political New Left movement had evolved out of the Beat Generation of the 1950s. The Beat Generation's origins remain a matter of debate, with popular opinion favoring the publication of Jack Kerouac's novel *On the Road* in 1957 as giving birth to the movement. Others, however, have laid claim to its origins, among them Kerouac's one-time friend John Clellon Holmes in his 1952 jazz novel *Go*, originally titled *The Beat Generation*, and inspired in part by Kerouac's first novel, *The Town and the City*, published in 1950. Kerouac claimed that he first heard the term "Beat" in the late forties, being used by Times Square hustler Herbert Huncke, who referred to the term in relation to a state of exalted exhaustion. Kerouac, influenced by his Jesuit upbringing, saw in this a connection to the beatific vision enjoyed by saints, and often hinted that the term was closely related to a Catholic-Buddhist search for truth.

The philosophy of the Beat Generation was one of restlessness. Movement was paramount. Their biggest fear was entrapment. Freedom to move, not only through landscape but also through relationships and cultural styles, was an attractive philosophy for youngsters who felt trapped by their parents' conformist, consumer-led post-war lifestyle.

By 1958 the movement had been hijacked by the very society it was condemning. The "beatnik," the collective term for the Beat Generation coined by *San Francisco Chronicle* columnist Herb Caen, and inspired by the recent launch of the Russian Sputnik-1 space satellite, had been sanitized following its immersion into popular culture.

Kerouac hated the idea of the "beatnik," who, in his view, were nothing more than an offshoot of the "cool hipsters" of 1948, with their black clothes and surly laid-back manner. He saw himself, and the genuine Beat, as the "hot hipsters," characterized by their energy and love of new forms of experience. Ironically, the man responsible for starting the movement that would, in part, inspire the 1960s New Left radicals was dismayed by their politics, which he saw as a Communist plot to infiltrate and ultimately take over America.

Consisting primarily of white youngsters under the age of thirty from affluent middle-class backgrounds, the New Left actively stood against social and racial injustice, the Vietnam War, the "affluent" society, the Great Society (a term made popular by Lyndon B. Johnson), Puritan morality and rampant technology. Critics noted that Puritan morality was replaced by a "free sex" ethic that would lead to an average half-million illegal abortions a year by the mid–1960s.

Minnesota Democrat Eugene McCarthy had announced his anti-war Presidential campaign on 30 November, 1967, and was attracting support from the various youth movements. His strong showing against Lyndon Johnson in the 12 March New Hampshire

Primary, in which he received 42.2 percent of the vote, prompted Deuel's entry into political activism and his vigorous support of Senator McCarthy in the 1968 primaries.

"Peter was prompted to political activism when McCarthy announced his candidacy in November 1967, and volunteered shortly after the Los Angeles McCarthy headquarters opened in January 1968," declared Beth.

McCarthy, a native of Watkins, Minnesota, and ex-college professor, gained his master's degree from the University of Minnesota and studied for a time at a Catholic monastery. Election to the House of Representatives in 1948 was followed a decade later by his election to the Senate. His strong Christian beliefs were a factor in the anti-war stance he took regarding Vietnam.

Deuel described McCarthy as the "philosopher-king" he wanted for President, and someone with "the vision and awareness of a philosopher, plus political acumen." Deuel's comments echoed a speech by Senator McCarthy delivered on 9 May, 1965, in which he said, "Some forty years ago G.K. Chesterton wrote that every time the world was in trouble the demand went up for a practical man ... usually what was needed to deal with an impractical muddle was a theorist or philosopher."

The late 1960s was a flourishing period for the idealist in an increasingly fragmented society where the individual sought meaning in groups that attempted to alleviate their feeling of alienation. A growing sense of alienation resulted in race riots in Deuel's birthplace of Rochester, New York, in 1964. Violence followed the arrest of a drunken man at a block party on the evening of 24 July. Rioting and looting threatened to spread to surrounding areas and was eventually brought under control, after three days, by the New York National Guard. Four deaths and approximately 1,000 arrests resulted. National Guard troops remained in the city until 3 August, and the state of emergency was finally lifted on 10 August.

Pamela Deuel recalled, "We were all quite surprised by the Rochester race riots. The burning in the streets and the violence was scary. I was living in Berea, Ohio, at the time, but I was a little concerned for my mother and father. Fortunately we were far enough away from Rochester in Penfield, but we didn't know how the riots might have escalated."

High-profile celebrities actively supporting McCarthy included Paul Newman, Joanne Woodward, Barbra Streisand, Walter Matthau, Myrna Loy, Martin Landau and Carl Reiner. Their presence at the discotheque–night club Eugene's, formed by McCarthy supporters, rallied support for the campaign.

Actress Leslie Parrish had starred in the classic political thriller *The Manchurian Candidate* (1962), alongside Frank Sinatra. An active campaigner for McCarthy, Leslie first met Peter Deuel shortly following the New Hampshire primaries.

"Peter and I were political acquaintances," related Parrish. "He joined us after we won in New Hampshire. I admired him. It wasn't easy being anti-war at that time. It could ruin your career. Peter didn't care and neither did I. We were out in the open. I was elected chairperson of McCarthy's Speaker's and Entertainment Committee."

"Peter was very serious about politics. He was just a darling man. I didn't know Peter's personal side. I knew his political side. All of us who got into the anti-war, civil rights movement knew each other's hearts very clearly. We didn't need to say how many times have you been married or where do you live. We knew all the important things about one another. Those of us in the political arena were very dear friends."

Leslie Parrish in *The Manchurian Candidate* (1962) (courtesy Leslie Parrish).

"My very first peace march was on June 20, 1967, in Century City. We just wanted to march past the hotel where Lyndon Johnson was staying. We had legal permits, and I felt very proud of being able to march as an American and to oppose the war peacefully. At a certain point the police stopped the march and waded into us with clubs. It was just a horrible scene. I was beaten up, and still suffer from the beating. These were terrible times. Something like that makes you very wary of your democracy and makes you wonder if you have a democracy.

"The police had been whipped into a frenzy by a mayor in Los Angeles saying, 'Commies will be marching in the streets.' So when the police saw us they just saw red. They where like a bunch of bulls with red flags and plowed into us. We were labeled as Commie sympathizers.

"I started out working at the headquarters on Fairfax. I got stuck with running the Speaker's Bureau because I knew a lot of actors. Five professors at U.C.L.A. promised to give us training and background on the war if I could get other actors together to make speeches. I wound up with 125 actors. Actors, writers, producers and artists used to meet in different places every weekend. I'd pick someone like Peter, who would be a draw at a party where they were trying to raise money. I had 200 calls a day and turned my home into a headquarters and had phones and offices all over the house. I paid for the whole thing myself, and every now and then I'd take an acting job to pay for more of it."

Phil Watson had a small storefront in North Long Beach from which he and his friends organized the putting out of bumper stickers and yard signs, as well as making numerous phone calls to determine support. It was on a visit to Westwood in the spring of 1968 that Phil Watson met Deuel.

"Those were times when you could feel the intensity of history in the making," recalled Watson. "We were there working for a man who we hoped would end the insanity of the Vietnam War. During the week before the California Primary we went up to Westwood to help organize some door knocking to get out the vote. Pete Deuel was there. At the time I didn't know who he was, but he said he was an actor, just as if it were any other kind of profession.

"He was charismatic for sure, but what I remembered most was how intensely he cared about what we were trying to do to change the direction of our country. He was really wired, and his energy was a little manic. At the end of the evening out in the parking lot after almost all the other volunteers had left, Pete talked with us for a good hour until midnight. He was just a regular good guy as far as I was concerned.

"Peter Deuel was absolutely sincere and didn't give off that air of being all things to all people that politicians and many public figures give off. The leadership style that he exuded was 'Here's where we are going and it's important.' He made us feel that we were all making an important contribution and didn't put himself above anyone. But he was a bit grandiose about the historic significance of the campaign, and there was some desperation — as if we were facing the awesome forces of darkness with pop guns. And he filled an empty space with his outspoken thoughts."

Deuel followed work campaigning in California in mid–March with a visit to McCarthy headquarters in Rochester for the primary on 18 June, 1968. The planned June wedding to Beth Griswold was called off. Their involvement in the campaign left no time for marriage. That could wait until the fall. But the relative safety of stuffing envelopes, handing out leaflets, speaking at shopping malls in Rochester and canvassing college campuses in California soon turned to violence for Deuel when the campaign trail took him to Chicago.

The National Mobilization Committee to End the War in Vietnam (MOBE) had decided to organize a massive peaceful demonstration in Chicago to coincide with the Democratic National Convention, which was due to take place during the week of August 28. However, the tumultuous events earlier in the year had set the tone for violent confrontation.

The "Tet" offensive, led by the Viet Cong and aided by North Vietnamese regulars, took place on January 30 and involved U.S. troops in bloody battles for control of their bases at Da Nang and Khe Sanh, the city of Hue and the grounds of the U.S. embassy in Saigon.

"I think we were all filled with such terrible pain as a result of the Vietnam War," commented Leslie Parrish. "It was such a horrible thing to be doing to some poor little nation that didn't want to do anything except vote. All they wanted to do was have a democracy like we did, only they called it Communism. Ho Chi Minh's Declaration of Independence was word for word taken from ours. So it was horribly, horribly sad to be committing this atrocity. And we all had difficult, impossible times with it. I know for myself I decided I wouldn't go to the beach again until the Vietnamese could go to the beach without getting killed. We were all throwing our careers aside, basically, and devoting ourselves to that."

Regardless of the fact that American troops kept control of their bases, with heavier losses on the Viet Cong side, President Johnson was beginning to realize that the situation was heading toward a stalemate. On March 31 he announced a suspension of the bombing and his decision not to seek reelection. Within days of Johnson's announcement, and Vice President Hubert H. Humphrey's decision to stand, Dr. Martin Luther King Jr. was assassinated on April 4 in Memphis, Tennessee, by James Earl Ray, a Southern white.

Riots followed in Chicago, and Mayor Richard Daley ordered police to break up peace marchers with unnecessary brutal force on April 27. Then on June 6, anti-war spokesperson Senator Robert F. Kennedy was assassinated in a Los Angeles hotel by lone gunman and Palestinian immigrant Sirhan Sirhan, who claimed he killed Kennedy because he resented his pro–Israeli stance. Kennedy had entered the Presidential race in New Hampshire and had won everywhere except in Oregon. Prior to Kennedy's death, a TV debate between Kennedy and McCarthy was held in San Francisco. In a poll taken by the *Los Angeles Times*, Kennedy was shown to have won the debate by a two-to-one margin. McCarthy supporters often bitterly opposed Kennedy's proposals, and he was seen as lacking the ethical purity of McCarthy.

Phil Watson recalls, "Eugene McCarthy had illuminated the shift in public opinion against the war for all to see. Bobby Kennedy had also broken with the party establishment, but was more disingenuously moving to capitalize on the anti-war sentiment without being as overt about it."

Beth Griswold was aware of mixed feelings at the news of Robert Kennedy's death. "The McCarthy volunteers at headquarters that night were in shock," she said. "McCarthy had just lost the California Primary, and the man who defeated him was shot while we watched on TV. The horror of the shooting had not really sunk in before people started talking about it meaning that McCarthy still had a chance.

"There was a crazy, sickening feeling among us that night. Over the next few days it seemed many were into the conspiracy theories. What government agency was responsible for this? Who was really behind it?

"While we were all shocked and deeply saddened by Kennedy's death, many of us were still very angry about his campaign practices. There had been some serious campaign spying going on that spring. There was one man hired by the McCarthy's national headquarters who got way up in McCarthy's Los Angeles organization. The rumor was that he turned out to be a Kennedy man from the start and had provided the Kennedy team with information on all McCarthy's campaign strategies and planning. He had also been instrumental in creating the strategy to convert McCarthy volunteers to Kennedy volunteers.

"There were still a lot of people angry about the fact that Kennedy had sat in the Senate and not come out against the war until McCarthy had tested the water. We were at McCarthy Headquarters watching the election results on TV, wishing we were the ones celebrating and deeply upset that McCarthy had lost the California primary to Kennedy. Most of us were horrified by Kennedy's assassination, but at the same time we were speculating that now McCarthy would have the votes of the California delegation and therefore the nomination as the Democratic candidate for President. Sadly, that did not happen. Instead, Kennedy's death affected us even more devastatingly, thrusting the Democratic Party into turmoil, widening the chasm between the pro-peace and pro-war Democrats, and ensuring the Republicans a better chance of winning in November."

Robert Kennedy's death placed fellow candidate Hubert Humphrey in a strong position, much to the chagrin of the anti-war movement, who considered him nothing more than Lyndon Johnson's lapdog.

The involvement of other protest groups in Chicago increased the already mounting tension. The Youth International Party (YIP) — Yippies announced a "Festival of Life" to coincide with the Democratic Convention. Founded in February of that year by Jerry Rubin, Abbie Hoffman, Ed Sanders and Paul Krassner, the Yippies combined the "lifestyle" of the hippies with "revolutionary" political tactics. "Allying" themselves with militants of Students for a Democratic Society and Senator George McGovern, they set the tone for conflict in Chicago by arriving in Lincoln Park on Friday, August 23, with a hog called *Pigasus* who, atop a platform of garbage, was declared their first choice for President.

Refusing to move from their spot in the park, they were finally expelled by the police without resort to undue violence. However, the night of the 24th saw the police resorting to tear gas in an attempt to clear Lincoln Park of demonstrators, who in turn hurled stones at the police. This was to be the first night of what was to be ever-increasing violent confrontation.

Police tactics were proving to be at odds with the official policy reported in the *Chicago Daily News* that same month:

> Don't hesitate to walk on the grass or to spread your coat and take a nap. Chicago likes its parks to be used by people so you won't see any "Keep Off the Grass." And you can feel safe in the park. It is well-patrolled by policemen, and many Chicagoans sleep there on hot nights.

"I was at the '68 convention as a McCarthy delegate," declared Leslie Parrish. "Because McCarthy didn't have a chance, I worked a lot with people in the streets. Not as part of the riots but taking people to the riots and showing them that kids were standing there and getting beaten up, having done nothing. I turned quite a few very rich, very staid political businessmen into very radical thinkers as a result of showing them the truth.

"At one point we chartered a 747 jet plane, the group was so large. I was part of the California delegation going to the Chicago convention. Peter traveled separately because he wasn't a delegate. It turned into an absolutely huge movement."

The escalation of tension reached a climax on the evening of August 28. The afternoon rally by MOBE at the Grant Park band shell received a poor turnout. Only 10,000 out of an estimated 100,000 demonstrators turned up. Early evening saw groups of demonstrators marching toward the central downtown area and the convention hall. The National Guardsmen had tried their best to block their exit from Grant Park, utilizing a barricade of barbed wire–covered jeeps. Despite being bombarded with clouds of tear gas, the demonstrators eventually reached the Hilton hotel headquarters.

Finding themselves denied access to the hall, MOBE demonstrators joined up with protesters from the mule-drawn Ralph Abernathy's Poor People's Caravan, who had a permit to march to the headquarters of the convention delegates. Chants of "The whole world is watching. The whole world is watching" were brutally silenced by yet another onslaught of choking tear gas. Suddenly, lines of sky blue–helmeted police charged the partially blinded, suffocating demonstrators, swinging their clubs and rifles, and spraying mace indiscriminately. The large plate-glass window of the Hilton Haymarket Restaurant gave way under the increased pressure of the retreating demonstrators and bystanders. Still the police continued with their orgy of violence as the people lay bleeding among the razor-sharp slivers of glass.

"National Guardsmen were pointing bayonets at us, and I saw a helicopter flying over our heads with machine guns pointed at us," described Leslie. "That was our government pointing those machine guns. We lived through a very strange experience which most Americans don't know about or aren't aware of. It changed us dramatically."

"Peter was in the Conrad Hilton hotel looking down on the confrontation and watching everything unfold before he went downstairs and joined in," recalled Beth. "When Peter came back from Chicago he told me horror stories of what the cops had done to the demonstrators and what some of the demonstrators had done in an attempt at retaliation."

At four o'clock in the morning on August 30 police stormed into the McCarthy headquarters located on the fifteenth floor of the Conrad Hilton and proceeded to beat up McCarthy's young workers. The reasoning for the raid was a report by the National Guard of objects being thrown at them from a window on the fifteenth floor. When confronted by reporters Paul Saan and Judy Michaelson about the incident, Senator McCarthy replied he would "have to consult with the police and get their version" of events. McCarthy approached the police and told them, "You can't just come up here and knock heads."

McCarthy had advised his followers not to come to Chicago, and had anticipated the violence that might occur, in an interview for the *Chicago Tribune* on 13 August, 1968:

> The pressure of large numbers of visitors ... may well add to the possibility of unintended violence or disorder. This would be a ... personal tragedy for anyone hurt or arrested, and a tragedy for those of us who wish to give the political process a fair and decent test.

Infiltration by government supporters was a major problem for protesting groups.

"In the beginning we didn't understand," explained Leslie. "We'd be planning a peaceful march or a demonstration and arranging to get permits. And some idiot would pop up and say, 'Let's get a bunch of skunks and release them in the room,' or, 'Let's get some snakes and let them go.' And I'd say, 'What, are you crazy? What a terrible idea. Just shut up.' We were infiltrated by all sorts of people who made weird suggestions, who made things disappear at critical times and who made little secret of the fact they were photographing us. It was difficult, when in the midst of the frenzy of the time, to say with certainty that this government agency or that one did it. Most of the problems became clear in hindsight.

"After the first time or two I was very aware we were infiltrated. I could tell that the person who stood up with the worst ideas was the government and they were trying to set us up. I would confront them with that and everyone would howl that I was being unfair. I had basically stopped working as an actress for the most part and did nothing but this stuff, so I was very aware. I could spot an infiltrator. They would just pop up in bushes and take my picture all the time. I knew it wasn't the paparazzi."

Beth Griswold, echoing the experiences of Leslie Parrish, commented, "I remember bomb threats that came in over the phone while I was directing calls on the headquarters PBX. The place was rampant with rumors — the FBI, the CIA, and others had all infiltrated McCarthy headquarters during the campaign. The rather straight-looking 'angry hippies' who would grab the spotlight at the rallies were really FBI or CIA agents assigned to cause trouble, grab the headlines with disruption and give the peaceful demonstrators a bad name. We were all sure that these same 'angry hippies' were also present in Chicago and were the cause of much of the 'violent behavior' blamed on McCarthy supporters. The idealism with which the volunteers entered the campaign had disappeared altogether by the time the convention was over. I had been a Youth for McCarthy volunteer, one of the many that worked for him but would never get the chance to vote for him."

Many of the McCarthy supporters had gathered around the band shell in Grant Park. Various speakers, including David Dellinger, Jerry Rubin and Tom Hayden, were present. Police surrounded the band shell on three sides. Some of the demonstrators became violent when police arrested and began to beat a teenager for taking down the U.S. flag from a flagpole. Further trouble ensued when a red t-shirt replaced the U.S. flag on the flagpole. Demonstrators and police exchanged blows in escalating violence. Tom Hayden, David Dellinger and Tom Neuman urged demonstrators to move out of the park and disperse. A series of bridges had to be crossed in order for demonstrators to make their way to the Hilton hotel, the Amphitheater or the Loop. As demonstrators headed for the Balbo bridge, eighteen National Guardsmen waited for them. Bayonets, rifle butts, tear gas, grenade launchers and .30 caliber machine guns were used as deterrents.

Eyewitness accounts of the violence stressed the insensitive and brutal tactics of the Chicago police, as they described scenes of police beating demonstrators with their clubs and spraying chemicals into their faces to disable them.

Extracts from the *Walker Report to the National Commission on the Causes and Prevention of Violence* made for harrowing reading:

> A priest who was in the crowd says he saw a "boy," about fourteen or fifteen, white, standing on top of an automobile yelling something which was unidentifiable. Suddenly a policeman pulled him down from the car and beat him to the ground by striking him three or four times with a nightstick. Other police joined in ... and they eventually shoved him into a police van.
>
> A well-dressed woman saw this incident and spoke angrily to a nearby police captain. As she spoke, another policeman came up from behind her and sprayed something into her face with an aerosol can. He then clubbed her to the ground. He and two other policeman then dragged her along the ground to the same paddy wagon and threw her in.

A study prepared by Professor Jerome Skolnik, head of the task force on "Violent Aspects of Protest and Confrontation," titled *The Politics of Protest*, (1969) concluded, "Nearly all violence that has occurred in mass demonstrations has resulted not from the demonstrators' conscious choice of tactics, but from the measures chosen by public authorities to disperse and punish them."

Mayor Daley, defending the police tactics, stated that the police weren't there to create disorder but "to preserve disorder." However, *Los Angeles Times* reporter Robert J. Donovan described the behavior of the Chicago police as "a prescription for fascism."

It came as no great surprise when Humphrey won the nomination on the first ballot. The backing of party leaders, including Chicago Mayor Richard Daley, helped him fight off the challenge of McCarthy and George McGovern with relative ease: 1,760.5 votes to McCarthy's 501. But the events of Chicago would ultimately spell defeat for the Democratic Party, and Humphrey's call for "a politics of happiness" would sound naive and insulting in a time of conflict for his country. Humphrey's contradictory words regarding the events in Chicago didn't help his cause. In his acceptance speech Humphrey remarked, "We have now learned the lesson that violence breeds counter-violence, and it cannot be condoned, whatever the sources."

Yet one week later he would say the riots had been "planned and premeditated," and to "quit pretending that Mayor Daley did something that was wrong."

"We were not thrilled with Hubert Humphrey. He had supported Johnson and had supported the war," commented Leslie Parrish. "We thought, we got rid of Johnson and now we have this guy. He's the same as Johnson. I couldn't even vote for him. There wasn't much about Chicago that was funny except the night that Hubert Humphrey was doing his acceptance speeches. I was in a room full of McCarthy delegates and McGovern people, and most of them were hanging out the windows with their rear ends turned toward the TV screens. Poor Humphrey was making his speech and we weren't listening or watching, with a bunch of bums turned towards us."

The McCarthy campaign had been doomed to failure almost from the start. Democratic convention delegates were selected approximately two years previous to the convention and would therefore have been pledged to Lyndon Johnson's ticket and platform.

Richard Nixon reflected this political truth when he was asked who would succeed Lyndon Johnson in 1968.

"We must assume that someone within the Democratic Party who represents the Johnson viewpoint will be the candidate," replied Nixon.

The protest movement that faithfully followed McCarthy with evangelical zeal was fighting within a closed system. Hubert Humphrey was a certain winner, following Robert Kennedy's assassination. Eugene McCarthy expressed his lack of support for Hubert Humphrey as Democratic Presidential candidate following the nomination.

The New Left had never won the general support of the American public, who were suspicious of its anti-government stance and support of Communist forces in Vietnam. When certain movements within the New Left adopted a more radical aggressive agenda, the support of the general populace collapsed. Liberal arms of the New Left turned to environmental, women's and consumer protection movements.

Deuel's first-hand experience of a riot-torn Chicago and the defeat of Eugene McCarthy resulted in his retreat from the party political scene to turn his attention to the increasingly persuasive ecology movement.

"It took guts to be in that movement, and that's why those of us who were in there loved each other so much. We formed a bond," described Leslie Parrish. "I think politicians don't realize the extent to which we cared. I imagine Peter went off by himself with his depression because I never saw it. He wasn't a person who joked a lot. I don't think any of us did. Our conversations consisted of politics and the movement and what would we do next. It wasn't funny stuff. We all had a certain amount of depression. We were determined more than depressed.

"Had McCarthy won, Peter would probably have gotten into politics on a deeper level. McCarthy was a really phenomenally brilliant man and extraordinarily well educated. I'm not sure McCarthy would have been a good administrator. I think he would have been a good visionary who would have had the big picture and would have handed off the rest to somebody else. He could certainly see right from wrong.

"The last time I saw Peter was at a small dinner with Senator McCarthy at Donna Reed's house. Peter gave quite an enormous amount of money that night. He was very, very serious about politics. He was just a darling man and adorable."

Frank Price recalled the attitude of studios toward the anti-war movement and his own political preferences at the time.

"Most television directors, writers and executives are, and were, liberals," observed Price. "Actors like Martin Sheen, Ed Asner and Mike Farrell come to mind. They worked regularly around town. Jane Fonda became a big star during that period. Hollywood was not a 'pro-war' place. Quite the opposite.

"The Hollywood of the 1960s and 1970s wasn't the Hollywood of the 1940s and 1950s. Television had destroyed the motion picture studios as they had once been, and the old guard–types like Mayer and Cohen were all gone.

"Roy Huggins was a strong Gene McCarthy supporter. I, on the other hand, was a strong supporter of Bobby Kennedy. Roy argued with me that Kennedy was the most dangerous man in America. He believed it. His argument became moot when Bobby was shot. I became a Humphrey supporter. The fanatics on the left would not support him. I pointed out to them that the alternative was Nixon. One of them, a good friend, told me that it would serve the country right if Nixon got elected. He got his wish. Humphrey lost very narrowly. The hard left did him in."

Beth Griswold, reflecting on McCarthy's defeat, commented, "In retrospect we realized McCarthy was too intellectual, too gentle a man to get elected President. He was a poet and a philosopher, characteristics Peter thought so highly of."

Deuel's relationship with Beth Griswold began to fall apart after the violent events in Chicago.

"Things were never quite the same with Peter after Chicago. He came back from Chicago almost 'shell-shocked' and distant," described Beth Griswold.

"Disillusioned, incredibly angry and frustrated, after all that work and emotion poured out towards such a good cause; not only for McCarthy but for the end of the war — and then to have Nixon headed for the White House.

"Some of the spark and some of the fight had been kicked out of Peter, and in many ways he gave up. Heck, we all did. Chicago may have marked the beginning of Peter's

(Left to right) Beth, Peter, and Beth's sister Mary celebrate Beth's birthday at her parents' house, early September 1968 (courtesy Beth Griswold).

depression. There were more times that fall when he seemed withdrawn and distant. We were 'slipping away' from each other, and, not understanding why, I was overwhelmed with all those emotions.

"We had postponed our wedding plans twice and were not even talking about it anymore. In early September I went home for a visit to celebrate my birthday with my family. My parents recognized my fragile emotional state, and my mother encouraged my dad to take me out to dinner for one of those father-daughter talks. He took me to my favorite restaurant. After dinner, my father asked me to look closely at my relationship with Peter and whether or not I thought it had any future. He interpreted Peter's disrespect for him and my mom as disregard for me. Dad surmised that if Peter really loved me and was committed to our future together we would have made new plans to be married. He encouraged me to step back to see if Peter would step up. Peter came to my parents' house for the last time on my 21st birthday. He bought me a deluxe Singer sewing machine. He knew I loved to sew, but it seemed like such a practical gift, more suitable for a wife than a girlfriend. My parents, even though they were discouraged about the future of my relationship with Peter, gave me a place setting from the china Peter and I had selected for our wedding.

"Looking back, it had been strained and uncomfortable during most of the visits with my parents that year. If Peter was with me, we hardly talked. If I was alone, they spent their time trying to talk me out of the relationship. My grandmother was a very uptight Victorian woman, born and raised in San Francisco. In her mind her namesake granddaughter should not be seen with some 'dirty hippie actor.' Peter was not rude to her or anything. She just couldn't stand his appearance or his profession. She and my parents were straitlaced Goldwater Republicans and knew it was these 'dirty hippies' that were ruining the country. So Peter never had a chance in her view.

Peter's birthday gift of a Singer sewing machine, early September 1968. Bottom left to bottom right are Beth's sister Anne, her friend Zemmie, Peter, Beth, and Beth's father Bob Griswold (courtesy Beth Griswold).

Plus, as far as she was concerned, I was living in sin and my parents were not doing anything about it, so she disinherited me. (She rescinded the disinheritance after I broke up with him.)

"I went back to L.A. with Peter, hoping to reignite our relationship. We were both kind of in a daze without the focus of the McCarthy campaign. That month we had a photo shoot scheduled for an upcoming article in one of the Hollywood movie magazines. We spent the day with the photographer walking around the Fuller apartment neighborhood, taking mostly casual shots of the two of us together. It was a fun day filled with moments when it seemed we were back in sync with each other.

"During our relationship his drinking was never the problem because Peter had stopped. The problem turned out to be another woman. I was of the mood that 'engaged' meant a monogamous commitment to each other. I understood he was around women all the time who were very attracted to him. And Peter had quite an eye for the ladies, too. It didn't

Peter and Beth at Plummer Park, mid–September 1968 (photograph by Curt Gunther, courtesy Beth Griswold).

seem to bother him (as it did me) when we would be at a party together and women would walk up and step between us, even if we were arm in arm or holding hands."

Curt Gunther, famous for his photos of the Beatles, followed Deuel and Griswold around Plummer Park and other areas close to Fuller, photographing them for the proposed magazine article. The article and the photographs were never published. Although the photos were supposed to show a happy, soon-to-be-married couple, the reality of the increasingly tense relationship was evident in many of the photographs. Deuel was hiding a secret from Griswold that would eventually destroy the relationship — an affair with a woman he met during his campaigning in Chicago. While Deuel was posing for the camera he was continuing the affair by phone, unknown at the time by Griswold. In the meantime, Griswold decided to move back home to northern California in late September 1968.

"In October, a few weeks after I moved back up north, Peter's disclosure of being involved with another woman at the Chicago convention and their extended affair afterwards was what caused me to realize our relationship was in serious trouble. He had been with her the weekend before, the anniversary of our first date. I finally understood the feelings I had in late August of the relationship 'slipping away.' We broke off our engagement completely. Even then, in spite of the fact that I felt betrayed by Peter's infidelity, I still held on to the unrealistic hope that we could work it out.

"Towards the end of our relationship, after I had that talk with my father and decided to move home, Peter had nothing but disgust for my folks and let me know in no uncertain terms. It was hard trying to defend them to him, and defend him and my feelings to them. Between a rock and a hard

Beth and Peter at Plummer Park, mid–September 1968 (photograph by Curt Gunther, courtesy Beth Griswold).

place describes it well. That winter of 1968, my mom had another nervous breakdown. Late 1968 and early 1969 was a bleak time for me.

"We kept hanging on to what was left of our relationship, Peter occasionally coming up north for the weekend and me flying south for Thanksgiving with his friends. We spoke on the phone a few more times, around Christmas and New Years. The last time I spoke with him was in February of 1969, around his birthday. He let me know he was sending the contact sheets of the photographs of us from September for me to keep. They arrived in March.

"That last evening on the phone I remember I couldn't reach him emotionally. I couldn't connect with him anymore. I remember him staying on the line with me when I began to cry — I tried, but I couldn't hold back the tears — but he was very calm, almost cold, and very distant. It was done, it was the end,

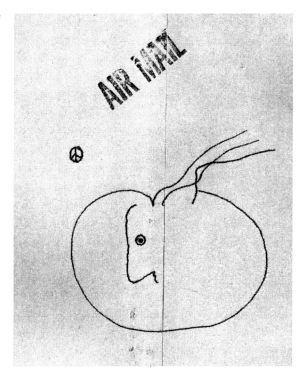

Peter Deuel artwork on envelope addressed to Beth Griswold, March 1969 (courtesy Beth Griswold).

and I knew once we hung up the phone we would probably never speak to each other again. I don't remember anything he said to me or even saying goodbye and hanging up the phone. He had moved on, and I was inconsolable.

"I cried for several hours after we hung up that last time. That was it. As painful as it was to look at those photographs, I'm surprised I kept them. But then sometimes I could look at them and just remember the laughter and the love.

"I remember hearing about Peter and Kim Darby sometime in early 1969. A friend of mine brought me a 'movie' magazine with some pictures of the two of them together. It was quite crushing. The pictures and comments of them together made it crystal clear that Peter was out of my life forever.

"It wasn't until years later that I came to understand what was happening to both of us towards the end of our relationship. We had been so 'into' each other in the beginning. I was so impressed with his free and exuberant self-expression. He was equally with my unaffected, grounded steadiness. ... a 'down to earth' kind of girl, he would call me. Near the end, I would shudder with embarrassment at some of his public displays and wince at his criticism of me. He would blast my unwillingness to be more expressive, more flamboyant and 'out there'— this 'down to earth' girl was now 'stuck in the mud.' In the end, we were repelled by the very qualities that attracted us to each other in the first place.

"My time with Peter was intensely emotional. When I look back on it now I realize what an incredible experience I had with such a marvelously unique individual. I only wish it had lasted longer and hadn't ended so sadly."

★ 6 ★

FORWARD MOTION

"A man cannot be comfortable without his own approval."

— Mark Twain

Following the violent events in Chicago, Deuel attended the wedding of close friend C. Davey Utter in Toluca Lake, California, together with brother Geoffrey, Donald Fanning, David McHugh and Jack Jobes.

"Pete came to my wedding dressed as a California Highway Patrolman," remembered Utter. "He upstaged the bride and walked around handing out joints. He loved to be the center of attention."

Deuel's next film project was *How to Steal an Airplane* (1968). Filmed on location in Lancaster, California, near Edwards Air Force Base in November 1968, the mediocre TV movie can have done little to lift his spirits. A pilot for a series that failed to sell, the story concerning the son of a banana republic dictator and the attempted repossession of a Lear Jet lacked depth and characterization. Peter Deuel and English co-star Clinton Greyn played Sam Rollins and Evan Brice in one-dimensional tones. The addition of French starlet Claudine Longet singing "Sadness of a Happy Time" did little to lift the boredom.

"The movie was filmed, in part, out in Death Valley towards Joshua Tree," recalled Beth Griswold. "I remember driving out to the set in the Toyota Land Cruiser in the heat. I was out on location while Peter was filming. Peter loved to play practical jokes, and he set up Sal Mineo on a date with me disguised as somebody else. He knew what he could do to rile Sal.

"He wasn't happy with the movie and he was frustrated with his part. He wanted some better parts. He was under contract to Universal, and he found it restrictive in that it dictated who he could work with and what he could look at."

Producer Jo Swerling, Jr., recalled, "The most memorable event which took place during production was the unplanned crash landing of the Lear Jet. The good news was that no one was hurt and we had completed all scenes using the jet. The bad news was that the plane was a total loss and the pilot had his license suspended. The insurance settlement was as large as the entire budget for the show."

Network executives shelved the TV movie until December 1971, hoping to salvage their efforts when Deuel was gaining a large following as outlaw Hannibal Heyes on *Alias Smith and Jones*. The TV movie was largely ignored by critics. Those that did bother to watch were scathing in their criticism.

82

Left to right: Geoffrey Deuel, Peter Deuel, C. Davey Utter and David McHugh, Toluca Lake, California, 1968 (photograph by Phillip Dixon, courtesy C. Davey Utter).

Left to right: Peter Deuel, C. Davey Utter, Donald Fanning and Jack Jobes (photograph by Phillip Dixon, courtesy C. Davey Utter).

The TV critic for *Daily Variety*, 14 December, 1971, wrote:

The film is on a cartoon level, peopled with pasteboard characters. Duel strives to rise above the silliness, but it's beyond hope.

Deuel hoped for better things with his next project. *Generation*, originally a Broadway play starring Henry Fonda, was adapted for the big screen by original writer William Goodhart. Duel played Walter Owen, an idealistic young man who marries Doris Bolton (Kim Darby) in her ninth month of pregnancy. Their one overriding wish is to deliver their baby at home. However, home consists of a cheap loft, and Doris' father (David Janssen) is firmly against the idea.

Kim Darby, born and raised in Hollywood, California, as Deborah Zerby, came to prominence playing opposite John Wayne in *True Grit* (1969).

"Producer Hal Wallis saw me on the Roy Huggins show, *Run for Your Life*," said Kim. "That's when he pinpointed me and thought I was the only one who could play the role on *True Grit*. He visited my home and told me he'd only ever been to an actor's home once before to ask them to do a role. And that was Richard Burton. So I felt in esteemed company.

Claudine Longet, Jo Swerling, Jr., and Peter Deuel in *How to Steal an Airplane* (courtesy Jo Swerling, Jr.).

"My room was lit with candles during our meeting. Hal's associates asked him how the meeting went. He said he thought it went well and that I'd accept the offer. Then they asked, 'Well, what did she look like?' Hal replied, 'Hell if I know. I couldn't even see her.'

"I initially turned *True Grit* down. I was in a deep depression because my grandfather had died. He was my best friend and I had just had my baby and was going through my divorce. My focus wasn't there and I had a pelvic thrombosis after I delivered my daughter. I stayed in the hospital and my daughter Heather went home before me. All of a sudden I was off to Colorado and I had all this baby fat on me.

"In the beginning of the movie I was chubby, but at the end I was very slight. The fat was just falling off of me. I loathed myself in *True Grit* and I can't stand the film. I was completely unfocused. I did feel ashamed of the fact I didn't get to know John Wayne better. I wish I had taken the time to spend more time with him."

Deuel and Darby initially met at Kim's Coldwater Canyon home. However, unknown to Deuel, she had been watching him from afar.

"I moved away from home when I was 18 and I had a tree house–type apartment in

West Hollywood on Hacienda Drive," recalled Kim. "Peter happened to be seeing the woman next door, Jill Andre. I was never introduced to him and didn't speak with Jill. I would see him come and go. He was very intense and, I felt, unapproachable. Peter was splendid looking and always gave me the impression he had a mission as he drove off very quickly after each visit.

"I called Peter to meet up with him at my home before we went into rehearsals on *Generation.* He had no idea I had been admiring him from a distance and didn't recognize me as the girl who used to live next door to Jill Andre. At that first meeting Peter was sitting on one end of the couch and I on the other. I found him to be very withdrawn with a real edge to him. Quite intimidating. We started to talk and I felt very, very nervous. It was so intense.

"He had a wedding band on and told me he had been in an engagement that broke up. He looked very sad and felt very bad about the break-up. He told me that Beth had said to him, 'Why can't you just be nice to me?'

"I knew that he was politically inclined and very bright. He made it obvious he didn't respect the way I lived because I drove a Mercedes, lived in Beverly Hills and had a nanny. He called me a 'Capitalist' and was quite blunt. My insecurities were just the feelings I got from him on that first meeting.

"Kim's house was a beautiful, charming home," described Pamela Deuel. "Kim was always quite fragile, and she would need the help of a maid, especially when she had a child. Peter objected to that, but he also loved what it could do for you. So I think he was tremendously conflicted and almost scared of falling into that materialistic trap."

Kim commented, "There may have been an element of 'I'll show you I'm a true artist and a dedicated, committed person' in Peter's spartan lifestyle. I think he may have used it to say, 'I'm authentic. You're not.' It was an immature view in retrospect, but at the time he thought it had to be that way for him to be artistic."

Director George Schaefer had high hopes for Deuel, saying he "...expects the picture will establish Deuel as the brightest young male star since Dustin Hoffman in *The Graduate.*" Schaefer had been working exclusively in television since 1951, directing and producing episodes for the dramatic anthology series *Hallmark Hall of Fame*, for which he won two Emmy awards in 1965 and 1967. In 1969 Schaefer directed his first theatrical release, *Pendulum*, starring George Peppard and Jean Seberg, followed by *Generation* (1969).

"I didn't audition for *Generation*," said Darby. "I met George Schaefer, Freddy Brisson and his wife Rosalind Russell in the Polo Lounge at the Beverly Hills hotel. It was just to say hello and to welcome me on board. The word off *True Grit* was very good and they never thought of auditioning me. Peter was up against Michael Anderson Jr. They went with Peter because he was considered more mature for the role.

"We went into rehearsals and read for two weeks. One week around a table and one week blocking scenes. It wasn't too far into rehearsals that our connection began. George told me to pay attention at one point. Nobody had ever told me to do that before. I guess I was distracted with Peter. George had originally instructed me I had to fall in love with Peter for the role and had an idea I was in love with Peter already. We were mutually attracted at the same time."

Chasen's Restaurant provided the venue for a party to mark the start of filming. Kim was preparing to get dressed at her home when her daughter's nanny received a phone call.

"Peter just called. Do you know what he told me?" asked the nanny.

"What?" replied Kim.

"He told me to tell you that he loves you."

"I just sat down on the bed and started to cry because I didn't know how he could possibly love me," exclaimed Kim. "I didn't feel worthy of being loved by him. But it was a wonderful way to get the message. Only Peter would have done something like that. I was very happy and so excited. Then I saw Peter at the restaurant and it all just happened. We were holding hands and sitting close together all that evening."

Robert J. Koster, whose previous credits included *Valley of the Dolls* (1967) and *Pendulum* (1969), served as assistant director and production manager on the New York shooting, and second unit shooting in Denver, Colorado. "We filmed locations on *Generation* in downtown New York, near what was called Houston Street," he recalled. "There's an exceptionally poor area just off Houston called Attorney Street. We had the whole crew down there and took over a town house that was really a slum. It was an awful thing. Really decrepit.

"The director, George Schaefer, picked the location because it was run down and looked perfect for what he wanted. Schaefer wanted to have that kind of verisimilitude. We rented that building from the city of New York for a few pennies a day. The owner of the building abandoned it, as a matter of fact. The ground floor had a clubhouse in it where gangs gathered and played pool and planned to kill other gang members and stuff like that. It was pretty awful.

"I had hired a detective service, Burns, and explained what the situation was and that we needed help with the gangs and to keep the building safe while we were filming. So they sent over two armed guards. They sat in the room while the gang was meeting. I wanted to start putting set dressing in there so we could use the place.

"About 11 o'clock at night the detective service called me and said, 'Look, I hate to tell you this but the guards have run off into the night and there's nobody guarding the building anymore.' I said, 'Oh my God. Maybe I should call Pinkertons.' He said, 'You go ahead and do that, we own Pinkertons too.' So I called Pinkertons but they said they wouldn't touch it. But the guy who answered the phone at the detective service said, 'I'll tell you what. I'm an off-duty policeman, and a bunch of friends of mine and I specialize in this kind of work. If you want it guarded, let me know and we'll send somebody down there at 6 o'clock in the morning.'

"I met this guy the next morning who was 6'4" and ate cows for breakfast. He was a huge man physically, as were all the off-duty policemen. And there wasn't a gang member to be seen anyplace. These guys had scared them off. I hired them and kept them on while we were shooting down there.

"We did have one problem with David Janssen. He was in his trailer and didn't want to come out and sign autographs for some of the locals. They got angry and started to shake his trailer. They were rocking it back and forth, and Janssen thought they were going to tip it over. I went over to one of the hired men and they got their billy clubs out and cleared that trailer in about five seconds. The police have the Tactical Patrol Force, which deals with the movie industry, and they're supposed to help people. But they didn't do much to help us at that time.

"The slum quality of the apartment building was part of the script and therefore essential to the scenes filmed there," continued Koster, but the city of New York apparently had different plans for the building. "The city of New York didn't want the building to be shown in a bad light. So the day before we were supposed to start filming they sent a crew in there and painted it all in bright colors that made it look very new and upscale. It was just bloody awful. And I had to send a crew in that night so the next morning it looked run down again. They painted over the new colors in drab, run down colors. And they made it look pretty darned good for one night's painting."

Koster, commenting on working with Peter Deuel, said, "Peter was a lovely guy. A very nice man. He was there with Kim Darby. They were obviously very much in love. He was a thorough professional and very well prepared. He knew when he was supposed to be there and he knew his lines. Peter was always on time. We never had any problems with him at all, or with Kim. One of the marks of that picture was the fact we never had any trouble with anyone. I've worked with some really painful people in my life, but Peter, Kim, David Janssen and Carl Reiner were wonderful. And George Schaefer was a truly excellent director.

Peter Deuel and Kim Darby, 1969 (courtesy Kim Darby).

"Peter Deuel and the cast stayed uptown. We were downtown. I had teamsters who drove them down to the location. They had trailers on the set or close by. In those days we didn't yet have motor homes. George Schaefer was very protective of them and he would rehearse between the scenes with them. It was a very professional crew. We were down there for three or four days at that particular building. And then we had a warehouse and two or three other locations downtown and a couple of locations uptown. They were in town altogether for maybe two weeks. Pete and Kim worked together very well."

Kim Darby recalled, "We stayed very close to each other during the filming. You could tell there was a romance. I remember us being very affectionate and demonstrative. It was just like being on a vacation. The set was very sparse. It looked like something Peter would have had in real life. We finished shooting in New York toward the end of *Generation*. All the looping was done back in L.A. Altogether we worked for three or four months on *Generation*."

Deuel took time between filming in New York to look up former girlfriend Jill Andre.

"We had dinner one night," recalled Jill. "He wasn't quite sure about how this was all happening and why. He thought things were moving so fast and he didn't really deserve it."

The film received a mixed reaction from the critics. Wanda Hale from the *Daily News*, 16 December, 1969, commented:

> The young people, played by Kim Darby and Pete Duel, are good enough to make one believe these high-minded rebels against the System exist.

Nat Freeland of *Entertainment World*, 12 November, 1969, was less enthusiastic:

> Kim Darby and Pete Duel never have a chance as the most unbelievably squeaky-clean hippies extant. Among the story elements that never get explained is why Pete Duel won't let a physician deliver Kim's baby.

In contrast to Freeland's viewpoint, in the official Avco Embassy Exhibitors Showmanship Manual for the movie, director George Schaefer stated that the characters portrayed by Darby and Deuel "...are the opposite of hippies, and closer to the American pioneer in pursuit of their goals."

Bridget Byrne, writing for the *LA Herald Examiner*, 21 December, 1969, was generous in her appraisal of the film:

> *Generation* is an enjoyable movie.... Kim Darby, looking as usual too young to be allowed out alone, is sweet and sensible as Doris. Pete Duel, as Walter, brings a convincing idealism to his role which defeats some of its rather sissy qualities.

Hamilton B. Allen, reviewing the film for the *Rochester Times Union*, 5 February, 1970, saw promise in Deuel's performance:

> One would bet that Pete is headed for stardom if his showing here is a measure of his potential.

Avco Embassy promoted the movie in a variety of outlets, including department stores, furniture stores and automobile showrooms. Suggestions for advertising copy in their promotional literature included, "There is no generation gap in our full line of clothing for everyone. And there is no gap in the brilliantly funny comedy *A Time for Giving*— Now at the Rialto!"

Motown Records also released a 45 RPM single, "Generation," sung by The Rare Earth. Although the film didn't receive the strong reviews and ticket sales its producers had hoped for, Kim Darby was nominated for a Golden Globe as Best Motion Picture Actress in a Musical/Comedy.

Peter Deuel and Kim Darby in *Generation* (1969) (courtesy Kim Darby).

"I thought it was a very sweet movie," commented Kim. "I was glad that our characters were in love in the movie because I've often played so many heavy roles where I'm with the wrong man or the wrong boyfriend. It was a perfect time making that movie."

"Even though *Generation* was a good film and had some substance, Peter felt it wasn't promoted properly," declared Pamela Deuel.

David McHugh commented, "Peter had wanted to progress from television, but his movie work was a disaster. We sat in this theater on West 57th Street in New York. There must have been 12 people watching *Generation*. Peter got up and said, 'What a piece of shit.' That only fed into his lack of self-esteem."

Describing Deuel's criticism of his own work, Jack Jobes commented, "Peter liked to criticize his work to draw attention to himself."

Kim Darby had recently divorced actor James Stacy. Their marriage had lasted only seven months. Kim was understandably reticent about committing to another relationship, but her relationship with Deuel had intensified during their time together on *Generation*. They were both in love and became unofficially engaged.

"We never exchanged rings. It was just a verbal understanding," declared Kim.

Peter Deuel had taken the decision to simplify his name for the credits of *Generation*. In a letter to Frederick Brisson, George Schaefer and Charles Forsythe at Avco-Embassy/Warner Bros.-Seven Arts, Burbank, California, dated 26 May, 1969, he wrote:

Dear Sirs,

Please be advised that I wish the name used for my credit in "Generation" to be PETE DUEL, as changed from Peter Deuel. I have spoken to Mr. Forsythe over the phone informing him of same. I realize this comes quite suddenly, or appears to. Actually I have considered the change for a long time and have given it much thought. Cut Well!

Sincerely,

Peter Ellstrom Deuel

"His agent advised Peter to change his name," explained Pamela Deuel. "Peter said he refused to change it legally but would do it for the sake of his profession. I was disappointed when he went by Pete because I love the name Peter."

Kim Darby recalled, "He used to write his name all the time on pads of paper and wanted it to be more simple. I think he just wanted his name to be different. It was part of taking away the identity he started with. To have his own individuality. He kept writing out his new name when he was with me."

When Deuel's work took him to Spain in July 1969 for ten weeks to film the *Western Cannon for Cordoba*, Deuel invited Kim Darby to Madrid to sample Spanish life and culture.

"I had bad jet lag," recounted Kim, "and I recall Peter gave me some milk and tea with lots of sugar and a biscuit in his trailer. I fell asleep on his bed and never felt safer. He was very comforting and placed blankets over me. Peter was the only man I could fall asleep with and feel safe. He liked Spain. We would walk for hours at night.

"On the way to see a bullfight we were mobbed by a crowd in the street surrounding our car. They thought Peter was a matador. We both found it hilarious. My father was a dancer and he used to perform a matador dance. So somewhere in my head I thought it was okay. But it's not okay.

"One evening I got terribly sick and I could not stop throwing up. I was a mess. Peter had grown very long hair and a goatee for the movie, and he had these love beads he draped over a chandelier. Because I was so sick he took my hair and put it in two pony tails. Peter had a very logical base about him. He went downstairs and had the concierge get a doctor, who arrived at 4 o'clock in the morning. I was sitting up in the bed. The doctor looked at Peter and his long hair and goatee and glanced at the love beads. Then he looked at me and back toward Peter and said, 'What have you done to her?' We both found that so amusing. All the time he was in Spain I don't think he was using or drinking. He took very good care of me there. He seemed to be softer and gentler."

Deuel had signed to the movie on 11 July, 1969. The Western movie starred George Peppard in the lead role of military intelligence captain Rod Douglas, assigned to General Pershing (John Russell) to capture bandito Cordoba (Raf Vallone) and sabotage the cannons he stole from Pershing. Peter Deuel was cast as long-haired, guitar-playing Andy Rice, who helps Douglas in his mission to disable Cordoba's cannon. German actor Dan van Husen featured in a small role and recalled working on the film.

"I was very young at the time," said van Husen. "A bit part in a big film. Filming took place near Madrid, in a town with a small 'Mexican' looking train station. It was an exceptionally hot summer. It was my first big-budget film and I was just amazed. I remember Pete Deuel, as well as Don Gordon and George Peppard. Pete Deuel was a quieter personality. More withdrawn from the others. I am sure he would have become a big name and would now be playing the great cameos."

Kim Darby, by contrast, recalled a gregarious Deuel.

"I was on the set when the filming was taking place," said Kim. "Peter was very happy and making friends. Peter and Don Gordon were close. He seemed to be having a terrific time. Peter's good friend Jack Jobes and his girlfriend were also around because they were visiting Spain."

"Peter stayed at the Hilton," recalled Jobes. "We all went out to dinner with Don Gordon and George Peppard. Kim arrived after I returned to America."

The film, originally titled *Dragon Master* and partly based on fact, was inspired by the successful Italian "Spaghetti" Westerns of the 1960s. It came at a time when the continental Western was in decline and received generally poor reviews. The *New York Times* called the film "sloppy in its sense of period and relentlessly plodding in its writing":

> *Cannon for Cordoba* is movie-making at its most mechanical and wastes a cast that includes much proven talent.

Lewis Archibald, writing for the *M.P. Herald*, 4 November, 1970, gave the film a generally good review and had encouraging words for Duel's performance:

> The always capable Don Gordon and the continually engaging Pete Duel give the best portrayals as members of Peppard's company.

The Hollywood Reporter review, dated 30 September, 1970, found the film to be "rather lackluster":

> Of the group, Minardos and Duel are the only ones attempting characterization, with Minardos coming off the better.

Motion Picture Exhibitor, 14 October, 1970, called the movie "a routine George Peppard adventure film":

> The cast performs adequately, with Pete Duel, Don Gordon and Nico Minardos, as the three U.S. Army men.

Box office, 5 October, 1970, stated:

> The characters are just like those found in at least a hundred other pictures, except for Pete Deuel, more hippie than historical as a long-haired guitar playing soldier.

Deuel and Kim continued their romance, but unlike previous girlfriend Beth Griswold, Kim decided living at Fuller Avenue was no place for her.

"There was havoc going on everywhere," recalled Kim. "He had a picture of Che Guevera on the back of his front door. The resemblance between Che and Peter always struck me as a bit scary. Both of them were very handsome. It was all so new to me. We didn't live together as such. It would have been very hard for me to live at Fuller with my young daughter. He slept over all the time at my place though.

"Peter and I rarely talked about the business. We were both doing so well it just didn't come into our conversation. We mostly talked about each other. Our acting never played a part in our relationship. I remembered Peter from *Love on a Rooftop*, but I was impressed with Peter because of who he was and not because of his work. Peter was very happy when we were together. He had a wonderful sense of humor. He did take such a delight in me and taught me about ecology. Once he caught me throwing some garbage and he told me, 'No, you must never do that,' and I took it back and said it was another 'Petey trick.'

"Peter introduced me to Janis Joplin's music with *Big Brother & the Holding Company*. I remember him running in the house and he had me listen to a new Bob Dylan album, *Nashville Skyline*. Peter said, 'You know what. He sounds really happy here.' Our song was the Beatles classic, 'Something.' It was special to Peter and myself. I loved to share special moments with Peter. We both watched Neil Armstrong walking on the moon together. Peter wasn't that heavily into philosophy. He wasn't heavy all the time. I always referred to him as a dancer. He was not only bright but he was extraordinarily funny. Music was the biggest thing with Peter. We were just wrapped up in each other. We didn't watch any TV."

Deuel and Darby's relationship opened up new areas of sexuality for Darby.

"Peter was a sexual person and a sensitive and inventive lover," said Kim. "Our relationship was sexually profound. Very charged, healthy and passionate. You didn't have to have big breasts or long blond hair with Peter. He liked femininity. Our world was just the two of us. We were very connected."

Kim Darby celebrated her 22nd birthday on 8 July 1969, on the set of *Norwood* (1970) with Peter Deuel in attendance.

"When Peter visited me on *Norwood* he just looked different. He wasn't taking care of himself and I wanted to distance myself from him. Peter's mood improved greatly when he was offered a role on *Cannon for Cordoba* the following month. But I saw the beginnings of a decline at my birthday celebration," declared Kim.

Darby never drank alcohol but decided to "have a sip" on her birthday. Her lack of knowledge regarding alcoholism led to a lack of understanding regarding Deuel's drinking.

"There were several ugly times when Peter had been drinking. I didn't know he was an alcoholic. I had not a clue. I was naive and had no idea there was such a thing as an alcoholic. Peter's personality was mercurial even when he was sober, but he acted so different when he was drinking.

"One time I was in New York with him and was getting ready in my room. My pants wouldn't fit me because I was putting on some weight. I was very anxious about it. Peter wouldn't normally say anything about it but he said hurtful things when he was drunk. I was so naive I wasn't aware Peter was ever drunk. Just that he could be hurtful. It was very confusing to get these mixed messages from him because I had no understanding the alcohol was affecting his behavior. I didn't pay attention to drinking. If somebody drank they drank. I didn't know it did the harm. I didn't think it was in the back of anything that he did.

"It was Christmas and I was sitting under the tree. Peter was very angry. Maybe we had an argument over something I can't recall. He just stood over me and kicked me on my thigh. Peter had a quick temper. There were just the two of us and I guess I went down to reach for something under the tree. It could have been some jealousy on his part. He must have been taking pills or drinking but I wasn't aware of it."

Kim's work took her to San Francisco for location work on *Strawberry Statement* (1970). Deuel joined her on location for two brief visits.

"We were at dinner and I was very friendly with my co-star Bruce Davison when Peter kicked me under the table. He didn't kick me hard, but he was telling me to stop getting too familiar with Bruce with his kick. Bruce and I had become very close during the making of the movie and Peter obviously picked up on that. He watched me very carefully and was extremely jealous when I was working with smart and attractive men. This time his jealousy was justified," remarked Kim.

Following the incident Deuel and Kim kept a distance from each other until Deuel wrote a note to Kim to "please come and see me." Kim and Deuel resumed their relationship. They had always exchanged gifts including Tiffany eggs decorated with their respective zodiac signs, Pisces and Cancer. On another occasion Kim had bought Deuel a Picasso lithograph and Deuel had bought Kim a small vase. Following their latest reconciliation Kim gave Deuel a gift of a yellow baby's sweater.

"I gave Peter this gift because I thought we would have children together," declared Kim.

New Year's Eve 1969 was a time to reflect on the passing year. Their relationship had survived despite incidents that had created increased tension. They both spent the evening at a friend's home in the Hollywood hills.

"We spent the entire evening in the kitchen with Peter's back against the counter. He was wearing a brown silk shirt and I was in his arms, my head on his chest. We never moved and just held on to each other for hours. He was so happy," recalled Kim.

On 6 February, 1970, Kim shocked her friends and colleagues by marrying an actor she had known for only one week. James Westmoreland, who also went by the name of Rad Fulton, had appeared in the short-lived TV Western series *The Monroes*. During the course of the one-season run, Westmoreland had formed a friendship with the lead actor in the show, Michael Anderson Jr. Anderson and his wife Vickie had subsequently introduced Kim to Westmoreland when they both crossed paths during dinner at the Anderson home in Beverly Hills.

"There was an increasing strain on my relationship with Peter," explained Kim. "I don't think that we came to a closure though. We hadn't officially split. He wasn't the Peter that I'd originally met. He'd changed and was much angrier. We weren't seeing each other, and Westmoreland looked clean and neat and stable and was very handsome and courteous. I have no idea why Peter changed. I saw signs of instability in him. He didn't care about himself and was letting his personal hygiene slip. His hair was very greasy and he was growing a goatee. He was in his bare feet and he was smoking. The way he looked he had a feeling of entitlement. A "fuck you, I can do what I want" attitude. He would take his hands and push his hair back off his face and run his hands through it and then shake his head. I think that meant he had combed his hair. The greasy hair was quite a turn-off. I don't know how I ever tolerated Peter's smoking because I can't tolerate it now.

"I had a leukemia scare at around the same time we were distancing ourselves from each other. He wasn't around. I don't think he ever knew about my health scare. I didn't call him for help because I didn't feel he would give me any confidence. He was going through his critical phase. I'm sure he would have walked into the hospital with no shoes and probably smoking. It bothered me that he went around with no shoes. I felt that if he had walked into the hospital ward I would have felt embarrassed. I felt that I couldn't depend on him to be upstanding and to behave himself in public. Peter had told Michael Anderson Jr. he was fucked up and loaded on drugs when we visited his home. A radio announcer, who was at Michael's home, actually mentioned it on his news program. Peter was embarrassing me. I don't think Peter gave a rat's ass about anything at that point. He was just flying by the seat of his pants. I don't think he had any boundary lines.

"I knew I had made a terrible mistake the second I exchanged vows with Westmoreland. My head was spinning. A day into my marriage I went into a decline and a depression and tried to get Peter back. I didn't tell Peter I was going to get married, and phoned him a couple of days after the ceremony to apologize to him and ask if I could see him, but Peter didn't want to talk to me anymore. He was just cold and had no room for me whatsoever. I dreaded phoning him, but I'd much rather talk to him than not talk to him."

"Peter introduced Kim to our family and friends as the girl he was going to marry," recalled Pamela Deuel. "I knew they were having trouble, which saddened me because I knew they loved one another. She was very soft-spoken, warm and natural looking. Peter was besotted with her. Kim was sweet and fragile, and Peter liked that role of taking care of her. She really wanted all of us to like her, and we did. Even though it was a troubled relationship, I had never seen him be the way he was around her."

Recalling the visit to Penfield, Kim commented, "When he took me back to Penfield he referred to me as his fiancée. Peter was expressing his love for me but that never transferred to an actual proposal or an engagement ring. The parents seemed emotionally distant. It was very unsettling. I experienced his father being extremely critical.

"Most of Peter's conversations about his family were of Pamela and Jennifer. They seemed to be his family. There appeared to be some distance between Peter and his father when I visited them in Penfield. I don't remember that Peter talked about his mother.

"Pamela was so gracious to me. We were sitting outside on the lawn with Pamela, baby Jennifer and my baby Heather. Peter was very happy. We went to see Pamela sing in a club that night. She had her hair up in curls, and Peter told me she looked like she had a lot of turds on top of her head. We couldn't stop laughing. Peter was in fine shape then."

"When I heard they broke up I was sick about it," described Pamela. "And then I heard that she married another man I was so angry. I never contacted her. I thought, 'How could you do this to Peter?' I remember seeing Peter shortly after they broke up. He was crushed. He loved this girl. If he hadn't had the drinking issue and she wasn't so troubled I think they would have made it back to each other. There was a sadness in both of them."

It was shortly after his break-up with Darby that Deuel decided to visit Las Vegas to watch his sister perform.

"In 1970 Peter drove from Universal after work on a Friday and arrived in Las Vegas for my last show," remembered Pamela. "I knew he was coming to watch me perform. When the curtain went up, there he was, sitting in the front. I was so thrilled and so proud of him. He was, at that point, starting to be recognized.

"He came that weekend to see me, but also because we needed to be together."

Kim Darby's marriage was dissolved a month later, in March 1970.

"Marrying James Westmoreland was a big mistake. I knew the second it happened; I knew even before the ceremony," reflected Kim.

Deuel didn't waste time pining after his lost love and started dating a secretary he met while filming *The Psychiatrist* pilot in the winter of 1969. Dianne Ray and Deuel officially began their relationship in February 1970—the same month Darby announced her marriage to Westmoreland.

Born in Los Angeles, California, Dianne Ray's parents had converted from the Catholic church to become strict Seventh Day Adventists. Unhealthy early years saw Dianne develop strep throat at four years of age, with accompanying heart trouble, rheumatic fever, dropsy and nephritis.

"My first recollection were my last rites," recalled Dianne. "Within 24 hours I was 100 percent better. Within two weeks I was home. I'd been in hospital for two months. It was a miracle.

"While I was still living at home I became a model for the wholesale clothes industry doing live catwalk shows. When I finally decided to move out I really floundered. I was very naïve, having been raised in that environment. Between modeling jobs I would ice skate. You didn't get paid well back then for modeling and I just got tired of people looking at me and not taking me seriously. They just saw that I was beautiful and treated me as a piece of fluff. I did a complete about-face and became a legal secretary. Then I went to work at the studios."

The attractive 5'7" brunette struck up an immediate mutual attraction with Deuel.

"Peter was very cute. He pursued me. The chemistry was there for the both of us. He came and visited the offices at Universal where I worked for both Norman Felton and Edgar Small as a secretary and an assistant. Peter talked me into trying to do production assistance on the location in Monterey.

"I'm reminded of the old song 'It Happened in Monterey' because that's where we first became very attracted to each other. We didn't get together at that point, but I moved into his Fuller apartment very shortly after we met. It didn't matter it was a one-room apartment."

Kim Darby accompanied Deuel to location shooting in Monterey, unaware of any burgeoning romance between Dianne Ray and Deuel.

"I was at Peter's side every second. I never met Dianne Ray to speak with. I remember sitting in Peter's lap in the lobby of this hotel in Monterey listening to 'Good Day Sunshine' by the Beatles. We liked it there and stayed several times."

When Kim eventually heard of Deuel's relationship with Dianne Ray she had second thoughts about his fidelity.

Pamela Deuel, commenting on Dianne Ray, said, "When Peter started dating Dianne my first reaction was that she was so completely different to Kim. Maybe it was a rebound. I found Dianne Ray to be very materialistic. I can't say I wouldn't be excited by a young handsome actor, making good money, who was interested in me. That's the good thing I can say in fairness to her. I didn't see them in good times. There always seemed to be strife between them. I think it was probably the chemistry in the newness of the relationship that initially kept them together."

"Peter was so dominating in his relationships with everyone that whenever he met somebody who he perceived could handle him and not cave in, he was very attracted to that," commented David McHugh. "That happened with me. I gave back what he gave to me. He respected that. Peter was making so much money he could buy anything. Peter did have a good heart and didn't mind paying his girlfriend's bills. Why not spread some of his money around? If not they're going to accuse you of being cheap. People resented Dianne because she was strong and stood up to Peter. She was a ballsy woman who took charge. Maybe that's what Peter needed. Maybe he saw her toughness as a sign of attention."

Peter Deuel also became acutely aware of how Dianne Ray's personality and physical presence differed from Kim Darby.

"Peter found it unbelievable at times how different I was to Kim," declared Dianne. "We were living on Fuller and having a fight. We were very vociferous. I told him, 'I'm leaving now.' He stood there with his arms across the door. I said, 'Peter, get out of my way or I'm going to push you.' He remained steadfast and said, 'I'm not moving.' So I pushed him aside and Peter almost went clear across the room. I'm not butch but I'm a strong woman. When a person pushes me I do have a backbone."

Deuel told Dianne to quit her job at Universal, a decision Dianne was happy to comply with.

"He was happy having me as a housewife, and I was happy doing that too. I never regretted quitting my job. I loved my job but I always wanted to be a housewife. I never found anything that was great after I quit my modeling career. I survived on whatever Peter brought in to the household. He paid the rent and all the basics of everyday life. I would charge my card if I needed anything. There was no conflict over my lack of income. He was happy that I was doing the cooking and shopping and taking care of the house. I never felt the need for more independence. It's not that I'm lazy, it's just that if I were in that situation now it would be fine again. I've always wanted be a housewife or a little American geisha. I kept a tidy home."

Deuel decided to repeat the birthday gift he gave to former girlfriend Beth Griswold a couple of years earlier.

"He bought me an expensive white Singer sewing machine for my birthday," said Dianne. "I asked, 'Thanks for the machine, but could we go out for dinner?' Peter replied, 'If you're hungry take a bite out of your fucking sewing machine.' It was so funny.

"Peter wasn't drinking a lot at the beginning of our relationship, but he always had marijuana in the freezer. Every now and then he would take way too many LSD's and I would have to take him down from that. He would take four at a time and I would have to sit him down and just stare at him and let him talk for four, five or six hours until he was back in his right mind. It was really frightening. And he'd run out on the porch on Fuller and scream something political at the top of his lungs and I'd coax him back in the house.

"Peter was very much my knight in shining armor. I thought that this was going to be a relationship forever and that I would take good care of him at home and feed him right and do the things he needed and we needed together. He would be my guy. I was very naïve."

★ 7 ★

EPISODIC TELEVISION

"Nothing recedes like progress."

— E. E. Cummings, *Jottings* (1951)

Deuel had starred in three theatrical movies under his Universal contract, but all received mixed reviews and made little impact at the box office. He was making a bigger impact in episodic TV, with a series of excellent performances. Best known to the majority of TV viewers for his comedic talents, the early cancellation of *Love on a Rooftop* had freed Deuel to work on serious, dramatic roles.

Deuel's two guest appearances on *The Virginian* would serve as his introduction to the TV Western. Loosely based on the novel by Owen Wister, *The Virginian* was television's first 90-minute Western. The show had been through many cast changes when Deuel made his first appearance in the sixth-season episode "The Good-Hearted Badman" (6:20). Original Shiloh Ranch owner Judge Henry Garth (Lee J. Cobb) had been replaced by John Dehner as Morgan Starr, and subsequently by veteran actor John McIntire as new owner Clay Grainger. Sara Lane (Elizabeth Grainger) had taken over from Diane Roter (Jennifer Sommers), who in turn had replaced Roberta Shore (Betsy Garth).

"The Good-Hearted Badman" highlighted Deuel's talents for convincingly portraying both a charmer and a villain. Jim Dewey was an outlaw in the mold of Deuel's later outlaw incarnation Hannibal Heyes, but with a darker edge. The story effectively detailed the lure of the outlaw for a young woman (Elizabeth Grainger) attracted to the handsome Jim Dewey. Sara Lane recalled acting with Deuel: "I was so fond of Peter Deuel. What a wonderful man. Of all the actors I worked with he was my favorite. I think some of the best work I ever did on *The Virginian* was on 'The Good-Hearted Badman.' Peter had a slightly reserved quality. Both men and women really liked him. Some actors are ladies men and not much liked by the men on the set, and vice-versa. Peter had a nice quality. It wasn't a charm that was sleazy. My acting was always lighter with Peter. He worked so well with women."

Beth Griswold related, "In the roles he had that he was most proud of it seems he was able to access and portray a vulnerability and tenderness that he found difficult to express in his personal life."

Deuel returned to *The Virginian* for a second time, the following season. "The Price of Love" (7:18) saw Deuel play Denny Todd, an unbalanced young man whose feelings of love and loyalty for the adopted "family" (Clay and Holly Grainger) of his youth lead to

Peter Deuel and Sara Lane in *The Virginian* episode "The Good-Hearted Badman" (courtesy Sara Lane).

violence and murder. Once again, Deuel's scenes with Sara Lane were very effective, displaying his ability to change mood with the slightest facial expressions. The intimate medium of television was proving to be suited to Deuel's subtle acting skills.

"He had a very expressive face and could telegraph emotions," commented Sara. "You can see that in the picnic scene on 'The Price of Love.' He was a good ensemble actor. When he tried his best he brought everyone along with him."

Sara Lane recalled a disturbing comment made by Deuel.

"We were sitting around the set one time and he asked me when I was driving down the freeway if I ever wanted to move the wheel a touch to drive into oncoming traffic. He wasn't talking about suicide but thinking about how easy it would be to do that."

Fans of Peter Deuel were becoming familiar with his ability to portray various shades of good and bad, without ever resorting to outright evil. His convincing portrayal of cold-hearted killer-on-campus Jonathan Dix, on the *Ironside* episode "The Perfect Crime" (1:24), came as a surprise to many of those fans. Even more surprising was the intensity of Deuel's acting in the final scenes as Dix suffered an emotional breakdown.

Frank Price, executive producer on the "Perfect Crime," recalling the evolution of *Ironside*, said, "The series was another case of the network not liking the early scripts and first shows that were produced by Collier Young. Early on, long before the series first aired, Collier Young was removed from the series, and I was asked to try to fix the problems with the series.

"The produced, but unfinished, episodes had severe problems. It was a detective show, and often the plot lines were incomprehensible. My job was to re-plot these detective stories and make the denouement of each seem credible. We shot a lot of replacement scenes and improved those episodes. I also restaffed the show and started developing new scripts and producing new shows. I believe I brought my old team, from *The Virginian*, of Winston Miller, Cy Chermak and Joel Rogosin, aboard.

"'The Perfect Crime' came at a time in Deuel's career at Universal when he was still seen as a promising TV actor. Unfulfilled potential was waiting to surface, given the appropriate project to highlight his talents. I never really focused on Peter Deuel until we did the screen tests for *Alias Smith and Jones*. He was in that category of aspiring young actor with no name value. Name value helped draw viewers to an episode. 'The Perfect Crime' was an episode in progress which I took over before production, in time to rewrite it to some extent, but not in time to bring in different creative elements. I liked Charles Dubin reasonably well as a director."

The Name of the Game provided lighter fare for Deuel. "The White Birch" (1:11) provided Deuel with little chance to display any acting skills of note. With Deuel hidden behind thick-rimmed glasses and an unconvincing Czech accent as resistance leader Chernin in Soviet-occupied Czechoslovakia, the pedestrian episode was notable for being one of Boris Karloff's final performances. Little else recommended it.

Deuel's second appearance on *The Name of the Game* featured him in a more central role as filmmaker Ted Sands, who exploits the destruction of the environment while claiming to protect it with his work. Filmed on location in September 1970 at Lake Arrowhead, situated 90 miles east of Los Angeles in the San Bernardino National Forest, Deuel shared scenes with his brother Geoffrey in an episode that attempted to tackle a serious issue but ultimately proved to be unconvincing. Peter Deuel admitted he had problems playing a character who exploited the environment, which was at odds with Deuel's real-life campaigning to protect the environment — a fact betrayed by some lackluster acting in the final scenes. Director Leo Penn's young sons Sean and Christopher accompanied their father on location to watch filming.

Deuel appeared as himself on the Dick Clark–produced ABC-TV Saturday afternoon rock 'n' roll variety show *Happening '68* on September 7, 1968, talking about his recent work on *The Virginian*, the TV movie *The Scavengers* and *The Hell with Heroes*. He then joined James Doohan and Gary Owens on the panel of the Band Contest. Deuel came across as confident but reserved, and seemed a little ill at ease with the "live" format of the show.

"Peter would get very nervous preparing for a live interview," observed Beth Griswold. "He much preferred getting in front of a camera to film a fictional show or movie."

Marcus Welby M.D. (*A Matter of Humanities*) served as the pilot for a new medical drama from Universal TV. *Dr. Kildare* and *Ben Casey* had been the templates for TV doctors in the 1960s. *Marcus Welby M.D.* would carry on the tradition — with one major difference. Marcus Welby would be a mature doctor with a young, handsome assistant, in the form of James Brolin as Dr. Steven Kiley.

Peter and Geoff filming *The Name of the Game* at Lake Arrowhead, September 1970 (photograph by Ronald Foster, courtesy C. Davey Utter).

"I was asked by Sheinberg to help sell *Marcus Welby*," recalled Frank Price. "The first job was to persuade ABC that Robert Young was the right person to cast in the lead. Marty Starger and the ABC people felt Robert Young was too old. They preferred Ralph Bellamy. I felt very strongly that Robert Young was ideal and that Ralph Bellamy was too cold to play Welby.

"Robert Young wanted the part, and he insisted doing a screen test to demonstrate how good he would be. Clearly it was unusual for an actor of his stature to do a test. I ran the test with the ABC people and argued strongly for using Young. Somewhat reluctantly, Starger agreed. Of course, Robert Young worked superbly as Marcus Welby and certainly was not too old. I also stuck close by during the filming of the pilot and helped in the process of getting the network order."

Deuel played Lew Sawyer, a college chemistry professor who, following a car accident, suffers from a medical condition — aphasia — which severely limits his speech. His wife Tina (Susan Strasberg) faces the dilemma of committing him to an asylum for treatment against her husband's, and Marcus Welby's, wishes.

Price admitted Deuel made no impression on him in the *Marcus Welby M.D.* pilot as he was too busy watching the performances of Robert Young and James Brolin. Their performances would, in great part, be responsible for the success or failure of the pilot. In this particular case the pilot was a ratings winner, and a long-running series followed.

Deuel guest starred in the 1971 *Marcus Welby M.D.* episode "A Passing of Torches" (2:16) as a Chirichua Apache suffering migraines after being told he must attend medical school. Although Deuel gave an intense performance as the young Apache, it would have been more authentic to cast a Native American in the role.

"Ethnic casting in Hollywood has gone through revolution and evolution," noted Frank Price. "There was a day when it was thought an 'actor' could play any character, regardless of ethnicity. Asians were commonly played by Caucasian actors, sometimes mixed in with actual Asians. I suspect this casting practice — that of casting the best actor rather than the correct ethnic type — came into movies from legitimate theater, where the artifice of stagecraft was respected highly. American Indians were portrayed by a variety of white actors, including Jeff Chandler and Anthony Quinn. In those cases, those movies were made in the days when the first consideration was the name value of the star.

"In my early stages in TV Westerns, when I inquired about using real Indians in some skirmish scenes involving Indian Warriors, the casting and production people explained to me that it was impossible to find real Indians to do the work. Iron Eyes Cody seemed to be the only available real Indian, and I liked using him because he seemed so authentic, unlike the made-up stuntmen.

"All of Hollywood's past practices started changing when ethnic sensitivities started boiling over in the 1960s. But it took some years as everyone sorted out what could or could not be done. It's probably best that we made the change so that Asians play Asians, Indians play Indians, etc. But I also have nostalgia for that belief that a great actor or actress can, with the proper make-up, play anyone.

"Clearly in today's smaller and more sophisticated world, we no longer accept some of the theatrical conventions that we used to. While I agree with the current approach, I have some reservations. And it's strictly about the fact that an actor's job is to 'act.'"

A few years earlier, in 1968, an episode of Universal TV's *The Virginian* had featured an all–Indian cast. Guest star Buffy Sainte Marie had insisted on a real Indian cast, and producer Joel Rogosin had agreed to her demands. The result was a milestone, with the first all–Indian cast in television history. Yet two years later Universal TV was casting Peter Deuel as an Indian and apparently reversing any progress the studio might have made in ethnic casting.

"Probably the difference between the casting on *The Virginian* by Joel Rogosin and the casting on *Marcus Welby* by David Victor is that Joel was a generation younger than David Victor," commented Frank Price. "David O'Connell, who worked as a producer with David Victor and did a lot of the casting, was also of the older generation, and therefore he too would have thought in the old way. Or maybe if Buffy Sainte Marie had been hired by David Victor and insisted on an all–Indian cast, David Victor might have made the same decision."

A successful pilot, *Dial Hot Line*, starring Vince Edwards as David Leopold, psychiatric social worker to the poor, evolved into the short-lived ABC-TV series *Matt Lincoln*. The show lasted sixteen episodes before being replaced mid-season by *Alias Smith and Jones*.

Peter Deuel starred in "Nick" (1:06) as Father Nicholas Burrell. Up and coming actress Joan Van Ark, who went on to achieve international recognition as Valerie Ewing on *Dallas* and the spin-off series *Knots Landing*, had fond memories of working on the *Matt Lincoln* episode with Deuel.

"Peter Deuel was classy, sensitive, caring and sweet," recalled Joan Van Ark. "He cared about his work and was bright and not at all a typical or generic actor. Pete was special and sexy, because he was smart and witty."

The Interns was a medical drama series centered on New North Hospital and a group of five interns under the guidance of Dr. Peter Goldstone (Broderick Crawford). In "The Price of Life" Deuel played Construction Supervisor Fred Chalmers, in need of renal dialysis treatment, who is passed over because of his family history of diabetes and his social standing. Mike Farrell was a regular on the show, playing Dr. Sam Marsh. He recalled working with Peter Deuel.

"He struck me as a very good, very intense actor who was strikingly handsome and doubtless had a big career ahead of him," said Farrell. "The character he played in the episode was a tragic young man with a terminal illness. I recall there was a scene in a courtroom in which his character mused aloud about how long a butterfly lives. The young woman with whom he was involved in the story answered that it was only a day or so, to which he responded something to the effect that 'at least I have more time than that.' I remember the scene as a bittersweet and touching one — the irony of which I thought about many times."

On 2 November, 1970, *The Young Lawyers* episode "The Glass Prison" (1:07) aired on ABC. A successful 1969 pilot was followed by an unsuccessful one-season series, with Lee J. Cobb replacing Jason Evers as the boss of a legal aid law practice in Boston. Deuel played jazz musician Dom Acosta, forbidden to see his wife and friends while on parole. Series regular Zalman King played lawyer Aaron Silverman, attempting to lift the harsh conditions of Acosta's parole. Deuel was becoming adept at playing conflicted, addicted and frustrated souls, and the role of Dom Acosta was no different. Barbara Luna played his wife Stella and recalled working with Deuel.

"While filming this very dramatic scene in which I portrayed a heroine addict, Pete was supposed keep me from running off to get a fix. He had to pull me toward him and wrap his arms around me, but in doing so, our belt buckles became entwined, causing us to be stuck together, which prevented me from running into the street so that

Peter Deuel publicity photograph, 1969 (courtesy Kim Darby).

I could get hit by a car! I kept struggling and trying to pull away but it was impossible. The director, having no idea that there was a problem, kept yelling 'Run!' At this point we could no longer contain ourselves and just burst into fits of laughter.

"I can still remember thinking, it's so good to see Pete laugh because whenever I saw him ... he seemed to have such sad Pisces eyes," reflected Luna.

The Bold Ones: The Lawyers featured Burl Ives, Joseph Campanella and James Farentino as partners in a law firm in a rotating star format similar to *The Name of the Game*. The 27-episode series was preceded by two *Lawyers* pilots. "The Sound of Anger" featured Guy Stockwell in the role taken over by Joseph Campanella in the second pilot, "The Whole World Is Watching." The topical storyline of a student radical accused of murdering a policeman during a campus revolt was reflected in the subsequent weekly series, which tackled socially relevant issues of prejudice, drug abuse and Vietnam in its three-series umbrella format of *The Lawyers*, *The Doctors* and *The Protectors*.

Frank Price recalled the reasoning behind the shift toward social relevance in Universal's output of the late 1960s.

"When you're dealing with dramatic shows, you want the shows to appear contemporary," explained Price. "So changes in society will get reflected in the shows. If you chose to ignore what was going on in society, you ran the risk of looking stupid and dated. A good producer tries to stay current on fashions and trends. Music taste changes, wardrobe taste changes, slang changes. When fads get old they die fast. The only nightmare one could have is to jump aboard some fad, focus a show on it, and then have the fad disappear before you get the episode on the air. That's an easy way to look hopelessly dated overnight. So you had to be cautious and not pick up the fads until they appeared to be lasting."

Deuel guest starred on *The Bold Ones: The Lawyers* in "Trial of a Pfc" (02.03) as Jerry Perdue, a Bronze Star–decorated Vietnam vet accused of the murder of fellow veteran Peter Calendar, portrayed by Jared Martin. Deuel gave one his best performances as the war-weary Purdue protecting his friend's reputation in court. Once again Duel displayed his talent for fine emotional nuances in a scene where Perdue recalls Calendar's atrocities, committed in Vietnam.

Jared Martin, recalling his impressions of Deuel remarked, "I was several rungs below Pete Deuel at that particular time. A lot of guys were working their way up through episodic television pointing towards their careers. I don't know if Pete was a few years older than me or had been out there longer. I do remember him having a couple of people with him on the set, which was kind of unusual. Sort of a coterie. And I don't know who they were.

"He had a kind of presence about him. At that time there was a buzz he was a comer. I knew his younger brother Geoff. Pete was a physically bigger guy than his brother. Geoff and I were roughly the same age and the same level and would go up against each other for the same parts. In terms of a network I wasn't close to either of these guys. I was at the opposite end of it. But I did work with them. I never hung out with Pete. I just know he was thought of as being someone special. He was one of the guys you would expect to make the jump from episodic TV into films.

"I was a three-day player on 'Trial of a Pfc' and Pete was the star of that episode. So I was brought in to act with him. And basically, if you're a three-day player you'd better know your lines, keep your nose clean and get in and get out. I remember liking Pete. He seemed like a relaxed, genial guy. A regular kind of guy."

Deuel ventured into unusual territory when he appeared in the religious daytime anthology series *Insight* in 1970. The low-budget Emmy Award–winning syndicated show was a product of Paulist Productions, founded by Father Ellwood Kieser. From its premiere in 1960 to its final episode in 1984, the 30-minute episodes were shot on video and highlighted various moral and spiritual issues. Producer Father Terrance Sweeney won three Daytime Emmy Awards between 1982 and 1984 in the Outstanding Achievement in Religious Programming–Series category.

In "A Woman of Principle," Deuel starred in an uncredited small role as a heavily bearded gay musician of little talent being tutored by a lonely woman (Audrey Totten) attempting to earn enough money to fend off eviction by her bullying landlord (Ed Asner). Deuel's acting was uneven and in stark contrast to his prime-time TV and movie work.

"Peter accepted *Insight* just to get himself out there and to get more experience. I think Peter just wanted to try new things," explained Pamela.

"We were all willing to work for Father Kieser. I appeared in one episode," recalled Kim Darby.

Another unusual venture from 1970 saw Deuel narrating the ecology documentary *Ah, Man, See What You've Done*. With a limited release to select audiences, the documentary highlighted environmental issues close to Deuel's heart.

The Psychiatrist pilot, "God Bless the Children," was successful enough to be included in *Four-in-One*, a rotating anthology format that highlighted a different series each week. Other shows included *San Francisco International*, *McCloud* and *Night Gallery*. Very similar in format to *The Eleventh Hour* TV series, which featured Jack Ging as young psychiatrist Dr. Paul Graham working under the supervision of older psychiatrist Dr Theodore Bassett (Wendell Corey), *The Psychiatrist* starred Roy Thinnes and Luther Adler in the young and mature psychiatrist roles.

Deuel played widowed teacher and former drug addict Casey T. Poe, who helps Dr. James Whitman (Roy Thinnes) tackle serious drug problems in San Sebastian's teenage community. Jerrold Freedman drafted an intelligent story, tackling an issue often avoided by TV networks, and struck up a friendship with Deuel during filming.

"We became friends when we did *The Psychiatrist* pilot," commented Freedman. "I wrote it and basically, although my name isn't on it, I produced it. I liked Peter. We were good friends for a brief time and we socialized a little bit. We just got to be very close. I thought he was a terrific actor. He was slightly older than me.

"It was just one of those times when we thought we were going to do really good stuff in television. And we did, actually. Casey Poe and Jim Whitman were named after two great American writers, Edgar Allan Poe and Walt Whitman. It was an inside joke. I created the character of Poe specifically for Peter.

"Norman Felton was the executive producer of *The Psychiatrist*, but he wasn't involved that much, even though his name was on the credits. When Norman Felton came to Universal he'd already done a psychiatrist show called *The Eleventh Hour* (1962). He was a very important producer in television at the time. The pilot that he was bringing in didn't really work very well. So I wrote a pilot that the studio asked me to do. They basically turned it over to me. NBC liked it, so we went ahead and made it. Daryl Duke directed it.

"It actually came from a *Life* magazine article about kids on drugs. Richard Levinson and William Link wrote the original screenplay. It didn't work for a lot of reasons. They

The Psychiatrist pilot "God Bless the Children" full-page advertisement in *Daily Variety*, March 27, 1970 (courtesy David McHugh).

weren't really tuned in to kids. NBC basically wasn't going to make it until I wrote the script. There was no real story. Nobody was based on a real person. It was just a milieu of the times."

Reviews of "God Bless the Children" were mixed. John Gail's review for the *Hollywood Reporter*, 16 December, 1970, stated:

> Duel gives a finely delineated performance of an ex-addict.... He is especially good in a head-on discussion with John Rubinstein, about drugs and youth.

Morton Moss, writing for the *Los Angeles Herald Examiner*, 15 December, 1970, noted that "the film has the claim to reality but not the feel of it." Although Moss thought Deuel to be an "expressive young actor," he felt the material Deuel had to work with "forces him and other members of the cast to express themselves in barnacled convention and clichéd situations."

The controversial (for the time) subject matter caused problems with NBC, who objected to a scene of Casey Poe shooting up in the back room of a church. Although they initially praised the offending scene, they subsequently decided the sequence was too shocking and stark for the TV audience. Executive producer Norman Felton, in spite of his strong objections, was told to cut the scene.

Frank Price, V.P. of Universal TV at the time, commented on the problems of network censorship.

"I always fought for the greatest creative freedom possible," said Price. "I got to know all the network censors, called 'standards and practices,' well. They were doing their job and it was a difficult one. The censorship was self-censorship by the networks. If they failed in the self-censorship, then the specter of government censorship loomed over them. Or, worse than Federal government censorship, individual community censorship, which would have made the 'broad' in broadcasting very difficult.

"Since I knew they were under pressure from various pressure groups, I always fought to make sure there was pressure from our creative side on the networks. And I defended our case in various forums and interviews over the years. I pointed out consistently that these pressures were nothing new. Euripides was driven from Athens for corrupting the morals of the youth.

"A good friend of mine, the chief censor for ABC by the name of Al Schneider, told me that the complaints to the network fell into a consistent pattern. Liberals were bothered by violence on television. Conservatives were bothered by sex. The majority of complaints about violence came from the New England states, the Northeast corridor. The majority of complaints about sex came from the conservative Southwest. I never got too disturbed about the fight. I just kept fighting.

"The censorship of a drug scene could be argued in two ways. It is best to present such scenes in their grim, excruciating reality in order to deglamorize such drug use. Or, do not portray such detail in scenes where they can function as an instruction manual and 'how to do it' kit."

The deleted scene was subsequently reinserted into the TV movie when it went into syndication with a new title, *Children of the Lotus Eaters*.

Deuel reprised his role as Casey Poe on "In Death's Other Kingdom," a title named after the T.S. Eliot poem "The Hollow Men." The original 90-minute format was reduced to 60 minutes for the short-lived six-episode series.

"In Death's Other Kingdom" centered on Poe, who, after expressing his candid views about the parole board in a group therapy session, is expelled from the methadone maintenance program run by Dr. James Whitman (Roy Thinnes). Deuel considered his work on two segments of the show to be among his best.

"Casey Poe was a very well written character and well directed," described Jerrold Freedman. "It was a close knit group of people that were making the show. They were very committed to making really good stuff. I had an Emmy nomination for *The Psychiatrist* pilot and for 'In Death's Other Kingdom,' which I also directed."

The reviewer for *Daily Variety*, 4 February, 1971, expressed a liking for "In Death's Other Kingdom," saying it had a "terribly strong theme concerning desperation." Calling the performances "exemplary," the reviewer noted, "Thinnes is particularly strong. Pete Duel offers solid work as tormented young man..."

Deuel wore his own beard and clothes in order to get into character for the episode. Reading Louis Yablonsky's 1965 book *Synanon, The Tunnel Back* helped Deuel understand the psychology of addicts. *Synanon* was originally founded in 1958 by Charles Dederich as a therapeutic society, before evolving into an alternate lifestyle and social movement in 1969, and a religious cult in 1974. The philosophy of *Synanon* was based on self-help and self-reliance. Central to the *Synanon* therapeutic system was the "encounter group" that involved members of the group abusing each other verbally. This encouraged honesty and an emptying of often repressed emotion common among addicts. The controversial therapy was often open to serious abuse, but in the 1960s it was seen as progressive.

The six-week format ultimately proved to be a failure with *The Psychiatrist* and *San Francisco International*, both being cancelled. Frank Price, commenting on the reasoning behind the anthology format and its mixed fortunes, said, "Jennings Lang played the leading role in coming up with these 'different' approaches. Sheinberg, as a result of the success of *Name of the Game*, thought this format approach was the magic bullet and used it over and over when he became head of Universal TV. *The Bold Ones* worked moderately well. During this period I was in charge of our ABC business.

"*Four-in-One* was just a collection of series with no common reason for being. My feeling was that there was some justification for the format when it attracted very important stars that wouldn't do a regular series. Then the individual episodes became important. The later versions of the format seemed to use actors that would have been series leads in regular series; they weren't that special."

Commenting on Peter Deuel's work on *The Psychiatrist*, Jerrold Freedman said, "Pete was easy to direct. He was a good actor. When he had good material he was great. And he had good material with us. He was very motivated. I really enjoyed working with him. He was very committed and was never a problem actor with us. I know later on in his career he became frustrated."

That frustration would become apparent in the television series that would bring him his greatest public recognition and financial success. But lack of self-control and common sense would result in a serious automobile accident that would be an indicator of the trouble that lay ahead in Deuel's life.

☆ 8 ☆

DRIVE AWAY

"Life consists not in holding good cards but in playing those you hold well."
— Josh Billings (1818–1885)

Peter Deuel had a history of alcohol problems, going back to his youth in Penfield. The temptations of the bars and clubs in Hollywood continued to feed his problem. On June 19, 1966, he was arrested on drunk charges by the Los Angeles police. On December 15, 1966, he was arrested again for resisting a police officer in the discharge of his duties, a charge that was later dismissed.

On November 6, 1967, he was arrested for a third time for using abusive language to a police officer after he pulled him up under suspicion of drinking and driving. After a night of drinking in Foster City, located approximately twenty-five miles south of San Francisco along the San Francisco Peninsula, Deuel ended up in the local jail.

Beth Griswold, recalling the events of the evening, said, "During one of Peter's visits, sometime in November 1967, we went to a private party in Foster City. Before the night was over Peter drank so much it was frightening. Instead of falling down and passing out, Peter got more and more belligerent, getting into arguments with me and some of the other partygoers, and began shouting expletives and obscenities. Around 1 A.M. I finally convinced him we should leave, but he would not give up the car keys and insisted on driving. He got behind the wheel and didn't get much more than a few yards out of the parking spot before I started pleading with him to stop the car, and he did — right in the middle of the street. We sat there shouting at each other and arguing about how drunk he really was and who was going to drive. I thought I'd almost talked him into letting me drive when a police car drove up behind us and an officer approached the car.

"The officer went through the routine and, even though he hadn't seen Peter actually driving, he was still behind the wheel, so the cops arrested him. Peter resisted arrest all the way! I had never heard some of the language he used as they dragged him to the police car and shoved him in. I drove the car to the Police Station, hoping I could convince them to let him go that evening. When I got there I could hear him yelling vulgarities from the lobby. By the end of it I thought they would keep him locked up for days for resisting arrest and assaulting several police officers. I felt so embarrassed for him. I finally left for home around 3 A.M. Peter spent the night in the 'drunk tank.'"

The following morning Deuel awoke to a head filled with a dull ache and a battered, bruised and badly swollen arm. He recalled being held back by fellow prisoners the night before, as he shouted and screamed in anger and frustration at finding himself locked up like a common criminal. He couldn't remember when he parted company with his shoes. All he knew was he would have to walk barefoot to hail a cab. Walking barefoot was a regular occurrence in his apartment. But that was out of choice.

"That was the last time I ever saw Peter drink alcohol," Beth remembered. "I was prepared to never see him again if he was going to keep drinking like that. But the experience changed him. For the rest of the time we were together he stayed away from it, aware of the devastating effect alcohol had on him."

Deuel realized he had to clean up his act or risk sabotaging all the good work he had achieved in his career to date. Fortunately for Deuel, the charges were resolved through a courtroom disposition. But he knew that if he was caught driving under the influence of alcohol again he would end up in jail for much longer than twenty-four hours.

Unfortunately, his love of alcohol led to a fourth, more serious incident on the night of October 24, 1970. Filming on the *Alias Smith and Jones* pilot would wrap on 28 October. It was time to get away from the pressures of the set and enjoy a drink or two. Relax with friends. Except one beer led to another and another and another. And Deuel was driving that night. His previous experience with the police should have taught him a lesson. Don't drink and drive. He chose to ignore it. And like all drinkers who drive, he exercised his right to put other lives at risk. The right to act with selfish abandon. That recklessness resulted in a drunken Deuel getting behind the wheel of his 1969 white Mustang with a passenger, fellow actor Jon Shank, who had a bit part on the *Alias Smith and Jones* pilot as a member of the Hole-in-the-

A pensive Peter Deuel, 1968 (photograph by Curt Gunther, courtesy Beth Griswold).

Wall Gang. As the Mustang turned left at the intersection of Hacienda Place and Fountain it passed in front of an oncoming 1956 Austin Healey. At the wheel was 21-year-old student Wayne H. Zitter. Accompanying him was his date for the evening, Diane Lachman. They were on their way home after spending the evening watching the comedy movie *Lovers and Other Strangers* (1970), starring Bonnie Bedelia. It was 1 A.M.

The Austin Healy collided with the Mustang, slamming into the right side of the vehicle and damaging the right front fender. The damaged Mustang continued southbound for approximately 300 feet on Hacienda towards Santa Monica Boulevard and Holloway before pulling into a driveway. Deuel and Shank both exited the vehicle on the driver's side and began to walk away from the scene of the accident.

Zitter had injuries to his chin, later requiring 22 stitches, and cuts to his head and legs. An unconscious Diane Lachman was removed from the car by Zitter and placed on the sidewalk. She sustained chest injuries, cuts around the mouth, with several teeth forced up into her gums, and the loss of several more teeth after striking her mouth on the dashboard of the car.

Dierdre Daniels testified that she ran out into Hacienda Place with her sister after hearing a "loud noise" from her apartment. She noted that a white two-door Mustang "slowed and it looked like it was going to stop and it all of a sudden took off very fast again. It wasn't going completely straight. It wasn't even on the right side of the street. It should have been farther on the other side." Daniels called the police and ambulance before placing blankets over the bleeding Diane Lachman as she lay on the sidewalk.

Meanwhile, California Highway Patrolman Morris Arnold had shouted after Deuel and Shank twice before they stopped approximately one hundred feet south of their Mustang. Arnold asked them both for identification and if they had been involved in the accident. Initially Deuel "did then and there willfully, unlawfully and feloniously fail, neglect and refuse to give the injured persons, or to any traffic or police officer at the scene of the accident, his name and address, and the registration number of said vehicle, and the name of the owner of said vehicle, and exhibit operator's license, and did then and there fail, neglect and refuse to render all reasonable assistance to the injured persons who were then and there in need of assistance by reason of said accident."

Arnold described Deuel as "short and stocky," wearing "a brown sports-type jacket, black trousers and some funny-colored shoes."

Officer Arnold asked Shank if he was a passenger in the car at the time of the accident and if Deuel was driving. Arnold received no response to either question. Arnold questioned Shank a second time, to which he replied, "Yes, Mr. Deuel was driving."

Deuel echoed Shank's response and said, "Yes, I was driving." After a brief pause, Deuel continued, "I've had some trouble lately and I left because I didn't know what to do."

Following questioning, Officers Arnold and Lerner, and Deuel and Shank, began walking towards the top of the hill and arrived at the scene of the accident. Deuel was turned over to Officer Myron McNeil. He advised Deuel of his constitutional rights, which Deuel refused to waive.

At the preliminary hearing on 23 April, 1971, at the Municipal Court of Beverly Hills, Officer McNeil observed that Deuel "was pale and he had perspiration on his forehead. His eyes were bloodshot and glassy. There was a noted slow reaction or constriction of the papillary — pupils when I shined my flashlight into his eyes. He was noted to be weaving in place while he was talking to Officer Arnold, appeared to be unsteady on his feet, and he had a strong odor of alcoholic beverage on his breath."

The police photographer was on hand to take photographs of Deuel at the scene of the accident being given a field sobriety test.

Deuel was arrested on suspicion of felony drunk driving and felony hit and run. Jon Shank, being a passenger, was released. At the West Hollywood Sheriff's station at 720 San Vicente Boulevard in West Hollywood, Deuel was offered the choice of a blood, urine or breath test. Deuel chose to be breathalyzed. Officer MacNeil conducted the test, witnessed by two officers, in the jail section of the station. Deuel registered a .170. A reading of .100 would have been sufficient to show diminished capacity.

Meanwhile, Diane Lachman was taken by ambulance to Citizen's Emergency Hospital on Santa Monica for a check-up and stitches to her mouth, followed by dental work the following morning.

Deuel paid bail bond of $1,225.00, and was ordered to appear at Beverly Hills Municipal Court on 29 October, 1970, at 8:30 A.M. on felony charges. Official court documents note he was charged under his birth name of Peter Ellstrom Deuel. He pleaded guilty as charged to three counts of the crime of Violation of Section 23101, Vehicle Code of California, a felony, involving Wayne H. Zitter and Diane Lachman, and hit and run. The hit and run count was later dismissed.

A preliminary hearing on 23 April, 1971, was followed by an arraignment on 7 May, 1971, and a First Plea on 21 May. Prior to his 21 June, 1971, court hearing, Deuel, writing to Los Angeles Judge Bernard Selber, stated:

> In recalling my feelings on that night, shame and terror literally fill my mind. Sitting here eight months later, it is very difficult for me to recreate the events of the accident or even try to find justification for my conduct, but I do not want Your Honor to know that I am a person basically interested in other people and I would not knowingly do harm to anyone. But knowing this has resulted from my drinking I have sought professional help and have been seeing Dr. Lee Gladden, a psychologist, and I started going to Alcoholics Anonymous. I am not drinking anymore. I am trying to find out the cause of my drinking which led me to this incident. I am searching hard for a meaningful life outside of my work and I feel I can prove to Your Honor that I will not be involved any further with the law, particularly with regard to drinking and driving.

In the Santa Monica Superior Court hearing, Deuel pleaded guilty to the charges of drunken driving resulting in an accident. By promising Judge Selber he would give up alcohol and stay away from bars and liquor stores, Deuel escaped with a sentence of 180 days jail, suspended for two years, and a fine of $1,000, which was waived. However, because it was his second conviction, Deuel had to serve a mandatory five-day jail sentence. Deuel met with his probation officer, David Folsoi, on 22 June, surrendered his driving license, and began his probation. Judge Selber granted Deuel's attorney's request not to revoke his passport or restrict his travel to his immediate area.

Judge Bernard Selber stated that Deuel seemed to be a basically responsible and humane person who "has been shocked by the horrible consequences of his drinking and has taken steps to gain insight into the problem to prevent it from controlling him."

Alias Smith and Jones writer and producer Glen A. Larson, commenting on how the DUI accident affected the subsequent series, said, "I don't think it had any effect on the show. The show never went out of production. He wasn't a household word at the time of the accident. But having those kind of things hanging over your head at any time is a load. They affect us all personally, and he wasn't a shallow guy, so he wouldn't just toss it off and say it's meaningless. I'm sure he lived with it and it was a problem."

Pamela Deuel commented, "That accident left Peter so scarred. His actions had led to the injury of this young woman and he felt awful about it. Peter walked away from the scene because he was drinking and he was scared. And he was thinking, 'Oh my God, what have I done?' Of course if he hadn't been drinking he wouldn't have hit her. So he did panic. And he said it was the worst thing he could have done. What if she had died?

"The alcohol made him act out of character and lower his moral stance that he had during the day. And losing his driving license made him aware of the accident every time

Hal Frizzell drove him to the studio. It impacted Peter's life because of the guilt he felt about hurting that girl. He told me, 'If I could relive that minute, that's one minute of my life I wish I could do over.'"

The demands and pressures of his work soon made it increasingly difficult for Deuel to adapt to a lasting, alcohol-free lifestyle. His youthful idealism was being eroded by an increasing sense of frustration at his seeming inability to correct society's and his own faults.

Pamela commented, "Peter went to a psychologist and therapy often. I do believe he was given medication for depression, but he wasn't clinically depressed or bipolar, in my opinion. The depression was a result of the combination of the alcoholism and epilepsy. He was so afraid it was going to become public knowledge. Peter first showed signs of being an alcoholic in high school. He just wouldn't leave it alone. He struggled with the drinking from early on. It first became an issue when Peter was around 16."

Shortly following his DUI accident a chance meeting with Kim Darby saw Deuel in an unforgiving mood.

"After Peter and I broke up, and after my marriage to James Westmoreland, I was on the Universal parking lot one evening," recounted Darby. "I was there to do some looping. I pulled into this space and got out of my car and looked up to see Peter seated in his white Volkswagen. It was winter 1970–1971. I just froze. I didn't say a word and he didn't say a word. We were probably about 12–13 feet away from each other. Peter was hunched over and dressed in a big jacket. His hair was straight and longish. It wasn't that I was scared. I just felt so guilty. My heart sank, seeing him again. He saw me before I saw him, and he waited until I turned around, and I just went rigid. I sensed the anger in him. After a few moments I tried to take my ring off. I kept it on my finger because I wanted to feel like I had something. I could pretend I had something. It was a pretty ring. He looked directly at me for a long time and then directly at the ring. It was awful. He backed up and he pulled away very fast. I turned as he drove off and said, 'Petey, Petey.'

"That was the first time I'd seen him after my marriage. I just wanted him so badly to forgive me and so badly to understand me that I did something that was a mistake and it was meaningless. And I had so much more meaning for him. And I just couldn't get him. I was so vulnerable up against that car and so self-conscious. I wanted to say so many things to him but you could see he didn't want to hear any of them. Peter was verbalizing without verbalizing. His body language was, 'Don't come near me.' He said that very loudly without saying a word. He must have stared at me for two or three minutes. I just locked myself up against the car. I wanted to plead with him. He was so angry with me. I had done something so wrong and he was never going to let me explain. I just wanted him to listen."

☆ 9 ☆

OUTLAWS TO MAKE YOU SMILE

"Peter didn't like light comedy roles after a while. But he got stuck because he was so good."

— Kim Darby

In 1970 Deuel starred in a 90-minute comedy Western, *The Young Country*. The film, a pilot for a prospective series, was shown in the *ABC Movie of the Week* slot on March 17, 1970. Roger Davis starred as Stephen Foster Moody, seeking the heirs to the $38,000 he finds on a dead man. Deuel featured as Honest John Smith, who, along with his lover Clementine Hale (Joan Hackett), endeavors to claim the money.

A cast that included Roger Davis, Joan Hackett, Wally Cox and Walter Brennan didn't impress the public or the network, and the pilot failed to make the transition to a weekly series. Roy Huggins served as writer, executive producer and director. He took the decision to replace Deuel in the lead role of Stephen Foster Moody after watching Roger Davis in a TV commercial. Fortunately for Davis, Deuel didn't object to the change in casting. Although bearing certain similarities in style to the future *Alias Smith and Jones*, most notably the music of Pete Rugolo, the show was a reflection of Roy Huggins' penchant for the comedy Western genre rather than any conscious effort to anticipate a new style of Western for Universal TV. Reviewers were reminded of Huggins' hit TV Western *Maverick* and compared the two unfavorably. Deuel's performance was subdued and lacking in energy and enthusiasm, although his love scenes with Joan Hackett presented a tender and sensual side, and provided his best work in what proved to be a mediocre pilot.

The 1969 hit movie *Butch Cassidy and the Sundance Kid* had captured the attention of writer-producer Glen A. Larson. The plot centered on Butch Cassidy, leader of the Hole-in-the-Wall-Gang, fleeing to Bolivia with the Sundance Kid and his girlfriend, Etta Place, following a bungled robbery of a Union Pacific train. Larson saw the potential for a comedy Western show based on the interplay of two charismatic male leads.

The Western genre had always looked to the lone hero or outsider as its staple character type, coupled with an ideological message concerning the triumph of law and order. However, Italian director Sergio Leone and American director Sam Peckinpah had reinvented the traditional boundaries of the genre, with the hero interested in nothing more than his own self-preservation. In a time of civilian protest and disintegrating faith in the police and government, it was inevitable that the traditional Western themes emphasizing black and white values of good versus evil should be seen as outdated.

Butch Cassidy and the Sundance Kid (1969) used the marginalized outlaw as its theme and transformed Butch Cassidy and the Sundance Kid into lovable rogues. Glen A. Larson borrowed freely from the film in his script for the *Alias Smith and Jones* pilot in 1971, with the help of co-writer Douglas Heyes. Frank Price served as executive producer on the pilot. Price was no stranger to Westerns, having written and produced episodes of *The Tall Man* prior to becoming executive producer on seasons two, three and five of *The Virginian*.

"Western television series were dying by the time we did *Alias Smith and Jones*," recalled Frank Price. "That's one of the selling points we used for *Alias Smith and Jones*. It was different and it appealed to a young audience. Traditional Westerns were getting destroyed by the demographics. Old people (over 49) in rural areas were the hardcore basis of Western viewers. They were male also. Advertisers liked to attract females 18 to 49 to buy their merchandise. *Alias Smith and Jones* drew a young audience and, because of the appeal of Peter and Ben, it drew a strong female audience."

Glen A. Larson was a former member of the Four Preps, a soft-rock group of the late fifties and early sixties who had 13 hits in the "Top 100," including *26 Miles* and *Big Man*. He was known to viewers for his work on the Robert Wagner show *It Takes a Thief* and the Trampas segments of the revamped *The Virginian* series, *The Men from Shiloh*. Price recalled Glen A. Larson approaching him with the idea for a new Western show.

"When *Butch Cassidy and the Sundance Kid* became a huge hit, Glen got the idea of how to do a series dealing with these historical characters," commented Price. "The movie was a one-time event that ended in their deaths and had no element that could make it work as a weekly series. Plus, they were outlaws and no network would put on a series glorifying outlaws.

"Glen's idea was brilliant. Just as the paper clip was brilliant and simple. Make Butch and Sundance have to work for the government in combating crime or else they get sent back to the hoosegow. That, of course, was the basic premise of the *It Takes a Thief* show starring Robert Wagner. No one else thought of using that kind of set-up to make these outlaws acceptable leads in a weekly series. But Glen did. When he pitched it to me, I was delighted and felt we would be able to create a young-appeal, comedic hit.

"As a longtime story editor and writer, I worked closely with Glen to develop the pilot story. Since I have always had a flair for comedy I suggested various comedic situations as we progressed. My suggestions included the situation in the beginning of the pilot where Earl Holliman and the Hole-in-the-Wall Gang are unable to crack open the safe they've stolen. And later, when they've dug the tunnel under the saloon, they plant too much dynamite and by mistake blow everything sky high.

"Generally I work very closely with writers and contribute any ideas that I have that can make the script better. The fact that the movie was a huge, popular hit helped make the concept appealing to ABC. Fox, which had done the movie, couldn't do a TV series on these characters because they would have to steal Glen's idea to make those characters work on TV. It was clear to all that it was inspired by the movie, but fictionalizing the characters and making them government agents made it sufficiently different to avoid suits. There's an old bromide: Steal from one source and you're a plagiarist; steal from three sources and you're a genius."

Writer and producer Douglas Heyes also contributed to the pilot script, using the pseudonym Matthew Howard.

"When Glen turned in the first draft," commented Frank Price. "I read it and then gave him my notes and suggestions. I think it was around this time that Glen privately asked Doug Heyes to read it. Doug felt he could help improve the script. I never personally dealt with Doug on the script. With each draft, I would again give my notes and suggestions. I looked always to find ways to make the characters look good and to make the events more entertaining."

Glen Larson, explaining the evolution of the show, commented, "*Alias Smith and Jones* is based on a true story. Butch Cassidy was offered amnesty by the government. A state attorney general got together with the Union Pacific because they decided, if you can't lick 'em, join 'em. Let's hire these guys. And they set up a rendezvous. A dust storm came up and delayed the attorney general from meeting with them. These guys got furious because they thought they'd been duped or it was a trap, and they went off and robbed a train. I took the reality base of making the deal with outlaws and added the factor they had to keep their noses clean for a year. And that's hard to do if you can't tell anybody because you've got wanted bills around every corner on every tree.

"So I took a story that really happened to Butch Cassidy. There was a time when we were going to do 'The Further Adventures of Butch Cassidy.' It was all real stuff. The closer you can get to the reality of it, the more interesting your show's going to be. So the idea that they weren't beyond granting amnesty to outlaws makes it more interesting. There was a lot of problems with the railroads and the banks, and a lot of people were feeling victimized by those things and turned to the outlaw trail for reasons they considered quite honorable. The effort was to present a contemporary Western.

"Television is often following on the heels of what is playing in the big theaters. It's like audience research. Roy and I had a lot of differences over that issue. He was made my boss and I didn't have the last word. But it made a lot of sense for Frank to bring in a guy who'd had the most successful lighthearted Western in the history of television. At that point you can see the difference in fingerprints in where I thought the show should be and where Roy thought the show should be."

An experienced writer and producer, Huggins created the hit shows *77 Sunset Strip*, *Maverick*, *The Fugitive* and *Run for Your Life* prior to working on *Alias Smith and Jones*.

"Roy was no stranger to comedic Westerns, *Maverick* being first at the gate," continued Price. "His skill in the comedic genre was one of the reasons I asked him to do the *Alias Smith and Jones* series. Although Glen Larson created the show, he was green and did not have the reputation or the experience to be an executive producer yet. The network naturally insisted on having me, or Roy. I'd planned on Roy doing *Alias Smith and Jones* all along. I put Glen with Roy so that Glen could get more experience and turn into a 'star' producer by being on a hit show.

"I ran something of a farm system at Universal. I liked to take very talented young writer-producers and put them on a show with a 'star' executive producer for a season or two. Once that showcase training was completed I could sell them to the network doing their own show."

Although Huggins wasn't involved in casting the pilot, he wasn't in agreement with the choices made.

Frank Price explained, "When we were debating which actors to cast in the pilot, I consulted with Roy Huggins regarding his preferences, since he had agreed to be executive producer of the series. Roy was not enthusiastic about my choices of Peter Deuel and Ben Murphy. Instead of Peter Deuel, he wanted to cast Steve Forrest. Roy felt Peter and Ben were too young to do the kind of stories, involving romances, that Roy preferred to do. The lead had to be an adult to be believable.

"We argued about it. I finally asked Roy: 'How old is Steve Forrest?' After some hesitation, he admitted Steve was 46. And I said, 'Peter and Ben are between 20 and 30. Roy, in the real world, who has more of a romantic life? A 46-year-old man or a 30-year-old?' He conceded the point.

"As you age in show business you have to be very aware of a weakness in your casting. Your contemporaries always seem to be the 'right' age for a leading man. Roy and Steve Forrest were contemporaries, and therefore Roy was misled into thinking Steve was the 'mature' choice for the role. I tried to keep an awareness that we always needed to cast young. My question would be: 'Would a 17-year-old girl think of this actor as romantic? Or think of him as someone the age of their grandfather?'

"Once Peter Deuel and Ben Murphy were in their roles, Roy became a big advocate for Peter Deuel, in particular, praising his performances."

Selling the pilot proved to be a stressful experience for Frank Price.

"Since I was trying for a mid-season sale and was up against an impossible deadline," explained Price, "once I took the film over in the editing stage, I had to take in hand what was a long, poorly edited film and fix it quickly. The director had dragged out his cutting time unconscionably, leaving me with very little time to meet our deadline.

"I recut it in a couple of days, and put together a temporary score with records I bought in a record store. When I was looking for music in the Universal library that could be used to create a temporary score, I was presented with perfectly awful music by our department. It was either standard Western music, suitable to *Laramie* or *Wagon Train*, or it was broad comedy stuff that would have worked with *Ma & Pa Kettle*. That's why I finally got in my car, drove in to Hollywood to Wallach's Music City, and started playing albums. I found a lot of Flatt and Scruggs that worked. I picked up perhaps ten albums with different selections.

"I then went on the dubbing stage and raced through putting music, sound effects and dialogue together in an effective blend. I think I did it in a day — a task that normally would take several days. I barely finished on the dubbing stage when I took the film for testing at the audience testing theater. We tested it and it went through the roof.

"I then took the film to the airport to catch the red eye, taking the film aboard as luggage. I arrived in New York City the following morning, took a limo to the network, and deposited the cans of film in their projection room. I then went to the hotel, checked in, showered and returned to the network for a 10 A.M. screening for the assembled top executives.

"It screened beautifully. They loved it. I had at least ten hit songs in the score I was using, including "Bridge Over Troubled Water." After the frantic and comedic action of the early part of the picture, I used "Bridge Over Troubled Water" when our two heroes had eluded the posse and we pick them up riding quietly into a Western town. It made a terrific transition. We eventually had a composer do a score. I was disappointed in it, but not disappointed enough to spend the money to replace it. It just didn't do the job I was hoping for. Nothing could top that hit-filled first score that I had on the picture for the audience testing and the network sale screening.

"I had never worked this fast before. It was great to see everything work so well in spite of the speed and pressure. Of course, what I did was illegal, since the record companies and composers would all want to get paid if they knew their material was used. My excuse was that it was a temporary score. So that music track was destroyed once the network had seen the pilot.

"I had a lot of fun doing the pilot. I was responsible for the *Alias Smith and Jones* title, which just popped into my mind. I also wrote the narration that opened it. We got Ralph Story, a popular personality in L.A. news programs, to record it. He had a dry, humorous delivery that was perfect for the material. I wrote it with him in mind, and I enjoyed my own wordplay. I added this to the pilot after we shot and edited it when it became clear we needed to tell the audience up front something about Heyes and Curry that would set the humorous tone of the picture."

James Drury took time out from his acting duties as the Virginian on *The Men from Shiloh* to guest star as Sheriff Lom Trevors on the *Alias Smith and Jones* pilot. Drury had also worked with Deuel on *The Virginian* episode "The Price of Love" (7:18) in 1969.

"Pete was a very intense, proud young actor," recalled Drury. "He was thrilled to be where he was and to do what he was doing. And he seemed to be enjoying it very much. I never have any memories of Pete being anything but happy and extremely grateful to be working with the situations he was in."

Alias Smith and Jones became a mid-season replacement for *Matt Lincoln*, which failed to attract an audience.

"The ratings week after week on *Matt Lincoln* were disappointing," recalled Frank Price. "It was clear to ABC, and it was clear to me, that the show would not survive. Rather than have our competitors sell a replacement mid-season show, I came up with *Alias Smith and Jones* as a candidate."

Frank Price had previously worked with Roy Huggins on the first season of *The Virginian* when Huggins replaced Charles Marquis Warren as executive producer.

"On *The Virginian* Roy also eliminated the turn-of-the-century elements," recalled Price, "moving the period back to the time before the great blizzard and placing *The Virginian* in the classic time period. Roy didn't feel it helped us on *The Virginian*, and he had the same feeling on *Alias Smith and Jones*. I agreed with him. Roy was playing it safe by avoiding the turn-of-the-century elements, but it was in the interest of quality. Those anachronisms can be very distracting to an occasional viewer who spots scenes and items totally out of place in a Western. Something like that can kill that valuable 'suspension of disbelief' that we strive for with the audience."

The characters were introduced in a 90-minute *ABC Movie of the Week* pilot on January 5, 1971, followed by a one-hour series on January 21, 1971. Set in the 1880's, *Alias Smith and Jones* centered on the characters of outlaws Hannibal Heyes and Kid Curry, who are promised an amnesty if they can stay out of trouble with the law for one year. Adopting the aliases of Joshua Smith and Thaddeus Jones in the hope of escaping recognition, they inevitably have trouble meeting the terms of their amnesty. Initial reaction was promising, if not enthusiastic.

Television reviewer Cynthia Lowry, of *Associated Press*, commented after viewing the pilot episode:

A good-humor treatment of the Old West. It might provide a weekly hour of mild amusement.

Rick Du Brow, of *United Press International*, wrote:

... *Butch Cassidy and the Sundance Kid* solved the generational problem with its cool, hip, contemporary tone puncturing the traditional western form. It's only logical that *Alias Smith and Jones* jumped on the bandwagon. Happily it succeeded in rollicking fashion.

Whatever reservations the critics might have had, the show was an immediate hit with the public — despite the fact that early audience research testing had proved difficult. ABC tested on "concepts." This testing took place before the pilot was ready for viewing. A written paragraph describing the show and its salient features would be read by test subjects. These would be gathered from the relevant demographics. The comments from the test subjects would be analyzed by the network to give an idea of the level of interest in the basic concept of the show.

"When I first took the idea to ABC and pitched it as a pilot, they tested the premise of the show through their audience research department," described Frank Price. "They reported later to me that the research results had come back poor. I asked to read the paragraph that they tested. Reluctantly, breaking protocol, they showed me the paragraph. I read it and ridiculed it, saying it didn't describe our show at all.

"I asked if I could write the paragraph on the premise and if they would retest it. Humoring me, they agreed. I wrote a lively description of the show. They sent this to research for testing. The test results came back. It was one of the highest rating concepts they'd ever had. So much for the vagaries of research."

Price had objections to the pilot airing as a *Movie of the Week*.

"I wanted to use the pilot as a special to kick off the series in its regular time slot," commented Price. "Network research felt it would get more audience sampling by airing in the *Movie of the Week* slot. They won."

The *Alias Smith and Jones* pilot had a 29.3 ratings share, which translated to 44 percent of viewers.

The weekly *Alias Smith and Jones* series would revert to a 50-minute time format, abandoning the pilot's 75-minute format, and with it the scope for greater characterization and plot development. Frank Price was in agreement with the shorter weekly format.

"*Alias Smith and Jones* had a basic premise that limited the storytelling opportunities," explained Price. "*The Virginian*, which ran to 75 minutes every week, had a loose format that allowed great flexibility in the kind of story told and the characters involved in each episode. We could do westerns, dramas, melodramas, comedies, farces, all in the interest of variety of storytelling.

"The premise of *Alias Smith and Jones* had these two good guy-bad guys forced to go straight and work for the law for some time to gain their parole. You can't stray too far from the premise. A light and comedic approach was desired, so a heavy dramatic piece would have been out of place. Doing a pilot is very different than trying to do weekly episodes. You've got much more time to prepare the script and much more money to spend to make it right. The shoot is twelve to fifteen days instead of five."

Girlfriend Dianne Ray, recalling Deuel's reaction to working on *Alias Smith and Jones*, said, "Peter was a very serious actor who did not want to do a series. He didn't want to be typecast. But he was under contract and they made him do it. He did say, 'It will be the death of me.'"

Frank Price recalled having no trouble with Deuel concerning his being obligated to appear in the weekly series.

"I don't think Peter Deuel tried seriously to get out of doing the series," Price said. "I don't remember having trouble over that. Had it come up in a serious way, and not just grousing with his friends or newspaper writers, that would have been a crisis which I would have had to deal with. We would have told his agents and his lawyers in loud and clear tones that we expected him to perform, and that if he didn't he would face strong legal action.

"We, the studio, were legally obligated to the network to deliver a series starring Peter Deuel which we had sold them, and the network expected us to live up to our responsibility to do that. We would have no choice but to insist he live up to his agreement. Nothing like that happened. When an actor agrees to do a pilot, it is clearly understood that he agrees to do the series if the network orders the series.

"Peter Deuel had the right to turn down the part in the *Alias Smith and Jones* pilot. I think he did it because he liked playing the role. But an actor can't do a pilot just because he enjoys it. The network and the studio invest hundreds of thousands of dollars in making a pilot that features certain stars. The time for an actor to turn down the role is before he appears in the pilot, not after that investment is made. Once the investment has been made, the actor has become difficult to replace at the least, and is, frankly, irreplaceable.

"Society works because most of us honor the agreements we make with each other. That's why we have contracts. Or at least shake hands. Doing a series is like enlisting in the Navy. If you don't want to serve for four years, don't enlist. You can get out of the Navy, but it's not easy. If you don't want to do a series then don't do the pilot.

"There are times that an unhappy actor has been released from a series, but it always produces great difficulty for the network and the production company. Pernell Roberts was unhappy in *Bonanza* and was eventually released, so that he could return to obscurity. Lee J. Cobb talked Norman MacDonnell into releasing him from the fourth year of *The Virginian*.

"We weren't generally ready to release an actor or actress who was interested in going to a rival studio. There would have been no amount of money that an actor could pay to get out of a series. Bad behavior would do it. That's what happened with Pernell Roberts. But a recalcitrant actor violating his contract by not performing would get sued by the network and by the studio. Once the *Alias Smith and Jones* series was underway, then the tough and grueling task of turning out an episode a week wore away some of Peter Deuel's enthusiasm. But I suspect the real problem was his depression, and with that kind of mental affliction, whatever he was doing would have been no good."

Jo Swerling Jr. had a close working relationship with Roy Huggins, going back to *Kraft Suspense Theatre*.

"On *Alias Smith and Jones*," recounted Swerling, "I was basically working under Roy Huggins and was the only person in the world with the title of 'Associate Executive Producer.' It was just something Roy dreamed up.

"I really liked Peter. I thought he was a very big-hearted, generous, hard-working, talented guy. I first met him when we worked together on *The Scavengers* pilot. He was so big-hearted he seemed to take on the troubles of the world — as if he wished with all his heart that he could solve them. But he couldn't and that was too much for him to take.

Peter came back extremely distressed and depressed by all the violence that took place in Chicago. He took things too heavily and seriously. That was part of his problem."

English actress Juliet Mills guest starred on the first-season episode "The Man Who Murdered Himself" (1:09).

"Working with Peter was a very happy experience," Mills recalled. "I found him to be a nice, easygoing, professional, charming and seemingly happy-go-lucky kind of guy. There was no game playing or flirting nonsense. He just got on with it."

Monty Laird, who had been taught trick shooting by Ken Maynard, served as stunt double for Ben Murphy. Work with Universal TV on *The Virginian* led to regular employment on *Alias Smith and Jones.*

"Pete and I hit it off when we first met," remembered Laird. "I originally met him in Joe Swerling's office when I was cast for a role on *The Virginian.* I worked on the show for two years, but, even though I was a stuntman, I had to be cast for each role. When I met Pete I was cast as a gunfighter in a *Virginian* episode with Joe Campanella. Pete and myself talked and had a cup of coffee together. I liked him from that first day.

"I was given a horse called Clay Bank. He was green broke when I got him. A part Thoroughbred and part Quarter. Pete was always watching me and Clay. One morning at work I went to saddle Clay but he was gone. I was asking, 'Where is Clay?' and Pete rode up on Clay with that smile of his and said, 'Hi pard. Thanks for my new cast horse. Now you have to start all over and get a new one.' He smiled and rode off. That is how he got Clay Bank."

With each episode taking only six days to shoot, Deuel soon found the pressure of working on a hit series to be both stressful and frustrating.

"Often a series is a compromise on many levels," commented Juliet Mills. "There's not the time, the money or the rehearsal. They just keep cranking them out."

Deuel was known to be a perfectionist and wasn't afraid of confronting producers or directors if he felt the script or acting was inadequate.

Deuel had threatened to quit *Alias Smith and Jones* during the summer of 1971 because studio executives had refused him a few days leave to return east to visit his sick grandmother. He was finally granted leave.

"Peter had bought my grandmother and grandfather a large-screen television so they could watch him on TV," recalled Pamela Deuel. "Sadly, grandmother Ellstrom was very ill and passed away in Altoona of heart failure that summer. Peter went back to see her and paid for all her oxygen before she died."

Born 11 September, 1936, in Ashland, Kentucky, Harold Frizzell worked as Peter Deuel's stand-in on *Alias Smith and Jones.* Following Deuel's DUI conviction in June 1971, Frizzell also served as his chauffeur, picking him up from Deuel's home in the morning and dropping him off in the evening.

Frizzell recalled, "Pete got very depressed when his grandmother died. They were real close and he'd call her Honey. She was the one who kept him off the alcohol. She was really a nice lady and a good influence. I tried everything under the sun to bring him out of his depression, but he started drinking again."

Frank Price, Vice-President of Universal TV at the time, discussed his feelings regarding Deuel's often negative comments to the press.

"I'm sure we called his agent and asked him to tell his client that he was doing himself

Harold Frizzell and Peter Deuel taking a break from filming on *Alias Smith and Jones* (courtesy Harold Frizzell).

and the show no good with interviews such as this. Actually, I sympathized with actors like Peter. Starring in a television series is an extremely difficult undertaking for certain very talented actors," commented Price.

"If an actor asked me point blank whether or not it was a good idea for him to do a series I was trying to persuade him to do, I could not look him in the face and assure him that it was. A starring role in a series means getting up before dawn to go to the set and working long, long days under sometimes very difficult conditions.

"There is very little time left to have much of a personal life. No matter how good the pilot script is, it will be followed by script after script that will vary in quality. Some will be good. Most will be ordinary. Some will be bad. All will need to be shot.

"Actors need to find a way to deal with acting in a script that they would ordinarily turn down if they were freelancing. Some actors have the resilience and mental attitude that helps them cope with this. Some find it extremely difficult. One of the reasons I was pleased to leave television to go run a movie studio is that I realized I was dangerously near the point of counseling some actors not to do a series. Not a good attitude for someone in my job."

However much Price sympathized with Peter Deuel's position regarding the stress of working on a weekly television series, he did draw the line at his publicly criticizing the efforts of others on *Alias Smith and Jones*.

"I think it was inconsiderate of Peter Deuel to demean the creative efforts of others," opined Price. "I don't think you get the best results from writers if you tell them everything they write is garbage. But, I guess it was Peter's intentions to let critics and fans know that his personal standards were superior to what was attained on the series. I think that's a dishonest position. Better to exhort everyone to work harder and then work harder yourself.

"Peter Falk was a difficult actor to work with because he did have sometimes unrealistic high standards. He, however, did not publicly berate the writers. He worked with them, and his criticism helped them raise the level of writing on *Columbo*. I don't know what Peter's motivation was, but there is a saying: 'Better to light one candle than curse the darkness.'"

Producer and writer Glen A. Larson expressed his feelings concerning Deuel's negative press comments.

"It all took place over a much shorter space of time than allowed for people to stop," said Larson. "I think we'd have wanted to deal with it a little more as time went by. It's a big job to mount a show like that, and sometimes there's a lag time between an interview and when you read it. And other things have happened since that interview. Pete definitely brought a dark side with him. But he was worth a little bit of the pain he delivered. Sometimes that dark, edgy side is what comes across to the camera as real and interesting. As opposed to being dull and boring."

Harold Frizzell had a simpler explanation for Deuel's comments to the press.

"Peter was just depressed when he was criticizing the show," explained Frizzell. "You can tell from the expression on his face on the show when he was in a good mood. He always had that little smirky smile. But it is true that he wanted to get into some good acting. He told me *Alias Smith and Jones* was just a paycheck."

Larson, commenting on his friendship with Peter Deuel and Deuel's reaction to fans, said, "I'd seen Pete Deuel in a show called *Love on a Rooftop*. He was an interesting guy on the screen and brought a real charm to the role, which was very important. I probably got to know him best as *Alias Smith and Jones* progressed because we wound up socializing a little bit. I had a boat and we went to Catalina Island one weekend. He had a girlfriend with him.

"There's a charming little island off the California coast called Avalon. I once wrote a song about it called *26 Miles*. Kids came up to Pete. They looked up to him in the way that I had adored Roy Rogers when I was a child. He was a cowboy star. But it wasn't where Pete's head was. He didn't really appreciate the fact that he was as adored as he was. The weekend we'd spent with kids coming up to him and worshipping him was really the tip of the iceberg. It was just starting. And he hadn't had a chance to really savor that yet or to really see where that was going to go.

"Yet on the trip he was great fun. We had a wonderful, charming time. Pete visited a few of the other boats in the harbor. A former colleague of mine who was in the Four Preps with me was on one of these boats. It was very ironic and unusual that another member of our group would be on the same island on that weekend. Apparently, he had some misgivings and was a little worried about some of the things Pete said. This guy was a doctor, and he later said Pete's comments betrayed some darkness and some dissatisfaction with where he was in life. Of course it was easy to say that after the fact. They didn't say it to me that day or within a few weeks' range of that. They brought it up to me much later.

"But that was a great trip and I got pretty close to Pete. He was very much into his lady and he was having a good time. He wasn't a shy person, and by the time the evening was over I think he was naked on the boat in the state room. So I suppose he had enjoyed the weekend frolic, and probably the drink ran out before he had a chance to regroup."

The average day on the set of *Alias Smith and Jones* began at 6:00 A.M. Deuel usually went into makeup around 7:30 A.M. and had to be on the set by 8:00 A.M., ready for the first shot of the day. A welcome break for lunch would usually be taken between 1:00 P.M. and 2:00 P.M. in the studio restaurant. The day would finally end around 7:00 P.M., although circumstances could extend the working day to 14 hours at certain times.

"He had to work hard on a show like *Alias Smith and Jones*," commented Glen Larson. "An hour production with all of the locations was a lot tougher than *Love on a Rooftop*, which was partly based on a play and a little more contained."

"The long hours on *Alias Smith and Jones* wore him down," related Don Fanning. "Away from work Peter wanted to have fun and not talk about work. He was a gregarious person. Working on the show was eating into his social life. I could see Peter was getting burnt out on *Alias Smith and Jones*. It was the usual complaints about scripts and shooting schedules. He enjoyed it initially, but as it went on it became more of a difficult haul."

Frank Price acknowledged that the long hours could place pressures on actors, but he also thought a perspective was needed when complaints about working conditions were aired by certain actors, including Deuel.

"Clearly it took dedication and stamina to sustain this kind of schedule," admitted Price. "However, it happens to be a pretty normal thing in television. Most series have a star, plus possibly some other supporting players. The fact that Peter and Ben shared scenes made it easier than it was for Jack Klugman in *Quincy* or Robert Wagner in *It Takes a Thief*. A lot of actors have done the grueling task of starring in an hour show."

Harold Frizzell amd Peter Deuel on the set of *Alias Smith and Jones* (courtesy Harold Frizzell).

"My grandfather, Richard Moran, worked as a slate picker when he was only nine years old. He worked on the slag heaps of the coal mines all day to help support the family, until he was old enough to go underground and mine coal himself. During World War II, my father, an electrician, worked on high tension wires a hundred feet above the ground in all sorts of weather, winter and summer, enduring bitter cold, searing heat and high winds. He was exhausted, but he got what rest he could and managed to bear up.

"Part of my job was to be sensitive to the needs of actors and to try our best to adjust schedules if anyone was complaining. Starring in a series was hard work. That was a given. But remember, it was not digging ditches. I'd try to keep it in perspective. There are really hard jobs in the world. Sand hog comes to mind. Generally, actor is not one of them. There's seldom heavy lifting involved. An actor needs to be there on time and say his lines.

"Actors tend to enjoy their work. They accept the conditions because they are being paid princely sums. The ongoing conflict the studio would have with actors was with the amount of money the actors were receiving. Generally, before an actor was in a leading role, he was happy just to get the work. Having the lead in a series means getting a regular huge check. Prosperity enters the actor's life, generally for the first time. Once the series is on the air and has succeeded, then actors, through their agents, show up to renegotiate their deal and get more money for themselves.

"Everything in life is, in some measure, a matter of economics. The longer time it takes to shoot a show, the more expensive it is. If it becomes too expensive, the network can't afford to put it on television because it's not worth it to the sponsors to pay additional huge amounts for the show. You pay actors based on the number of days you are using them. Double the time you need from them and they'll double the amount of money they demand.

"We tried to produce shows that were designed to be done in a reasonable amount of production time, so that a good product could be produced. The schedules were not too grueling for practically all the stars that made series."

Deuel's increased visibility as a successful actor was offset by an increased feeling of alienation.

"We would talk about his being lonely and alienated in acting," recalled Pamela. "Being naive and new to the business myself, I found it surprising in a negative way because he was enjoying celebrity stature and starting to make good money. The future should have looked very bright for him. I tried to understand that. Peter said, 'But it's not really me.' I replied, 'But every person who has a part on television goes through that.' But Peter felt lonely, and he was melancholy."

"Peter's serious nature became more pronounced later in his career," declared Don Fanning. "We were at a restaurant in Stockton, California. A little girl approached us with awe in her eyes, saying, 'Are you Joshua Smith?' Peter replied, 'Yes darling, I am.' She was so enthused. At the next table a group of teenagers asked, 'Why is she interested in you?' Peter said, 'I'm on television.' They replied, 'Yeah? Who cares?' There were two extremes.

"Peter told me, 'Sometimes I get nice little children and sometimes I get people who say I should get a real job.'"

The melancholy didn't reflect on any dissatisfaction Deuel felt having co-star status on the show.

"I think anybody who's an actor would rather be number one than just a co-star. But I didn't ever get it from Peter that this bothered him because he saw the show as a vehicle

Peter and Grandmother Deuel, Penfield, May 1971 (courtesy Deuel Family Collection).

for his talents," related Pamela. "He was not happy as the series progressed. But he felt more trapped with his contract than sharing billing with Ben Murphy. Peter always got his name billed first anyway."

Deuel obtained respite from his melancholy when his niece Jennifer visited the set of *Alias Smith and Jones*.

"One time he took me to Stockton where they were filming on location on *Alias Smith and Jones*," remembered Jennifer. "He always took me riding and took me out on the set. I was the apple of his eye because he didn't have a kid and was totally spoiled. Uncle Peter was always positive around me and always made me smile."

In the summer of 1971 Jennifer had her tonsils removed in a simple procedure that led to severe complications.

"A couple of the stitches ripped and I was bleeding profusely into my stomach and had to be rushed back into surgery," recalled Jennifer. "My uncle Peter flew out from California because he was so concerned about me. He would love to play with me and get me laughing and have a great time. My grandmother told Peter I needed to rest, but he ran downstairs in his underpants doing this crazy dance and running all over trying to get me to laugh. Just trying to make me feel good."

It would be his final visit to Penfield, and the joyful and carefree play with his niece would soon be replaced with the long hours of work awaiting him when he returned to the set of *Alias Smith and Jones* to begin filming on the second season.

☆ 10 ☆

NATURAL RHYTHMS

"Ecology and spirituality are fundamentally connected, because deep ecological awareness is ultimately spiritual awareness."

— Fritjof Capra

Deuel would relieve the stress of working 12 to 14 hours a day on *Love on a Rooftop* and *Alias Smith and Jones* by loading up his Toyota camper with a tent, stove and provisions and going on camping trips far away from the hustle and bustle of the city.

"There was always a loner streak in him. He would say, 'I'm taking my Toyota and going off to the woods, or to drive across the country,'" recalled Jill Andre.

Deuel's love of nature and the great outdoors was nurtured through fondly remembered summer vacations on Lake Little Hawk in central Ontario, Canada.

"When we were children we had the advantage of being born and raised during that time in America when women did not work outside the home," described Pamela Deuel. "And even if there was a modest income, women just didn't do it. We certainly weren't wealthy, but we were better off than a lot of people in town."

"We would go up as a family a few days after school got out for the summer. Just getting out of Penfield was a big deal. We would stay on the lake for the summer. Dad wouldn't stay the whole summer, obviously. He'd go up for a couple of weeks because, being self-employed, he didn't get vacation pay and had to come home to make some more money.

"My parents first went up to the lake in 1943. They found the place through my Dad's sister's husband. My uncle. He was a great fisherman and had heard from friends at a wedding in Toronto that there was this great little lake 150 miles from Toronto. It probably took six hours to get there because in those days the roads were terrible. It was a very remote little lake at the time, with only half a dozen cottages down by the lodge. My folks went up a few months later with my uncle and his wife. They all fell in love with the place, and my grandparents built a place there.

"From 1945 on we went up every summer and stayed in a little log cabin down by the lodge. That was the only place we went in the summer, except for 1959 when we went to Alaska. Being the oldest, Peter was kind of the pioneer of the family. And we all learned to fish. The boys chopped the wood and carried the water in the pails. I can see Peter coming up carrying these galvanized pails. And you had to carry several in order to do the dishes and stuff. We had no running water or electricity at first. It was quite wonderful, with the woods and the lake that was so crystal clear and clean to swim in. The only lights we had at night were these kerosene lamps, and we played cards.

"We loved Penfield. It was a great little town to grow up in. It was like something out of an old movie. But it was wonderful to get out of there for the summer with the family. We'd take the dogs and the cats."

"I went to Little Hawk Lake every summer from August 1964 to my teens," added Jennifer. "I recall going out on the boat with uncle Pete. It was a wonderful time."

Deuel became increasingly dismayed when, on visits back to Penfield in between assignments in Hollywood, he noticed the woods he played in as a child being flattened by bulldozers in order to make way for new housing. While Deuel recognized the need for increased housing as city dwellers moved into the countryside in the 1960s, the idea of his childhood town of Penfield changing its essential character as a small country town depressed him.

Peter Deuel, 1967 (courtesy Deuel Family Collection).

"Even when I was a small boy, I worried about people and factories moving in and taking over and eventually destroying the woods and the fields," described Deuel in late 1971.

Deuel's love of the outdoors and concern for the natural beauty of the environment being destroyed to make way for new homes and shopping malls resulted in Deuel becoming actively involved in the growing ecology movement in the late 1960s.

Beth Griswold, recalling Deuel's love of nature, said, "In the spring of 1968, Peter and I went out camping in Death Valley. Peter described the qualities of the desert air. When the bats hit our sleeping bags in the middle of the night, Peter spoke of the quiet rhythms of the desert night. We went up to Big Sur and looked at property, hiking the hills with the realtor. He would describe the smells and sights and it would let me 'see' it better. He was wonderful in that way and so thrilled with nature. He loved the earth.

"Peter also looked into buying property in Hawaii, on the Big Island. Not a big house but land where he could hike and be out in nature. He spoke of the 'sensuality of the tropical air.'"

The environmental movement gained momentum in the 1960s due in great part to Rachel Carson's book *Silent Spring*. Published in 1962, the book highlighted the dangers of pesticides to the environment and humans, and earned strong opposition from the pesticide industry, who attempted to censor it. Carson was continuing a tradition started by Henry David Thoreau over a century earlier in 1845 when he retreated to Walden Pond in an effort to simplify his life and commune with nature. He could be called the first environmentalist, although he was heavily influenced by Ralph Waldo Emerson, his book *Nature* (1836) and the Transcendentalism movement. Emphasizing the spiritual and transcendental nature of creation, as opposed to the material and knowable reality, the Transcendentalists mixed spiritual doctrine with a love of nature. Thoreau took the movement a step further with his deep connection to the environment removed from what he saw as mankind's corrupting influence.

On a political level, many viewed Thoreau as contradictory, with his stance wavering between non-violent resistance and violence. But his legacy was influential in the 1960s, and he achieved iconic status among the youth of the day. Peter Deuel was one of his admirers, as Thoreau's environmental and political views centering on reform and non-violent resistance took hold. Deuel often talked about his need for simplicity in his life in a manner that reflected Thoreau's philosophy. Deuel achieved that simplicity in his early years at his West Hollywood Fuller apartment, but the stresses and complications involved in maintaining a successful career in Hollywood and a simple lifestyle began to unravel after Deuel began work on *Alias Smith and Jones* and moved to Glen Green.

Despite the passing of the National Environmental Policy Act and the formation of the Environmental Protection Agency in 1969, and the passing of the Clean Air Act in 1970, Deuel would often become depressed about the deteriorating state of the environment, both on a physical and political level. He argued that over-population could be controlled if couples limited themselves to one child. And if they refused, then the issue should become a matter of law. Air pollution was a problem that was a prime concern for Deuel. Los Angeles was infamous for the cloud of smog that covered the city, and Duel commented that "you can grab it by the handful."

Campaigning for recycling in an age when such matters were often seen as trivial, Deuel signed "Peace and Ecology Now" on many of his autographs.

Dianne Ray commented, "Peter was very earthbound and into ecology and recycling. So was I. Most of the foods that I made for us were vegetarian because I was a vegetarian when I met him. I ended up not being one while I was with him. He was very conscious of the earth and the world and politics. Some people won't vocalize it because they don't want people to think badly of them. Peter was very open about those things. And that was a good thing, because in his position it could have hurt him. He was way ahead of his time.

"He was very sad about what we did to the Indians. We both read, cover to cover, *Bury My Heart at Wounded Knee*, which is the history of how we treated the Indians. I'm part Cherokee, and a part of his interest in Indians came from that, but he was appalled at the way we treated the Indians. He wasn't politically connected with any Indian movement but was passionate to help them."

Deuel's love for the land transferred into a land purchase he made consisting of 20 wooded acres in Tuolumne County, California. Situated in the lower Sierra Nevada Mountain range, at an elevation of 8,500 feet, the land is adjacent to the Stanislaus National Forest. U.S. 108 cuts through the area, with nearby Dardanelle serving as a tourist stop for campers and hikers.

"Peter bought the land around 1969 and 1970," recalled Pamela Deuel. "He would go up and camp there sometimes. He had hoped to eventually build a cabin and have a rough road go in, even though it was very rugged territory and had no water access. That was the environmentalist in Peter."

Actor Mike Farrell recalled talking with Deuel about his environmental and political concerns a year after Deuel guest starred on *The Interns*.

"I got to know Pete only a little better a year later when we were both doing shows at Universal," said Farrell. "He was starring in *Alias Smith and Jones*, and I was playing Tony Quinn's assistant in *The Man and the City*. As luck would have it, our stages were right next door to each other and we used to drop in on each other from time to time and talk about the state of the world. The one conversation I recall clearly was about the dilemma of atomic energy and the nuclear arms race. Pete was very aware of political and social issues, and very concerned about where we were going."

David McHugh, commenting on Deuel's concern with the environment, said, "He was passionately upset at the environment and read Paul Ehrlich. But when a person is accusing everybody out there of abusing the environment, and you're smoking four packs of unfiltered cigarettes a day and abusing your own body, you lose credibility. Because he did identify with Native American culture — and they were very respectful of the environment — he really embraced that. He told me he had Native American blood in him."

Jack Jobes saw Deuel's concern for the environment as another passing phase: "Peter liked to make a fuss for the sake of a fuss. He would believe in a lot of different causes and then he'd go home and drink and socialize."

Deuel's love of camping wasn't always matched by expertise, as Jobes recalled. "We camped out in 1967 at the Monterey Pop Festival. Peter was shooting *Love on a Rooftop* at the time. Peter told everyone, 'You've got to sleep out under the stars.' I ignored Peter's advice and borrowed this pup tent and told Don Fanning to join me.

"'Don, trust me. When that fog comes in you'll be soaking wet.'

"Geoff and Peter slept on the ground in sleeping bags. When I got up in the morning, large puddles of water covered their sleeping bags. Camping with Peter was usually a disaster. He had no idea. His supplies usually consisted of beer, cigarettes and peanut butter."

Leisure time for Deuel was essential to his well-being. His love of the outdoors was matched by his love for adventure and speed. A member of the Sports Car Club of America, Deuel competed in his first Novice meet in 1969 in California, driving a white Formula Ford Lotus 51. He placed fifth. Acquiring the Novice License to compete in a Novice meet race began with a Novice Permit and six hours of Novice training track time. This was followed by a Novice Log Book and License. After competing in two regional SCCA races, the driver's completed Novice Log Book was mailed to the National Office to upgrade to the Regional Racing License. A National Racing License was obtained after competing in four Regional Races. This would usually take two to three years. The 1969 Regional Points Standings for the California Sports Car Club listed "Peter Deuel" in the Formula Ford class with a points total of one.

"He was into street racing with Uncle Geoff," commented Jennifer. "Uncle Peter loved cars. My first vivid memory of my uncle is when I was 4 or 5 years old, around Christmas, when he was visiting Penfield. I was living with my grandparents at the time because my mother was traveling with her band. He had a new Mercury Cougar. We went for this incredible ride at high speed and tore up our gravel driveway when we returned home."

Judy Carne introduced Deuel to the tranquil grounds of the Self-Realization Fellowship Temple in Pacific Palisades, California, in 1971 to raise his depressed spirits. A mixture of Hinduism, Buddhism and Christianity, together with a blend of psychology and self-help, made the Fellowship appealing to counterculture advocates in the 1960s, who equated Eastern philosophy with enlightenment, and sitar music with spirituality. The Beatles' visit to India in 1967, and George Harrison's enthusiasm for the spiritual beliefs of the region, had transformed the culture of the East for many youngsters seeking alternatives to orthodox Christianity.

"I can honestly say he was just exploring many things, as we all do when we are young," commented Pamela. "But he had a basic fundamental Christian belief, I believe. I do remember one conversation that we had when I was living in his guest house those last few months of his life. We were talking about my mother's sister and husband who lived in Altoona. They were very strong, loving, Christian people. Non-judgmental and not false like the people who use religion for other reasons and are phony. They had a tremendous influence on my life as a young girl.

"Peter said, 'The way they live is really the way to go.' We were both sad and missing them. He was kind of torn. He wanted to be very current and go with the new ways of thought, but he also had a traditional streak in him."

Dianne Ray declared, "Peter never attended the Self-Realization Fellowship. Neither did I."

Relaxation was also found in the company of his two dogs, Carroll and Shoshone, named after Alice in Wonderland author Lewis Carroll and a Native American Indian tribe. Beth Griswold, recalling her time living with Deuel in 1968, noted, "Peter didn't own any pets when I knew him. Sometime in May of 1968, when I was out canvassing for McCarthy, I knocked on the door of a family whose cat had a litter of kittens. After we talked about voting for McCarthy in the primary election, they asked me if I'd like to take one of the kittens home. I knew Peter liked animals and I thought he'd be as happy as I was. Both Peter and I enjoyed having her around the apartment. She was with us until August. When I returned from a short visit up north, Peter told me she had run off. He had searched for her but never found her. I was very sad over her disappearance and blamed Peter for not keeping her inside while he was away during the day. It turned into another experience that would push us further apart."

Pamela Deuel recalled, "Peter wanted an Australian shepherd. Shoshone was the love of his life. Carroll was a Cockapoo — part cocker spaniel, part poodle. She was a blond butterscotch color. Peter told me he heard the neighbors opposite him on North Fuller yelling at this dog and then he'd hear the dog yip. And he'd seen them, more than once, hit the dog. Finally Peter went to these people and, not wanting to cause any trouble, said, 'Please, if this dog is a problem, let me have her.' I'm sure he paid them something for taking the dog. She was so afraid and skittish because she'd been abused for so long. If she saw someone strange she'd just run and yip and go into the bathroom."

The two dogs were regular visitors to the *Alias Smith and Jones* set and appeared in the background of two episodes.

"The dogs stayed in Pete's dressing room and were taken for walks every two hours by a driver. The dogs were Pete's buddies," commented Monty Laird.

Deuel would often insist his dogs accompany him to a party if he was invited.

"Peter would say, 'May I bring my dogs?' and if they said, 'No,' he wouldn't go," described Pamela Deuel. "Shirley Jones and Jack Cassidy always said he could bring the dogs. But I have to admit if I was having a lovely dinner party and some friend asked to bring their dogs, I'd say no. It was like a

Peter Deuel and Shoshone, May 1969 (courtesy Deuel Family Collection).

get-out clause for Peter, and there were many times it was successful."

Dianne Ray's dog Champagne joined Shoshone and Carroll after she moved in with Deuel at his Fuller apartment.

"I had a little toy poodle called Champagne. We called her Champy, but her full name was 'Mon Petit Babet Champagne Carrion I.' Carrion was the man who gave her to me long before I met Peter. Shoshone was his dog, Champagne was mine and Carroll was ours," declared Dianne.

In the spring of 1969 Peter and Geoffrey Deuel and David McHugh were involved in the rescue of a dog from New York's Hudson River.

"I was doing graduate school in New York, and one of my relatives let me have a little room in a penthouse on 93rd and West End Avenue," recalled David McHugh. "Geoff and Peter were staying there with me. We went out to dinner in this little Greek restaurant on Broadway. We were just hanging out and smoking pot. As the evening wore on we had some drinks and went into a little pizza place on Broadway. A sweet, shy Italian teenager asked us what we wanted to drink. His bullying father came out and started shouting at the boy and took our orders. When he returned to the kitchen, Peter, who was an incredibly funny guy and had the gift of mime and imitation, started making fun of the father. The boy started to laugh because Peter was so hilarious. I was chewing on a piece of pizza and laughed so hard that I choked, and, being stoned, that made us laugh that much more. I took a tissue and blew my nose and tomato pizza came out. We must have been laughing for 15 minutes before we decided to go to Riverside Park and smoke some more pot.

"All of a sudden this hysterical woman approached us. 'Pierre has fallen in the river. Please help me.' We thought Pierre was her boyfriend. So we agreed to look for Pierre and asked where he fell in. She ran a couple of hundred feet along the river wall. Geoff, Peter and I all started to look for Pierre. It was pitch black and I suggested everybody shut up and listen. Than I heard this yapping from this small white dog that could fit into a woman's purse. The dog was lodged in a brick near the wall, and the water was overlapping it. Every time the water receded the dog would get hysterical, yapping. I jumped over the fence and told Peter and Geoff to hold my right arm. I went way down with my left hand to try to rescue the dog. I remember saying, 'You little bastard, you better not bite me.' I finally grabbed it by the neck and pulled it up and handed to Geoff and Peter.

"Meanwhile a police car showed up because the cops were going down the Westside highway and saw three guys running after a woman. We explained what had happened. The woman was crying and very appreciative about the dog. The police drove her back to her apartment because the dog looked like a drowned rat. Peter ended up taking the credit for the rescue because he was a star and the story was worthless if he wasn't the hero."

Throughout his life, Deuel continued to write poetry. While the poems were few in number, their personal nature exposed aspects of his character that he often chose to hide from public view. Written in November 1963, "Musings of an Eastern New Yorker in Southern California" displayed a yearning for simpler times borne out of a realization that the homely pleasures of his childhood were now a part of the past.

How I miss the crisp, golden smell of fall.
Pheasants half clucking, half honking their silly call
In back of the house.
The haze of leaf fires hanging in the air
Are comforting fuzzy for annual thumb suckers.
Occasional boom of shotguns, fired not in hatred.
A wide eyed anticipation of bringing home

A trophy for the little woman.
The little woman creating a masterpiece out of
Cold dead fowl, stale bread, bitter cranberries
And dirt encrusted potatoes.

A sharp crunch of thick green grass, underfoot.
Starched and glazed the night before.
By now the moles and woodchucks have retired,
Leaving the birds to forage alone.
We would build a fire and smile
Once more in wonder of the coming freeze.

"Love," written in 1965, was a deceptively simple poem that effectively described the transcendent nature of love.

An infinitesimal piece of star break,
That drifts into consciousness,
Entering into pastel ways,
To become simply,
Love.

"Soldier," a.k.a. "The Work Resembled a Smash of Cottage Cheese and Rotten Fruit — Food for Thought," also written in 1965, was an early pointer to Deuel's strong political beliefs. The poem, strong in its condemnation of the Vietnam war, was striking in the depiction of a soldier solving his problems with a violent act of self-destruction, and served as a poignant pointer to Deuel's personal situation six years later.

Madam, your son has just been shot between the eyes,
please tell us in your own words why he died.
And madam must produce an answer or,
her son has disappeared
like so much peanut butter and jelly
on a Saturday afternoon,
eleven years before.

Get off my back Corporal, he's dead,
I'm sorry.
What do you mean, why?
And Corporal must produce an answer or,
his buddy has disappeared
like so much PX beer
eleven months before.

I'll be straight with you soldier,
you've lost that leg.
But with luck your right arm will be as good as new.
And because soldier couldn't find the answer
polished for him 11,000 miles away,
he took a .45 and
decorated the wall with his brains.

Written in August 1969 at a time when Deuel was involved in the ecology movement, "We Got" saw an increasingly disillusioned Deuel in a pessimistic mood.

We got filthy air and air is all.
We got rotten rivers and water is air.
We got strangled streets and beer can highways,
crowded rooms and fume filled flyways.
We got crap on our minds.

We got commercial this and billboard that,
neon thin and neon fat.
Yeah, we got beauty but it's all in books,
or on some screen or where no-one looks,
because it's too far out of town.

Now, what are we gonna do?
The sky is blue but you have to look
straight up to see it.
And air is all,
all we got.

"Glen Canyon Eulogy" addressed Deuel's interest in the plight of the Native American and placed the blame for the destruction of the indigenous culture and tradition of America on the "white skin."

> Now I weep with unknown brothers
> For our land I never knew.
> Land once taken, gone forever.
> Raped and stolen from our view.
>
> Time and distance,
> Culture different,
> That decided I not see
> Land now taken, gone forever,
> By the white skin.
>
> Weep now white skin.
> By the white skin.
> You and me.

Deuel presented his friend, actress Leslie Parrish, with a number of his poems. Many have never been seen since he first gave them, in confidence, to Parrish.

"I own some of Peter's poetry," said Parrish. "It is very, very angry and full of swearing. The poems show he was really one angry man. But that's not how I think of Peter at all. He was calm, very quiet and very gentlemanly as far as I knew him. He was serious and self-contained. He let out some of his anger in his poetry. It was a release. It's somewhere to let go of all the pain.

"Poetry is so personal, and Peter did me the honor of sharing it with me, and I feel that was really special. I respect his confiding his deepest thoughts with me by keeping the poems private. I'm sure he didn't write the poems for me, but I'm sure he knew I'd understand."

"Peter would often call me by my given name, Elizabeth," declared Beth Griswold. "He thought it was more poetic and wrote a poem for me with that name as the title. The poem defined my name in all that I meant to Peter. It was beautifully written and touched my heart so deeply. Weeks after the last time we spoke, and after I thought I had come to terms with the finality of our relationship, I took out the poem and, feeling so angry and so very sad, ripped it to shreds. I blocked out that memory for years, having convinced myself that the poem had disappeared during one of my many moves. It wasn't until I began reviewing my history with Peter for this book and started re-experiencing some of the intensity of the feelings I had for him that I recalled destroying his poem."

Pamela Deuel, commenting on her brother's poetry, remarked, "I'm not particular fond of them. I can see Peter was talented in that regard, but they have an awful lot of anger in them."

Deuel narrated selected poems and discussed his views on the environment on the 45 RPM record *Pete Duel: Ecology*, produced in 1971 by his business manager, John Napier, for Deuel's own production company, "Duel Productions Inc."

★ 11 ★

HOPE AND DESPAIR

"Peter appeared to sabotage his own success and created drama and trouble where it didn't exist."

— Pamela Deuel

With season one of *Alias Smith and Jones* completing filming on April 5, 1971, Deuel turned his attention to the *Hollywood Television Theatre* production of "The Scarecrow." "The Scarecrow" was the fourth production by *Hollywood Television Theatre* and a dramatization of the Percy McKaye play, first performed at the Middlesex Theatre, Middletown, Connecticut, on 30 December, 1910. Involving witchcraft and sorcery in 17th century Massachusetts, the story has a scarecrow transform into a "nobleman" and turn to God to become a real man.

Deuel played Richard Talbot in a production also starring Gene Wilder as Lord Ravensbane, a.k.a. the Scarecrow, Blythe Danner as Rachel, and Will Geer as Justice Gildead Merton. The KCET Los Angeles production for PBS provided Deuel with relief from the light-hearted Hannibal Heyes and a chance to exercise his dramatic acting skills in a serious drama. Deuel prepared for the part by reading *The Devil and Daniel Webster*.

Rick Du Brow, writing for the *St. Paul Pioneer Press*, 9 January, 1972, noted:

It is a frequently delightful witchcraft fairy tale for adults and children. And whatever its occasional faults, "The Scarecrow" offers a good deal of witty, sometimes poignant fun.

Pamela Deuel commented, "Peter felt he did really good work on "The Scarecrow" and was very happy with it. I think he got to see a preview screening." In late April Deuel made an appearance at the San Bernardino County Sheriff's Rodeo where he presented the Tex Tan trophy saddle to all-around champion Mike Quick. The rodeo had been founded by Sheriff Frank Bland in 1963 and had a tradition of inviting Western stars of the day.

The success of *Alias Smith and Jones*, and the rewards of appearing in a hit TV series, meant more financial security for Deuel. The formation of "Duel Productions Inc." demonstrated that Deuel was looking to the future and to his finances. Frank Price explained the reasoning behind production companies.

"There are tax advantages to forming a corporation," observed Price. "One advantage is simplicity. An actor has to pay his agent, his manager, his lawyer, his personal assistants, his accountants, his business manager and his personal trainer (if he has one) out of the money he receives for his work. It makes more sense for his check from the studio to be issued to his corporation so he receives the gross amount of money contracted for. Then his company issues checks to all these other people, whose fees come off the top, and the actor has to pay taxes on the amount he actually receives from his corporation as personal compensation.

"Roy Huggins' production company was Public Arts Inc. It would make a deal with Universal or other studio to provide the services of the corporation's only asset, Roy Huggins. Public Arts would have no independent status unless Roy left Universal and set it up as a complete independent. Huggins' name was only evident on *Alias Smith and Jones* as executive producer, and on the Public Arts Inc. end title credit. His writing contribution was hidden under the pseudonym of John Thomas James.

"Roy's pseudonyms varied a bit, depending on how many sons he had in his second family. John, Thomas and James became John Thomas James. And that was the pen name he used regularly once James was born. Roy's son Brett is his oldest child. Katherine Crawford being Brett's sister and Roy's only girl. Brett is, of course, immortalized as Brett Maverick. Roy took pains to write the stories and take credit for them because of the residual payments such credit created, which I believe went into accounts for the boys."

In the summer of 1971 Deuel and Dianne Ray made the joint decision to move from his tiny Fuller apartment to a house on Glen Green Terrace in the Beechwood Village area of Hollywood. Deuel had become attached to his small apartment home, but after eight years it was time to move on to more spacious surroundings. His brother Geoffrey would move into Fuller and keep the small apartment in the Deuel family for a few more years.

Dianne Ray, describing the Glen Green home, said, "There was a front porch with an indoor front porch and a very long living room, part of which we converted to a dining room. You could sit in the huge country kitchen. I loved it. The house was styled in Maple Oak. From the kitchen through the dining room and living room you walked into a small bedroom off to the right, a bathroom to the middle and our bedroom to the left. The bedroom had a large, three-sided bay window that overlooked the back yard where the terrain was raised. It was lovely. We didn't need to have blinds on the window because nobody could see in. Up on the small hill was a little workshop we called the studio that served as a guest house."

"At first I thought Peter was going to buy a house," recalled Pamela, "but he was satisfied with just renting that place. I remember him saying, 'I don't want to rush. Looking for a house to live in is a big investment. I want it to be just right. On the weekends I'm just so tired and I need to relax.' Buying a house with Dianne would have been a huge commitment. He was also against the Hollywood stereotype and the Beverly Hills homes. Finding a little house on Glen Green tucked up against the trees pleased him. It wasn't extravagant in any way."

Alias Smith and Jones survived the mass culling of many favorite television shows in the spring of 1971. Thirty-five out of 77 prime-time series were cancelled in an effort to bring a greater sophistication to television by ditching "hayseed" comedies such as *The Beverly Hillbillies* and *Green Acres*. Westerns were also targeted as attracting the wrong demographics. Despite strong ratings that saw it placed number 16 in the 1970–71 season, Universal's long-running Western *The Virginian*, under it's ninth-season incarnation as *The Men from Shiloh*, came to an abrupt end. The popular *The High Chaparral* also became a victim of premature cancellation. *Alias Smith and Jones'* young leading cast, which attracted teenage viewers and an international following, spared it from the axe, despite average ratings in the USA.

ABC attempted to boost the popularity of *Alias Smith and Jones* as it headed toward a second season with a summer re-run of *Love on a Rooftop*. The attempt worked, with *Love on a Rooftop* gaining respectable ratings, thanks in part to Deuel's ever-growing fan base.

Season two of *Alias Smith and Jones* began filming on 23 June, 1971, with "Jailbreak at Junction City" (2:02). The second segment of the season was quickly followed by a parting of the ways between Deuel and Dianne Ray, following a heated argument.

"I confronted Peter about an incident that occurred on the *Alias Smith and Jones* set," declared Dianne. "We decided to split up. In retrospect it was more of a trial separation than a split. I never moved my belongings out of his house. We just needed our own space. Peter was working out a lot of anger aimed at himself."

Following the July separation, Dianne lived at her sister's apartment, attached to a house owned by a Reverend. Deuel attempted to reconcile with Dianne in late September 1971.

"Harold and Peter visited my apartment, and Peter pleaded with me to return to him," said Dianne. "I said, 'You need to make up your mind who you are and what you want.' He made it very clear that he wanted me as we sat at this big picnic table overlooking L.A."

Meanwhile, Kim Darby was attempting a reconciliation with Deuel following her disastrous marriage to James Westmoreland.

"In October 1971 Peter drove to my house at Oakdale Road in Studio City, in his white Volkswagen," recollected Kim. "I was expecting him. He was completely drunk. Harold Frizzell wasn't with him. Peter was driving the car. I was shocked to see him in such a terrible state. He was barefoot, with his shirt open. He kept slipping on the floor and I had to keep holding on to him. I was flabbergasted and undone that he couldn't stand up. I didn't want him to go. I wanted him to sit or lay down.

"I told him that I loved him and was sorry and didn't really understand how I made such a mistake marrying Westmoreland. I wanted Peter to come back, but he was unresponsive. I couldn't really talk to him about my marriage because Peter wouldn't listen. I had even slimmed in the hope he would love me again. I dropped some paper on the floor to get his attention. He looked at me and said, 'That's a Petey trick.' I didn't want him to leave and get back in his car in such an inebriated state. It was a 25-minute drive from my house to his and involved going on the freeway. I was scared for him but I didn't know what to do. I just wanted Peter to stop being where he was. But he wasn't hearing me at all."

Dianne sensed Deuel had been seeing Kim Darby again and confronted him one evening when he returned from a day's shooting.

"I have this sixth sense of when somebody has been screwing or flirting around," explained Dianne. "I just looked at Peter and asked him what he had been doing. He told me 'Nothing.' I said, 'C'mon Peter. I know.' I decided to get out of the house and go for a ride to clear my head, and went to put on a hunter's coat that we both wore. When I placed my hand in one of the pockets I pulled out an antique Rolex watch. I knew instantly that it belonged to Kim Darby because it was an expensive woman's watch."

Kim Darby had given Deuel the watch on his previous drunken visit to her home.

"I gave Peter my watch to remind him I was in his life and loved him, even when he was so drunk," recalled Kim. "To be careful and not to forget me. And I hoped that he would forgive me and would come back."

"I was angry at Kim for trying to get back with Peter," exclaimed Dianne. "But my view was, if any woman could take my man away from me she could have him."

As season two of *Alias Smith and Jones* progressed, Deuel looked increasingly bored with the role that was bringing him international fame and recognition. The fresh-faced Deuel of season one was slowly being replaced by a jaded and, at times, by-the-numbers performance. The smile often lacked conviction, betrayed by dull eyes and a distant look that told the viewer Deuel would rather be somewhere else.

Dianne Ray commented, "Peter was nearly always negative when talking about *Alias Smith and Jones*. When he came home from a day's shooting he would have dinner, watch television, read and play with the dogs. It wasn't a terribly exciting life because he always had to get up at 5 o'clock in the morning. He usually was taking or drinking something to keep him from getting exhausted. At one of the wrap parties Peter's shrink and I were talking, and he asked me how I thought Peter was doing. I told him I thought he was doing quite well and that his attitude was better. He looked at me and looked toward Peter and said, 'No, he's not doing so well.'"

Jo Swerling Jr. recalled problems with Deuel and his timekeeping.

"The only thing about Pete that used to give me concerns was that he had a tendency not to be on time in the morning," said Swerling. "And as the line producer, which in fact is what I was, budget schedule was a large part of my responsibility. He'd be 30 to 45 minutes late. We usually scheduled our day's work with a lot of pages. We had a six-day shooting schedule. In some cases five days. You had to do a lot of pages a day. There were 10- or 12-page days that were difficult, particularly when you're dealing with horses. You just can't afford to have an actor come in late.

"I recall pulling Pete aside and asking, 'Can't you help us out here? It doesn't look good and I don't think you want to look bad in the eyes of your colleagues.' Pete got a little defensive. And I said, 'The crew wants to go home on time. They have families and this irritates them. They don't like it.' And that disturbed Pete a lot. He was well liked by the crew, but getting in late doesn't sit well with them and after a while they start resenting it. I tried to point this out to him.

'But the crew loves me,' declared Pete. 'Yeah I know. But they're not happy with you right now,' I replied. But he didn't say he would do better in the future. He was miffed and went off a little bit hurt."

Harold Frizzell, commenting on Deuel's often late morning arrival on the set of *Alias Smith and Jones* during the second season, said, "That's when Peter was drinking pretty heavy. He'd just take off and go to somebody's house. But he'd always call me and let me know where he was going to be, and I'd go pick him up in the morning. Roy Huggins and Jo Swerling weren't pleased about his turning up late on the set, but there wasn't too much they could do about it."

Describing the relationship between Murphy and Deuel, Frizzell explained, "Pete and Ben were just working buddies. There was no great friendship. They weren't close. I got along with Ben fine, but Peter was closest to me. He would open up to me and tell me things he wouldn't tell anybody else. Peter treated me good. One Christmas he gave me a little paper bag with a string tied around it. He said, 'Here. Merry Christmas.' I opened it to find a Rolex watch with an inscription on the back that read, 'To my right hand man.' I still have that watch. He also bought me a Bowie buck knife for my birthday because he knew I liked to whittle."

Dianne recalled, "Peter told me that the fact Ben Murphy barely knew how to get on a horse, much less ride one, when they first started filming *Alias Smith and Jones*, really bummed him out. The chemistry off screen was non-existent."

In the fall of 1971 Deuel started to wear a ring on his wedding finger, with the inscription "Fuck" in capital letters. Monty Laird commented, "If I remember it was a friendship ring. That's all I know about it. He did not talk about it much."

"I never did see a ring on his finger. He never even wore a watch," declared Harold Frizzell.

Frizzell, commenting on Deuel's drinking, said, "A lot of times he'd call me on the weekend and we'd take off and get something to eat and mess around together. I'd say, 'I won't go drinking with you because I don't drink. Pete, you know better than that.' I told him that one time and that was it. A lot of times he wouldn't even drink around me. He quit drinking there for quite a while."

Despite his best efforts to control his drinking, old, destructive habits would resurface. As Dianne Ray recalled, "Every morning he would wake up with a terrible hangover, and I'd fix breakfast and have to drag him out of bed to come and eat so that he could go to work. He'd end up waking later and later. This one time he took so long getting up his breakfast was cold by the time he got to the table. He complained about the eggs being cold and the plate not being heated. I told him that was the very last time I would make breakfast for him. And I was true to my word. I didn't allow Peter to push me around. He really tried hard to push me around. And I'm too much my own person to be pushed around.

"It was interesting. His eyes would be grey with no shine in them when he left the house. But the minute he hit that set his eyes lit up and cleared, and the adrenalin ran and he was good. It was the adrenalin rush that shot through him and would straighten him up.

"Peter was jealous of my family and friends that loved me, and of their ability to care about each other. I think he wasn't used to this in his own life. He treated my sister and my best friend Lynne Karoll so badly every time they came over to visit that they finally said they wouldn't come over anymore while he was there. He would be nasty to them and say awful things. It would have been preferable if he'd just ignored them, but he didn't. Peter didn't like her because she loved me. He couldn't stand anyone loving me because he couldn't get that feeling in his own heart.

"Peter could be verbally very abusive — sometimes when he was drunk and sometimes when he wasn't. When you are an alcoholic, even if you don't have a drink you can be nasty. Because you feel under stress to have a drink, not having that drink doesn't necessarily make you feel good.

"Underneath it all, and even though he was mean to my family, Peter was basically a nice guy. I know that sounds contradictory. I would never allow anybody to treat my family or friends that way again, but I was young and in love and he was my prince. I didn't know any better. Peter closed up on emotional issues and wasn't good at communicating in general except on the screen. Part of his problem was that he experienced deep emotion, both high and low."

Lynne Karroll commented, "Dianne and I were best friends and I saw him a lot. I had been living in Mexico and moved back to L.A. in the spring of 1971. So I knew Peter for about nine months. We would get into arguments about anything and everything. I annoyed him because I found him annoying and showed it. There wasn't much reverence there. We were kind of back biting. I reminded him of his privileged background, and we'd argue about small, petty things. I kind of ticked him off.

"One time I said to him, 'One of your great problems is you would like to have a problem and be the struggling and starving young actor. You didn't have to struggle to get where you are and that's pissing you off.' And it pissed him off to hear me say that. But it was true. He had a good deal of success very quickly. I think he wanted more to have struggled, image-wise, than to actually have done it.

"When Dianne went to New York he hit on me. And I thought, 'Is this a test or what?' There's a lot of ego involved, and the fact we didn't get along and fought all the time. It was a case of, 'Let me see if I can score here.' When Dianne came back I told her, hoping it would blow the relationship.

"My opinion of Peter as a person really wasn't that high. I can't say that he was a terribly nice guy. He was very talented and such a good-looking guy with a lot of charm. Very interesting, but not a very nice man."

Pamela confirmed, "I know Peter wasn't an easy man to live with at this point in his life. Peter could be annoying. When he was into one of his narcissistic states of mind he could be really mean and nasty. I'm sure Peter wasn't nice to Lynne Karroll at all."

Beth Griswold commented, "From my perspective, Peter rarely showed any vulnerability. Any display of tenderness towards others was reserved for his sister and any animals that crossed his path. Only a very few times did I glimpse that part of him."

"Peter would throw his weight around and I would only buy so much of it," declared Jack Jobes.

Deuel's seizures were returning on a more regular basis, in part due to his heavy drinking, and in part due to his failure to take the medication required to keep them under control.

"Peter's medication was dilantin and phenobarbital for epilepsy," remembered Dianne Ray. "Peter didn't have to take them all the time — only when Peter drank too much and burned up the B2 and B12 vitamins in his system. That would cause seizures. He had a grand mal seizure at his parents' house when we visited Penfield. It was the first one I had seen. As he came out of it he couldn't remember anything. It robbed him of his memory for quite a while and resulted in depression. I'm not sure that he had any medical advice at that point because nobody would say he had seizures. People looked at you differently in those days, and he did have a reputation to uphold as an actor. I respected that."

Harold Frizzell commented, "The heavy medication made him drowsy and sleepy and look like he was on dope. Peter's seizures scared him, but he wouldn't take his medicine. I told him, 'You got to take your medicine.' When he went into a seizure, that's when I had to give him the shot in the stomach. It had to go all the way through the stomach muscle into the stomach. It was quite frequent because Pete would drink a lot and that would bring on the seizures. And I'd tell him, 'Pete, you can't drink.' I couldn't count the times I had to give him the shot. Probably twice a week.

"He kept a refrigerator in his trailer to keep his medicine in it. It had to be refrigerated because of the bacteria. Pete would get really depressed over it. I said, 'Pete, you can keep it under control if you keep taking your medicine and stop drinking.' But he'd get depressed and start drinking. And that made it worse.

"Peter had about eight or nine seizures during his time on *Alias Smith and Jones*. I'd smack him on the face, and he'd look at me real funny and I'd say, 'Get to the dressing room, now!' I'd come back on the set and they'd say, 'Man, what's the matter with you?' And I'd say, 'Well, he does stuff that I don't like and I smack him.' I could tell when he was going into a seizure. Peter would start twitching his thumb, and his eyes would start going into the back of his head. He went into one in his trailer. I carried a piece of wood with me that I'd carved out with my knife. And I'd always stick that in his mouth. It would keep him from biting his tongue. When he came out of them he'd be really exhausted. I took him home from the set quite a few times and told everyone he was sick and had the flu. It wasn't really fun for me to be on that show because of the circumstances that I had to go through.

"Roy Huggins and Jo Swerling never knew he had seizures. Pete told me, 'You keep it quiet. I don't want anybody on the set to know.' I replied, 'Why should I? This is between you and me and nobody else.'

Jo Swerling Jr. confirmed Frizzell's comments, saying, "I was not aware Pete had grand mal seizures. It never happened on the set. I would go to the set at least once a day, depending on where we would be shooting and what the condition of the production was at the time. For example, if we were behind and there was some feeling the director wasn't sufficiently prepared or was making up shots that were too elaborate and supervision was needed on the set, I might go and stay all day. That didn't happen all that often, but when

Peter Deuel outside his trailer with Harold Frizzell (courtesy Harold Frizzell).

we were shooting on the back lot or on the stage I'd go down there many times during the day."

Deuel's constant fear of a seizure while filming was coupled with a back problem. Pamela Deuel explained, "He had some residual pain from that horrible car accident in 1958 when he broke his hip. Riding horses was terrible for his back and wasn't a pleasant experience for him. I knew he took pain killers for it, and that some of the time they strapped him up when he was riding on *Alias Smith and Jones*. He would take his shirt off at the end of the day and I'd see the strapping."

Dianne confirmed, "He complained about pain in his back. He just lived with it."

"Peter did tell me that the doctors had told him he would probably be crippled within 15 to 20 years because of major damage to his hip," said Connie Meng. "He was in great pain and it was getting worse, and he was worried about his career because of it. I think the pain from his hip added to his depression. Constant chronic pain can be so debilitating. You can't function if you have to take heavy painkillers."

With a struggling relationship, health problems, increasing dependence on "uppers" and "downers," and a continuing battle with alcoholism, Deuel approached the final months of 1971 with some trepidation. But he still had hopes for election to the board of the Screen Actors Guild. If elected, he could focus his attention on the future with a renewed hope for change.

☆ 12 ☆

A SUDDEN COMPULSION

"Public opinion is a weak tyrant compared with our own private opinion. What a man thinks of himself, that it is which determines, or rather indicates, his fate."
— Henry David Thoreau, *Walden* (1845)

Over the weekend of 23 and 24 October, 1971, Deuel spent two days in Bowling Green, Kentucky, raising money for the March of Dimes Telerama at Channel 13 ABC studios. Deuel's stand-in and chauffeur, Harold Frizzell, accompanied him to the event, which raised $40,018.

Deuel also attended a Channel 12 Toys for Tots Telethon in New Bern, North Carolina, in the fall of 1971 with *The Partridge Family* actress Susan Dey. In an apparently playful moment, Deuel was photographed at the charity event holding the butt of a gun between his index finger and thumb, and pointing it to his temple. In the early hours of December 31, a gun would be found laying at the feet of Deuel's lifeless body.

Monty Laird had supplied the gun, at Deuel's request. The conditions of his court sentence precluded him from owning a gun, but in asking Monty Laird to provide him with one he could circumnavigate the law.

"Peter told me he bought the gun because there had been prowlers around the house," explained Harold Frizzell. "I would have said no if Peter had asked me to buy the gun. But Monty probably didn't even know about Peter's problems. I stood up to Peter and would say no many times. He respected that."

It wasn't the first gun he had owned, as Jennifer Seymour recalled, "He had owned a rifle and shotgun." David McHugh also commented, "Peter always had a gun."

Ballots for election to the board of the Screen Actors Guild were counted in the first week of November 1971. Duel had applied in the hope his election could provide him with the platform to make a difference in the working conditions of actors in Hollywood. Charlton Heston had decided to retire as president of SAG in the summer of 1971. Vice president John Gavin ran in his place.

The conservative nature of SAG and centralization of power angered many actors who found themselves without a suitable platform to express their demands for improvement within the film industry. In the late summer of 1971, the Concerned Actors Committee (CAC) was formed in the hope of breaking down the conservative barriers of the SAG and promoting a more democratic election process. Bert Freed ran against John Gavin, with CAC member Donald Sutherland running for vice president. Peter Deuel ran alongside

Dennis Weaver and others as one of 13 board members. The CAC wanted to change the way television residuals were paid, along with demanding better wages and working conditions.

Frank Price, recalling the studio relationship with SAG, said, "Relationships with SAG were professional and routine. Studios made a point of staying away from any internal Guild disputes between the factions. From both the studios' standpoint and the working actors' standpoint, having a radical faction take over was not good. That naturally would lead to impossible demands on the studios, strikes, and unemployment for the working actors.

"In general, most actors are sane enough not to elect the radicals. The radical groups never seem to understand the reality of the entertainment business. It is an international business. If the guilds make things too difficult in Hollywood, then more movies and series will be shot elsewhere. The Canadian or British actors guilds can be easier to deal with than the Hollywood militants."

Deuel returned to California from Kentucky with high hopes of being elected to the board. He awaited the outcome with anticipation of becoming an active voice in the Hollywood acting community. He hoped his frustration and anger would give way to action and change.

When the telegram finally arrived he opened it and read that he wouldn't be taking his seat on the board. That moment when depression replaced hope stayed with Deuel throughout November. One evening he pinned the telegram to a wall in his home and took aim with his gun.

"The rejection telegram affected Peter very badly," recalled Dianne. "He shot at it in an angry, drunken manner. It wasn't done in a jovial manner. You don't pick up your gun and shoot at the wall in a jovial manner. It scared me that Peter was using a gun in the house, but I never felt threatened by him. If he was the type of person to turn on me I would have been dead now."

Pamela Deuel stayed in the guest house overlooking the back of the Glen Green property for a few weeks in December. She used the space to rehearse with her pop-jazz band and recalled one particular evening when her brother arrived home from a day's shooting at Universal.

"I would often fix dinner for Peter," began Pamela. "He was always sober and was working the AA program. He never had a drink around. However, this one time I recall he had come home from the studio and still had the heavy make-up on. He came into this little kitchen, where I was making this spinach salad, and he was going to have dinner with me. He gave me a hug and asked about the band. He was wearing the famous blue shirt he wore on *Alias Smith and Jones*, with the long-sleeve white undershirt. He just stood there. I could see he was very down.

'Petey, what's going on?' I asked. 'Talk to me.' He replied, 'Honey, I'm probably going to kill myself.' I put my arms around him, started to cry, and thought if I squeeze tight enough everything would be fine. But he remarked, 'No. Now don't you worry.' Still shocked by his declaration, I pleaded, 'Petey, I can't make it without you. You're everything. Jennifer and I need you.' He said calmly, 'No. You're strong. You'll be fine.'

"I took Peter seriously when he told me this because he was sober, but it was a terrible moment because I knew I couldn't talk him out of anything. He was going to the doctor every week and liked him. And I thought if Peter could stand there so casually and tell me, he was certainly telling the doctor. I can't say, as his baby sister, that it occurred to me to help him. I should have known that it was a cry for help.

"I wasn't aware that he had a gun in the house. If I'd known that, because I had access to his house at that time, I don't know that I would have taken it away, but I probably would have done something about that. I heard about the telegram incident, but I didn't even know that Peter owned a gun, and I thought maybe somebody was there and they were messing around with a gun. I knew Peter had gotten his gun permit when he was Grand Marshall for the San Bernardino County Parade. But I also knew his felony record precluded him from owning a gun. It made me sick when I found out Monty gave him a gun, because Peter was drinking at the time. I thought, 'What a stupid thing to do. Friends don't do that.'"

Deuel also expressed his intention to end his life to C. Davey Utter.

"Peter told me he was going to commit suicide at a party a few months before he died," said Utter. "I saw him moping in a corner and I went over to him and asked what was wrong. He said, 'I'm going to kill myself.' I told him, 'Don't do that, it's a bad idea.'"

Jack Jobes deflected Deuel's talk of suicide with humor.

"Any time he talked to me of suicide I'd try and turn it around," explained Jobes. "I recall saying, 'Oh great. Can I have your stereo? If you're going to kill yourself I need a stereo.' He started laughing, and I started laughing and said, 'Now, what do we do?' I don't know if he seriously meant it, but it was too self-indulgent for me. It was absurd. I would pull him right out of it."

Dianne Ray, recalling a phone call from Geoffrey Deuel, said, "Geoffrey had called me to tell me he had a friend who was a psychic and that something horrible was going to happen over the holidays with the gun. His friend had seen pools of blood in a dream. I told Geoffrey to talk to his brother about his friend's dream. Sadly, in retrospect, Geoffrey telling his brother about the dream may have created a self-fulfilling prophecy in Peter."

December 1971 saw a hectic schedule for Deuel. From the 1st to the 24th of December Deuel worked, with the occasional break, on three back-to-back episodes of *Alias Smith and Jones*. "Twenty One Days to Tenstrike" (2:16) was completed on December 7th, followed by "The Men Who Broke the Bank at Red Gap" (2:17), which began filming on the 9th and finished on the 16th.

On December 3rd Deuel and Murphy found time to appear on The Merv Griffin Show with Joe Flynn, where they briefly discussed filming "Twenty One Days to Tenstrike" (2:15). The light-hearted banter and superficial approach exhibited by so many American chat show hosts resulted in an interview where little of significance was revealed behind the laughter. Deuel told Griffin that his smoking annoyed Murphy. Murphy told Griffin that he exchanged dates with Deuel, to Deuel's annoyance. But the serious topic of Deuel's growing frustration with *Alias Smith and Jones* was only hinted at when he mentioned the long hours of filming and the problem of the series going to another season, thus creating possible problems with the one-year amnesty storyline.

The continued stress of working long hours, coupled with heavy drinking, was affecting Deuel's health.

"Peter was coming into a big seizure near to Christmas on the *Alias Smith and Jones* set," described Harold Frizzell. "I smacked him out of it and took him to his dressing room."

Jack Jobes recalled, "He was getting help at the time and making tremendous progress.

In mid–December we had a discussion at the round oak table at Glen Green. We just drank coffee. We laughed, cried, bitched, moaned and just aired it all. It all came out. Peter said, 'I was always jealous of you because you just had a natural ability. You were always the President at college.' I knew there was animosity between us but I had no idea why. I knew after that night we had taken this enormous turn in the road for the better. That night he told me he would get work for me on *Alias Smith and Jones*, and representation. He was definitely on the mend and turning a corner."

Deuel phoned his brother in late December. He was feeling lonely and wanted someone to talk over his problems with. Despite his upbeat meeting with Jobes, Deuel was still struggling daily with his alcoholism and increasing dependency on "uppers" and "downers" to counter the effect of the drinking.

"The alchohol exacerbated Peter's attention deficit disorder. he had bouts of great enthusiasm followed by depression," commented Dianne Ray. "I suffer from that so I recognize he had that. It's genetic."

Country singer and actor Bill Anderson worked with Deuel on his final completed episode, "The Men That Corrupted Hadleyburg" (2:18), filmed between December 17 and 24.

Peter Deuel on the set of *Alias Smith and Jones* late 1971 (courtesy Kim Darby).

"I do recall he was very nice to me on the set and tried to help me relax," commented Anderson. "I guess he sensed there was a big difference between being an actor and a hillbilly singer!"

Christmas Eve saw Deuel attending a party given by Lynne Karroll at Shoreham Towers.

"I was dating a veterinarian, and the Christmas party was at his place," declared Lynne. "I introduced Peter to 'White Russians'—a mixture of vodka, Kaluha and milk or cream and ice that you whip up in a blender. It's kind of like a lethal coffee and chocolate-flavored milk shake. He carried on drinking those 'White Russians' through the holidays. I'd say there definitely was a binge."

Following a two-day break in filming, Deuel began work on "The Biggest Game in the West" (2:19) on December 27. On the same day, Deuel completed a deal with fellow performers to own and develop land as a co-operative in Fresno County, California. That evening he talked with his sister on the phone.

"That Wednesday before he died I spoke on the phone with Peter for the final time," recalled Pamela. "It was a loving and sweet conversation. We were looking forward to Mom and Dad visiting."

"He was so excited," described Jennifer, "and said, 'I just can't wait and I love you so much. You're my girl.'"

During the day of December 30 he worked as usual on the set of *Alias Smith*

Lynne Karroll, Dianne Ray's closest friend (courtesy Lynne Karroll).

and Jones. The crew reported that he appeared to be in good spirits, although executive producer Roy Huggins had noted Deuel's behavior had been "manic" over the previous couple of days. It was while Deuel was at lunch in the Universal commissary that he was handed uppers. A fan on the Universal tram tour took what turned out to be the final photo of a smiling Deuel at 3 P.M. as he walked back to his dressing room between filming. A few days of filming remained on "The Biggest Game in the West" (2:19) segment.

Following completion of the day's work, around 7 P.M., Deuel had arranged to go the theater with Dennis Fimple to watch *A Clockwork Orange* (1971), the controversial and often disturbing and violent movie by Stanley Kubrick. A recall from the studio to loop scenes for "The McCreedy Bust: Going, Going, Gone" meant he had to cancel his plans and return to the soundstage at Universal. Deuel was driven home by stand-in/chauffeur Harold Frizzell. Inviting Frizzell in, Deuel and he watched the latest *Alias Smith and Jones* episode, "Miracle at Santa Marta" (2:14), on ABC. As usual, Deuel was dissatisfied with the quality of the segment. A basketball game between the Los Angeles Lakers and Seattle Supersonics relieved his mood.

Harold Frizzell recalled, "Dianne Ray was in the bedroom, and Pete and I were in the living room watching the show. When I left the house Dianne was still in the bedroom. It was about 10 o'clock when I left. He was sober and in a real good mood. He gave me a hug and told me he'd see me in the morning. I told him I had to get home to get some sleep because we had a 7 o'clock call. And I'd always have to get up around 6:00 A.M. to get to his house at 6:30 to pick him up.

"I said, 'Why don't you come home with me so we can get up in the morning?' And he said, 'Oh, I'll stay around here.' Peter's final words to me were, 'I'll see you in the morning.'"

Frizzell recollected, "My phone rang around about 11 o'clock and I picked it up and said hello. Nobody answered. I think it was Pete. I said, 'Pete, is this you?' Then it got real quiet and he hung up. So I figured that must of been him."

At some point later in the evening Deuel and Kim Darby talked by phone.

"I talked about being lonely and wanting to be with him," recalled Kim. "That's all I talked about. I was in tears. He seemed distant, but I received more of a response than I did when Peter came over to my house, drunk, in October."

Dianne Ray, commenting on the sequence of events, said, "I never saw Harold Frizzell at the house that night. Peter was fidgety and nervous and obnoxious, but you wouldn't call him in a bad mood. Peter was in the other mind that alcoholics get when they drink too much. He was drunk, smoking dope and loaded on street whites. Totally gone. He would get the diet pills on the *Alias Smith and Jones* set. He was taking them regularly when we were going through some hard times together. He didn't like the show that night, but he never did. He was fed up with all the idiots around him. His relationship with Ben Murphy wasn't terribly good."

Deuel began to open the Christmas presents under the tree. He had planned to wait until his family arrived, early in the New Year, but with his willpower weakened by alcohol and drugs, he decided he couldn't wait. Deuel excitedly walked back and forth between the living room and bedroom, waking Dianne to show her the presents, one at a time.

"Dianne told me he was like a kid at Christmas," recalled Lynne Karroll. "He was in and out of the bedroom all the time."

Dianne continued, "He was listening to Bach that night before he retired to bed. We were trying to work things out sexually because he was drunk, and both of us were arguing. We always slept together naked. Suddenly Peter jumped out of bed and went to the bottom drawer of the vanity and got his gun and sat on the floor with his legs crossed, stroking the gun and playing with it like a little child. I asked him, 'What are you doing?' and he just looked at me with this smile on his face. I became a little frightened at this point. And that's when he jumped up and ran through the bathroom which connected the bedroom to the next bedroom, and into the living room. He briefly stopped and turned around at the end of the bathroom and said, "I'll see you later," in the manner of a little kid. Then he departed the bathroom, hopping, half-running and excited. I heard a shot and immediately went into the living room. It went through my mind that he might have shot at the telegram again.

"He went right out and did it. It was all done very quickly. The gun was at his feet. Lots of times Peter would feint and I'd push the gun away, and he'd say, 'Ha! Got you.' He loved to see if he could be a good actor about it, and I thought that was what he was doing. So I reached down and pushed the gun away from his feet because I was terrified of guns. That's when I got gunpowder on my hands. And that's when I saw that he was in trouble. I first called 911 and then John Napier, his business manager. He told me, 'Now, his insurance policy won't pay if it's suicide. So don't say it's suicide.' Peter was facing the small dining room alcove when he shot himself. It was in front of the Christmas tree across the room. The kitchen was on the left, the small bedroom he ran through into the living room was on the right.

"Peter's eyes weren't open, but I tried to revive him by rubbing his chest. I didn't know anything about CPR. He was in the midst of a death rattle, a gurgle, and I thought that he was trying to say something, because obviously I'd never experienced that before. I put on Peter's jeans and an old shirt and I ran out on the porch so the police or medics knew it was the right place. I was looking for an ambulance because I thought he might still be savable if they could get to the house in time. The police arrived first, followed sometime later by the ambulance.

"I think Peter was on a blackout for most of the night," concluded Dianne. "You can carry on a perfectly fine conversation and not remember it the next day. He just had so many drugs and so much to drink there's no way he couldn't have been in a blackout."

"Somebody told me that Peter said, 'It doesn't hurt' immediately after he shot himself," said Jack Jobes. "I cannot tell you if it's true for certain, but I do recall I was told that."

Dianne recalled, "All the dogs were in the house when Peter died. They were frantic. Somebody showed up at the house shortly after Peter's death, and I told them not to let the dogs out. But they did. They found Shoshone and Carroll, but they couldn't find Champy. My best friend, Lynne, and her boyfriend went around to all the pounds and finally found my dog."

John Konstanturos served as head of the investigation into Deuel's death.

"You are asking me about something that happened 35 years ago," said Konstanturos. "I will do the best I can. At the time, I was in the process of being promoted to captain and was on temporary assignment because somebody else had retired. My background wasn't in detective work, but I had done a lot of investigative work in areas such as organized crime and riots. My specialty was dealing with major disasters — earthquakes, floods, riots, brush fires — and that included a lot of investigative work. That's where I spent the major part of my career.

"My job title was Assistant Commanding Officer of Hollywood Patrol Division as a lieutenant. Then they moved me into Hollywood detectives for several months. My duties included narcotics and homicide, although I did not have a background as a homicide investigator. Traditionally, one of two lieutenants would get involved in a homicide investigation to assure things were going all right and handled properly, asking questions and trying to stay out of the way of the more experienced investigators. But there was also a supervisor, a detective sergeant, now known as a detective three, who was managing and overseeing the investigation from more of a hands-on place.

John Kanstanturos, head of the investigation into Peter Deuel's death (courtesy John Kanstanturos).

"My responsibilities included interacting with the media and primarily keeping them off the back of the investigators and away from the crime scene. Additionally, I was responsible for coordinating with patrol and outside agencies."

Talking about the apparent delay in the police arriving at the scene, Konstanturos stated, "Those things are hard to measure. The call might have gone to the wrong place and it was eventually forwarded. It might have gone to on-duty patrol people. Detectives are not on duty at those hours. They have to come from home. It could have been reported to patrol, and by the time the patrol got hold of an investigator it was 1:20 A.M. That would be the most plausible reason."

Deuel was announced D.O.A. at 1:33 A.M. Following a quick survey of the house and weapon, officers labeled the death as "homicide pending." The initial police report, included as part of the Chief Medical Examiner-Coroner Medical Report, noted first observations upon arrival at the scene of Deuel's death:

Information from Sgt. Estrada, Hollywood Dets., L.A.P.D. at scene.

A female and decedent were in decedent's bedroom in decedent's residence, located at 2552 Glen Green Ave., L.A., during the early A.M. on 12–31–71.

Decedent left the bedroom at approx 0030 hrs. and the female, who was in the bedroom, heard a "pop" coming from the living room. The female went into the living room and found decedent down on living room floor. The female summoned L.A.P.D. R.A. # 35. D.O.A. 0133 hrs. Decedent naked, on back on living room floor covered with a blanket. G.S.W. to head. T&T. A .38 cal. revolver near decedent was removed by L.A.P.D. prior to coroner's investigators arrival.

A hole in the wall approx. 15 feet from decedent; and a hole in the window approx. 12 feet from decedent, both holes in living room area. Numerous empty beer cans and empty liquor bottles in residence. L.A.P.D. has in custody: the female (suspect), 1 .38 cal. revolver, and 2 spent shell casings. No bullets recovered that were fired. L.A.P.D. carrying as homicide pending further investigation.

John Konstanturos recalled the scene at Deuel's house.

"The thing that stands out about that incident is that I can still see him lying on the ground nude, except for a pair of underwear briefs," said Konstanturos. "His body was adjacent to and almost underneath the Christmas tree. During the preliminary interviews at the scene (before the interviews at the station) that I was involved in, everybody was quite visibly upset and feeling badly that they hadn't done more. According to witnesses, Deuel had been very depressed, was drinking heavily and was drunk when he fired the bullet.

"As I recall, the gun was very close to his body. The detectives thought he was sitting there on the floor next to the Christmas tree and just decided to do himself in and fell backward. He was so close to the tree. It was not a direct thing but more like a 45-degree angle. One leg was slightly pulled up, his arms were off to the side. He was on his back. I do not believe his eyes were open. The other thing I recall is Peter Deuel wearing an outsized ring. It had a flat surface with the word 'FUCK' in large lettering on the front."

Lynne Karroll commented, "It's a weird twist regarding that 'F' ring because Dianne and I never saw him wearing it."

"Peter was definitely naked that night," recalled Dianne Ray.

Konstanturos continued, "They did not cover his body with a blanket while I was there. They usually leave it for the coroner. The police take their photographs. They won't call the coroner in until they are ready, and by the time the coroner gets there they're pretty well wrapped up with their part of the investigation. Usually it's a routine thing to take powder residue tests and fingerprints, and also check to see what kind of residue was on his head.

"Most of what they use in the crime lab is technology and electronic equipment, and that stuff gets outdated. Back in 1971 it was probably in pretty good shape.

"I know that Ray felt badly because she knew Deuel was depressed and didn't do more. I think she took a lot of guilt and shame on herself. It seemed that she was a victim of her own mind. She came across not as depressed but as despondent — someone who clearly was sorry she couldn't have done more.

"People who feel guilty will usually make excuses, but Ray's excuses were more along the line of not doing something to help Deuel, rather than worrying about what the police thought. There are many indicators to look for in these investigations, and that was another one. She was not trying to shift the blame onto somebody else. She was somewhat despondent about being in the other room and not knowing he was going to shoot himself. She was not worried about what the police thought. She was more worried about what had happened to her boyfriend. She wasn't making excuses.

"I didn't get the impression they were afraid of him. We never saw or heard anything that indicated they feared him or that they feared for their lives. It is unfortunate, because he was very talented."

Dianne Ray spent six hours undergoing interrogation at the Hollywood Precinct before the police finally released her at 7 A.M.

"The police were horrible to me," said Dianne. "They started grilling me at the house. They wouldn't let me see Peter and put me in the other room. When they were interrogating me I heard a policeman leak Peter's death to the news. No one could find me for six hours, and they thought Peter had killed me too."

The interrogation was conducted in a series of sessions, interspersed with periods of rest. The questioning gnawed at Ray's already frayed nerves.

"They asked me what I did that night, and I told them we opened some Christmas presents. Then they asked me where the wrappers were. After each session they went back to the house to check on my story. They would come back and question me again and again, and I would tell them the same story over and over. They got a little tired of the truth I guess, because they found everything I said matched in the house, because I had no reason to lie. At that point they hadn't tested Peter's hands for gunpowder. Rather than let me go they wanted to make sure I didn't do it. If they had examined his hand they would know.

"And then they did the good cop-bad cop on me and stood behind me and said, 'We know she killed him.' The other came around and said to my face, 'Why are you crying? We know you did it!' I got so scared I stopped crying. I was naïve. I'd never been through anything like that. In a time of stress your mind becomes focused on survival — when you're sitting in the police station and they're saying, 'She did it.'"

Richard Wright, also present in Deuel's home at some point that night, but not mentioned in the initial police report, was questioned at the Deuel residence. But he wasn't asked to go to the police station.

"Until a few years ago I had no idea Richard Wright existed or that he was there," said Pamela. "I was never told that. Dianne never mentioned it. Never. I don't get why he was omitted from police reports. I wish we knew what the scenario was."

John Konstanturos recalled Richard Wright being questioned at the scene.

"I do recall Dianne Ray and Wright saying Deuel was very depressed, upset and for the most part wanted to be alone, which wasn't unusual for a guy like that anyway. Deuel was rather quiet and, it appears, a bit of a loner. He just wanted to be with his grief," said Konstanturos.

"I have no idea what the lady and the other gentleman were doing. For all I know they might have been asleep. They might have been in bed making love. I don't know what was going on, and I don't believe that they told us. But they were not in the same room. We wondered if he fired those other shots before he killed himself, why didn't they try to stop him. Yet they were not surprised. Evidently such behavior by Deuel was not unusual," concluded Konstanturos.

Dianne denied that Wright was present in the house when Deuel died, stating, "There was no one in the house when it happened. I can assure you of that. We were alone. He may have been the person who came over that night and let the dogs out after Peter died, but everything was a blur after I discovered Peter's body. Wright was of no consequence to anything that happened that night."

Commenting on how she first heard of her brother's death, Pamela said, "I was asleep in my bed in California. It was about 6:30 in the morning and my father called me. He had taken mother to the doctor because she was having some stomach problems. They showed mother into a room and the receptionists said to my father, 'Dr. Deuel, I've just heard something terrible on the radio, but it must not be true because you wouldn't be here.' And he asked her what it was, and she said, 'Well, I heard that Peter died.' He didn't have Geoffrey's or my phone number with him, so he left mother to see the doctor. And he drove back to Penfield. It probably took him fifteen minutes.

"He dug up our phone numbers and phoned Geoffrey, but he was busy. Then he got me and woke me up. Then I started calling Geoffrey and finally got through. I said, 'Is it true?' and he replied, 'Yes.' The precise moment that he answered the phone with me on the other end is when somebody walked in and told him. I talked with Geoffrey, and we decided that Geoff should call and tell Dad.

"Then Dad had to go back to the doctor's office and tell my mother. I just couldn't believe it. I went outside by the pool. And then I drove over to Fuller. Jane was there with C. Davey Utter and Jack Jobes. I do remember Geoffrey decided he should go to the police station, while I should stay at Fuller to greet any people that might come over."

Ray left the station, accompanied by Geoffrey Deuel and girlfriend Jane Soehner, after satisfying the police of her innocence regarding Deuel's violent death.

Dianne explained, "Geoffrey was never in the police station. He just came to pick me up that morning. He was cold to me. After we left the police station they took me back to the Fuller apartment. I could see already that this was no longer a good relationship with his family. My girlfriend Lynne showed up shortly after that and took me away to her apartment on Shoreham Drive."

Konstanturos commented, "There was little evidence or reason to suspect Ray. Whenever somebody is at the scene they're automatically going to be interviewed. It's very uncommon to have the questioning last six hours without a break, but it's very common to have six hours of investigative interviews.

"Sgt. Estrada was experienced with homicides and was used to regularly supervising homicide investigations. He was a very thorough investigator, with high integrity. While a lot of the interviews were going on at the station, I was out at the lobby holding the media at bay. The media was for the most part fair-handed. There was a little bit of inappropriateness. I remember talking on the phone with the captain of the detectives at that time and seeing bright lights suddenly coming on behind my back. A woman with the media stuck the microphone in front of me and started asking me questions while I was on the phone."

Pamela recalled her father being notified of her brother's death by John Napier, Duel's business manager.

"John said that Dianne told him that when Peter said, 'I'm going to kill myself,' she replied, 'So, go ahead.' I think had I been afraid that he might use the gun on me I wouldn't say, 'Well, go ahead.' I think I'd be real still, like a mouse. She told John Napier that that's what she said — 'Go ahead.' And Peter walked out into the living room. Peter then said, 'I'll see you later.' John does not exaggerate or lie. He's a very private person, and he loved Peter like a younger brother. I saw him at the funeral and he couldn't control himself.

"Maybe in the midst of that fight Peter had the ridiculous thought he'd get back at Dianne. We can think crazy when we're really inebriated. I'm not blaming her for Peter's death, but I don't think she helped him particularly."

"I can assure you, Peter never said anything except, 'See you later,'" insisted Dianne Ray. "John Napier has the right to his opinion, but he's wrong."

Deuel was officially pronounced dead at 3:15 A.M. by R.A. number 35. At 4:23 A.M. Deuel's liver temperature was taken. It was 93 degrees. Shortly after, his body was finally removed from the living room.

"The detectives cannot have the coroner or anybody else interfering with the scene until they've finished and made a thorough examination of everything," explained Konstanturos. "The detectives and the photographers are all called in from home and have to do a thorough investigation and keep as many people as possible, including me, out of their way. Of course, they would have allowed me to stay as long as I wanted, but I tried to get out of their way as a common courtesy. They have to move quickly and take care of a lot of things at the time, including people that are doing interviews. There are people there who are crime scene specialists, forensic specialists. They have to phase and time all that, and the coroner is one of the last ones they allow to come in.

"I made sure that the connection between the coroner's office and the detectives was intact, and that everything they were responsible for in the exchange of the deceased was done properly."

On admission to the mortuary, the body was placed in Crypt number 15 to be examined by the Chief Medical Examiner, David M. Katsuyama, M.D. Initial investigation was for "Homicide, Gunshot Wound to Head. Through and Through." Sergeants Edwards and Jaques from central detective, L.A. police department, were present when the body was examined.

At 5:35 A.M. the preliminary examination was completed by the County of Los Angeles Department of Chief Medical Examiner-Coroner. The autopsy was concluded at 11:30 A.M. and the Coroner's Report signed. Describing the gunshot wound to the head, the coroner noted, "Entrance is of contact-type and explosive type. ... small, unburnt powder flecks are also noted in this immediate area." The coroner also wrote, "A slight abrasion is present on the right posterior aspect of the elbow. Slight abrasion is present on the lateral aspect of the left hip area.... Slight ecchymosis is present over the medial aspect of the left leg just below the knee." Toxicologist Sharon Lynch noted on 31 December, 1971, that blood barbiturate was absent.

The body was released to Glasband Willen Mortuary in Hollywood on 31 December, 1971, upon the signature of the father.

The police revised the status of the case from "Homicide Pending" to "Probable Suicide" after investigators discovered a spent bullet in a wall in the hallway of the house. It had been fired "about a week ago" by Deuel at the framed telegram of rejection from the Screen Actors Guild. The bullet that killed Deuel was later found on the floor of a carport across the street after it had passed through the living room window.

"It appeared to be suicide," concluded Konstanturos. "Experienced investigators have what some would call a sixth sense, but mostly it's experience. They can't always tell if somebody is lying or not. They have to conduct a thorough investigation. But you can usually get a reading, not always, on whether somebody is genuinely despondent. There are little things you look for. For example, if people are blaming themselves for not doing something earlier. Somebody that killed somebody usually does not do that. But that doesn't prove anything. It's an indicator.

"My recollection was that they all had been drinking. Not just Peter. When I was working in narcotics, vice and organized crime related to narcotics, I had never been involved in the prosecution of a conspiracy where sooner or later somebody in the group either gets a guilty conscience or gets upset and comes forward. Almost all conspiracies that are successfully prosecuted are because a member of the original conspiracy has either become an outcast or gets mad, or somebody in the group is fearing for their life from somebody else in the group. Almost all conspiracies self-destruct over time. That has not happened yet — 35 years later.

"Sometimes the alcohol accelerates a feeling of depression. Just about all of our behavior is a manifestation of our thoughts, and our thoughts under alcohol clearly become distorted and exaggerated. Whether it was the rejection telegram or some person or some other thing that upset him, who knows? It could have been made 10 or 20 or 100 times worse in his mind than if he had been sober. Add depression to that, and you have a very dangerous combination."

"I was given the lie detector test after Peter died, at the request of Geoffrey and his attorney," declared Dianne. "He used to represent me until Peter died. I failed the test but blame it on the stress I was under at the time, and the questioning. They asked me, 'Have you ever considered killing anybody in your family?' Nobody believed me, but at that point I didn't care. I knew I was telling the truth. I was terrified of going to jail for something I didn't do. I just shut all my emotions off because I was terrified. They couldn't get a reading on me at all for the second lie detector test.

"Geoffrey wanted to talk with me about why Peter's nose was broken. I said I had no idea. 'Have you called someone to ask if you put a bullet in your head, does it break the cartilage in your nose?' I asked Geoffrey. 'If you want to discuss this, Geoffrey, I'm sitting in my attorney's office right now. And that is the only place we will have a discussion, ever. You're welcome to come.' Geoffrey told me, 'The reason I wondered how he broke his nose is because my brother told me you were very strong. You had an argument one day and you pushed him and he almost flew out of the window.' I never hit anyone, so I don't know where that came from."

Lynne Karroll accompanied Ray to the Glen Green home the following morning.

"I got a phone call early in the morning from Dianne's sister, who was on the east coast," related Lynne. "She said, 'Where's Dianne?' And I told her she was with Peter, because I'd talked to Dianne the night before around midnight. She had said, 'I'm going to bed because Pete's still drinking.' Then Dianne's sister told me Pete had been shot. She'd seen it on the news. I called and told Dianne's mother so she wouldn't hear it in the news.

"I arrived at the house at midday the next morning. The police kept Dianne overnight. I picked her up at Geoffrey's house and kept her with me the next few days. She told me she had to go and pick up his clothes. So I went with her. There was a police officer there. I covered Dianne's eyes and walked her in without letting her look. We went through the crime tape and picked up the clothes and left."

Dianne recalled, "After Peter died I opened his Christmas present. The box was covered in his blood. It was a beautiful Espresso Pot from Tiffany's."

Deuel's violent death marked new directions for everyone connected with him. Nobody would remain untouched, and many would develop open wounds that would take decades to heal.

☆ 13 ☆

PUZZLEMENT

"I could visibly see the deterioration in Peter's physical appearance in the final months of his life. He really did age in that year. The depression and stress took its toll."

— Pamela Deuel

Many of Deuel's close friends and working colleagues were shocked and puzzled by his tragic death. Although some did see warning signs.

Harold Frizzell recalled, "Peter was awful good to me. He was a quiet, caring person. He'd just go into work and do his dialogue. I never saw Pete lose it on the set. I did see trouble ahead, though. His main problem was alcohol. I got to see him at the funeral home. It was sad. That year when the show was going to wrap he was going to go home to Kentucky with me. We had plans to go fishing."

Beth Griswold commented, "I never thought that Peter would take his own life until I heard that he had started drinking again. The announcement of his death was a real shock to me, and a very difficult time. I heard the news over my car radio.

"We were in Arizona, on our way to Dallas for the NFL championship game between Dallas and San Francisco, to be played on New Years Day. My husband played for San Francisco, and if we won, we'd be on our way to New Orleans for the Super Bowl. My husband's brother was driving, with his wife beside him in the front seat. I was in the back seat with my dog, Beau. It was in the morning of New Years Eve day when I heard the radio news broadcast that "Peter Deuel has been found dead, in his Hollywood hills home, a suspected suicide." The newsman also said it was still under investigation. It was just a brief statement, and then he went on to other news. I couldn't believe what I heard.

"I asked my brother-in-law to turn up the radio and then to start searching for another newscast. He and his wife couldn't understand my shock and instant grief, as they knew nothing of the relationship I had with Peter. Even though I felt uneasy talking about it under those circumstances, I gave them a very limited history of my life with Peter.

"We were in the car for over 15 hours that day. I waited for the news to come on to hear more about what had happened, but there was very little information besides the brief statement I had already heard. We arrived in Dallas late that evening. When I saw my husband he asked if I had heard the news. I told him yes, but I was still in shock and so sad I found it very painful to try to talk to him about Peter. He knew how I had felt about Peter, that he had been the love of my life. It was something I shared with him early on in our relationship, before we were married. So we didn't speak of it. I never gave myself the chance to grieve that night, or for the next several months or even years.

"When San Francisco lost to Dallas on New Years Day, we drove on to my husband's home town in Mississippi and stayed at his parents' house for the next few weeks. From there we went up to Boone, North Carolina, where we spent the next few months. It was impossible for me to go to Peter's memorial service. I tried searching the newspapers for more information about what had happened with Peter, about the investigation into his death. But I couldn't find what I needed to know."

Jo Swerling Jr. recalled, "My reaction to his death was shock and disbelief. I remember it well. I got a call about 4 o'clock in the morning on New Year's Eve of 1971. My wife and I had planned a trip to San Francisco with another couple to celebrate New Year's Eve. We were going to spend the weekend there because New Year's Eve was on a Friday.

"I got the phone call from Dorothy Bailey, who was Roy Huggins' assistant. Dorothy had actually had a little bit of a romance with Pete in the early days of the show. There was a closeness there that transcended her position on the show. She had been called by some relative of hers who worked the night shift at some facility and heard it on the radio while driving into work at about 3 o'clock in the morning.

"Dorothy was almost hysterical on the phone. I felt that the first thing I should do is get her quieted down. So I said, 'Look, I'll come on over there as quickly as I can.' I was to learn about ten years later that my wife was not happy that I was going to do that and read things into it. I went to Dorothy's apartment and got her calmed down and called Roy from her apartment. This is around 5:30 in the morning. We didn't like calling Roy at that early hour, since Roy had a modus operandi of staying up all night working; he would go to bed at 5 o'clock in the morning and come into the office around noon.

"One of my major responsibilities, working with Roy, was to try to cover all the bases in the morning so that I wouldn't disturb his rest. And I fielded any curves that came in and either took care of them or put them off until he came in. It would be my judgment if some problem were serious enough to wake him up. And I got to be pretty good at that. Obviously this was a terrible crisis, and I called Roy and he said, 'Why don't you go over and break the news to Ben and then get a hold of the production manager and tell the crew not to come in. I'll get up and come in, and we'll talk and see what we're going to do.'

"So Dorothy and I went over to Ben's apartment and told him. Ben's reaction was interesting. He said something to the effect of, 'That son of a bitch. I was afraid he would end up doing something like this.' He was kind of pissed. It was not the reaction we expected. I understand it, but it came as a bit of a surprise."

Pamela Deuel, commenting on her brother's "romance" with Dorothy Bailey, said, "Dorothy Bailey was a lovely tall girl with long, beautiful thick brown hair. Peter took her out a couple of times. She was madly in love with him and they were dear friends, but it wasn't reciprocated."

Bridget Hanley recalled, "My husband Swack socialized with Peter, and they had kept in touch. My daughter was born the year Peter passed away. When we got the call about Peter's death, Swack, I believe, was in Arizona doing a film. I couldn't understand how Peter could deprive himself of the gift of life and deprive the world of his glorious talent and his wondrous spirit. He just was a bright light. I don't think Swack ever knew the dark side.

"When Swack heard, his first reaction was of great rage. Not at Peter, but at the event.

He said to me, 'Pete must have been so angry.' I remember great tears. I had only seen Swack cry a couple of times before. I think he felt like Peter's father and really loved him.

"Peter was very open and like a litmus paper. It's so sad because he was so joyful and such a presence. And funny and warm. I never saw any depression. For a number of years after Swack heard the news I would catch him shaking his head from time to time, and I knew he was having a 'Peter moment.' He just didn't understand."

"It came as a complete astonishing shock to me when I heard the news that he had killed himself," recalled James Drury. "I couldn't believe it. I had never seen him in a situation were he was depressed, but then I didn't socialize with Pete. We didn't hang out or anything like that. We just had a great time on the set. I always remember enjoying the work with him. He was always prepared and ready and knew what he wanted to do. He was very professional and had great talent. He wasn't at all depressed doing the *Alias Smith and Jones* pilot."

Fellow actor Mike Farrell commented, "His suicide was a shock, needless to say. I'm touched by the memory of our times together even now, as I recall those days. Such a waste. The death of someone so young and beautiful is truly a tragic thing."

Monty Laird, recalling his final memory of Deuel, said, "I was horseback riding with him the last day I saw him. I think of him often. We liked the same things in life. Those were the best years of my life when I did the show."

Writer Jerrold Freedman commented, "His death was shocking. I had friends who lived near him, and I had visited his house. You never expect something like that. Why did it happen? Was it an accident? Who knows?"

Actress Celeste Yarnall recalled, "I visited both Peter and Ben on the set of *Alias Smith and Jones* several times. Peter was a very special person — extremely charming, sensitive and kind. We were good friends and went out to dinner a few times, where we had deep philosophical discussions. He was quite intense and serious. I liked Peter a lot, and was shocked and saddened by his death."

Actor Jared Martin was equally perplexed by Deuel's tragic death: "I must admit I was totally shocked when he committed suicide. Just subjectively I thought, 'What the hell is this guy doing committing suicide? He had so many things to live for.' In retrospect there was probably some substance abuse involved. I didn't see his dark side. His death was an utter shock, and there was a huge buzz about it among actors."

Juliet Mills commented, "I was absolutely shocked and appalled when I read about his suicide. I found that very puzzling, having worked with him less than a year before.

"I don't remember anything about Peter that was depressed or eccentric. He certainly didn't look like an alcoholic when I worked with him. He was lovely to work with. Looking at the episode again today, it makes you realize just how young Peter was when he died. It was ironic that my episode was called 'The Man Who Murdered Himself.' One has tremendous sympathy for Peter."

Frank Price remarked, "One of the big hidden problems with a number of actors was substance abuse. It's not easy to deal regularly with people who are taking mind-altering substances, whether it's pills, booze or cocaine. There's not much you can do about it. You're not the police. God forbid that you should suggest that someone's using unusual substances. That would be met with outraged denials and accusations of McCarthyism. So you ignore it and pretend you're dealing with rational people.

"Pete seemed charming, agreeable and pleasant, with a sense of humor. Fortunately, most actors stayed away from the drugs. But some indulged a lot. Actors are crazy enough without the stimulants. But mixed with the disapproval of substance use was the empathy for the troubled people who chose the profession, with its terrible insecurities. That's what the drugs are trying to hide."

Pamela Deuel was aware of her brother's substance abuse problem.

"Peter got into a vicious cycle of uppers, downers and booze," observed Pamela. "The depression was increasing. But uppers were common in those days. Everybody carried them around and appeared to be using. It had to be a terrible thing, what it did to Peter's brain chemistry. Alcohol is the number one element in his life that was very destructive. Jennifer was absolutely devastated by Peter's death. Jennifer did come out to live in L.A. after the funeral, and we tried to pick up the pieces of our lives."

"The sadness and annoyance for me about Peter's death," described Jack Jobes, "was the fact he was walking around town with a snub-nosed .38, and his 'friends' should have said, 'No that's not a good thing to do Pete; I'll take that.' Peter was a charmer — self-confident and outgoing. Alcohol was his problem. It's a powerful depressant. I find it very difficult to believe that Peter killed himself. The depression brought on by alcohol was a major factor, coupled with discord in his relationship."

The only person present in the Glen Green home when Deuel died, Dianne Ray, heard no conversation or argument prior to the gunshot, and no evidence of forced entry was found by the police. Deuel's blood level of alcohol was listed as .31.

"No drugs were found, to my recollection," recalled Konstanturos. "It was primarily alcohol. There were quite a few empty bottles and beer cans."

"I truly believe that he really didn't mean to die," commented Dianne Ray.

"I honestly don't think he meant to go through with it," declared Lynne Karroll, "as odd as it sounds, because a gunshot is final. I don't ever pretend to know someone well enough, but I was physically around a great deal, and my best friend Dianne was living with him, so I had some insight into this thing. All of us thought it was not something he meant to be final. It wasn't a premeditated event. It was a spur of the moment thing, and Peter expected a 'take two.'

"It was as close to an accident as it could be, I think. Dianne has always felt that way. There were no signs this was going to happen. If Peter had missed, he would have had zero memory of it the next morning. He liked to get high, and I'm sure drugs were part of the picture. It makes it sadder by a hundred times because I don't think Peter wanted to kill himself. It was so bizarre and sudden. Peter wasn't wallowing in despair. I've known people who have been wallowing in despair and who have committed suicide. And this wasn't that. His career was rising. There just wasn't a good reason.

"I don't think it was a case of him saying, 'I don't want to be here any more.' I don't think he seriously entertained the thought that he was going to be gone. There was never that black depression. I think it was a dramatic moment and he screwed up. And he screwed up a lot of lives along with it. My friend Dianne is the least of it. Anyone terribly close to someone who does something like that — it takes them down too.

"I remember someone after the funeral saying they didn't think he was stable, and that acting is a business that attracts neurotics and feeds their neuroses. I think there was a good deal of that. But I don't think there's an actor alive who's stable. I didn't see some steady deterioration into gloom and depression before he killed himself. Not at all. And I was around a lot."

Harold Frizzell had a different opinion of events, commenting, "He just couldn't face up to his fears of going into a grand mal seizure and never coming out of it. He just got tired of it. That's my opinion. Peter would avoid talking about his epilepsy and tell me, 'That's enough of that, Hal. We don't want to talk about that anymore.'"

An ongoing civil action claim to sue for damages and expenses in connection with Duel's DUI accident in October 1970 was also a factor, according to Pamela Deuel.

"The impending court case involving Diane Lachman, combined with how terribly guilty he felt about leaving the scene of the accident for that period of time, weighed on his mind," recounted Pamela. "And then to know that he could lose everything he had. There was an awful lot going on that was possibly terrifying to him."

Deuel's memorial service was held on Sunday, 2 January, 1972. Three thousand mourners filled and surrounded the Windmill Chapel at the Self-Realization Fellowship Lake Shrine in Pacific Palisades, Los Angeles.

"The Self-Realization Fellowship was a weird place," said Pamela. "At the front of this little chapel there were about six framed photographs or drawings of the different religious figures, including Jesus and the Buddha. My mother looked at me and was just sickened to think that this was where her dearest firstborn's service would be. She looked at me and said, 'Well, at least there's a picture of Jesus up there.'"

Fellow actors and friends attending the memorial service included Kim Darby; Shirley Jones and husband Jack Cassidy; actor Jeff Corey, who had also served as Duel's drama coach; actors Kent McCord and Henry Gibson; actresses Thordis Brandt, Elizabeth Allen and Leslie Parrish; actor John Anderson; and director Richard Benedict.

"Nobody recognized me at the service," declared Kim Darby. "I had a severe eating disorder. When Peter died I was right behind him, dying. I had a grand mal seizure four days after hearing of Peter's death. I was in terrible shock and wasn't functioning at all. I just went to bed and lay there. I didn't have any interest in anything, and I felt that the only person that really loved me was gone."

Pamela Deuel, one the few people who did recognize Darby, commented, "Kim was dressed in black from head to toe and stood in a corner by herself looking very sad."

"I was so terribly upset, the Memorial Service was just a blur," recalled Leslie Parrish. "I heard about Peter's death at a particularly bad moment and I cried for days. He was such a dear and handsome man, and so kind. I think you can divide people into two groups: one that cares intensely — Peter was in that group — and the other that just kind of flies along accepting all the joys of democracy but not paying the dues. Peter paid the dues. Some of us just couldn't stand the pain.

"Peter never showed any signs of depression with me. That was a total shock. I know how depressed you must be to blow your brains out, but I couldn't see it. Had I any idea that he was as depressed as he was I would have done anything to help him. I'd go at 3 o'clock in the morning and talk to him if he was depressed. I was doing that for people. I had other friends who committed suicide. Another was the singer Phil Ochs, who was just horribly depressed about the political situation.

"You feel trapped in a series, which is why I never did one. I knew I could not stand the feeling of being committed to something for so long and be unable to get out. I sympathized with Peter's viewpoint. I turned down many successful series because I knew I couldn't stand it. Doing one week of a series was enough for me. It was not the greatest work if you were serious about acting.

"Peter was carrying the series, and there was no way out for him, which is probably why he did what he did. That's one way out. But the way Pete let go of his pain was not right. It was not the way to do it. It just broke everybody's heart."

Alias Smith and Jones producer and writer Glen A. Larson stated, "I got a chance to see him prior to the actual service at the funeral home. It was very moving and troubling, obviously. The SRF spiritual retreat was quite a pretty setting, but it was not a pretty situation."

Pamela Deuel, clarifying Larson's statement, recalled, "I remember seeing Peter for the first time, when the family viewed him, at a funeral home in Hollywood. There was an open casket for one evening. It wasn't for the public but for people who knew him. The casket wasn't present at the SRF memorial service. We all were in such shock.

"I looked at Peter and prayed to God that this was a nightmare and I was going to wake up. It was terrible. I just couldn't believe it. I kept touching him. It wasn't creepy. The hair covered his bullet wound. Peter looked perfect. I didn't look at his left side because we all knew the mark was there. The fact it didn't blow his head apart was interesting. The bullet just passed through and didn't affect his face. I've often thought, 'If only it had gone a little lower.' But it would have been terrible if he had lived and ended up brain-damaged. Peter would have really hated that."

Frank Price decided not to attend. Explaining his decision, Price said, "I am not religious and have had far too much experience with funerals in my childhood, since my mother's family was in the funeral home business. One of my lasting unpleasant memories as a kid was the smell of formaldehyde and dead bodies in the mortuary. So I rarely attend funerals. And I was not motivated to change my normal preference by any desire to play hypocrite and show up at a Self-Realization event.

"I've heard psychiatrists say that repressed hatred creates deep depression, and that can lead to suicide. I took Peter's death as an act of hate against everyone around him. He sure made an impact. I could sympathize with his struggle with whatever demons he wrestled with, but I could only be angry at him for destroying himself and his rare talent. Because he had talent and good looks, he was given fame and money far beyond what most people dream of. He didn't value it and threw it away. Apparently his life mattered more to the rest of us than it did to him."

Pamela Deuel, commenting on Sally Field's absence from the memorial service, said, "To my knowledge, she did not come to his service, and she never wrote to my parents after Peter died. My mother and Dad commented on that because they knew that Peter loved her as a friend, and that they were good 'buddies.' And we found that very strange that she didn't acknowledge his death."

Ben Murphy also declined to attend. "I was disappointed that Ben didn't turn up at the SRF service," said Pamela. "I can't blame him. It was a terrible thing for him, too, and he was probably in shock."

The L.A.P.D. were also absent from the memorial service.

"We have to operate like a business," remarked John Konstanturos, "and we don't have the manpower to attend any memorial services unless it's part of the investigation — if there's someone there we need to talk to or observe, for instance. The investigators and Sgt. Estrada didn't feel we needed to attend the SRF memorial service."

Glen Larson, commenting on Deuel's personality and possible reasons behind his tragic death, said, "He did have a dark side, and there were goblins going on in his head about what he wanted to do and where he wanted to be. I think it was probably an accident — the culmination of too much drink and of stress in his personal relationship. His relationship with the lady was not everything it should have been, and that was a problem. My perspective was that is was not a relationship that was giving him a lot of comfort. That was the root of where things went wrong. I was never convinced his death was a wholly deliberate thing. He had serious amounts of alcohol that night, as he did on the weekend trip to Catalina. It's more likely that he was just walking the edge and had an argument, and was just not in complete control of his faculties. It's not something that he would have done by design, saying, 'Okay, this is it; I've decided to check out.'

"It was probably various issues — his own unhappiness with his career, exactly where he wanted to go, when he was going to get there. I wasn't inside their house. The public side was pretty well managed. It's quite clear that that last night he was probably in a depressed mood. But I certainly don't think it was by design. We'd spent too much time together, and there was not enough indications he was going to go in that direction. It's a great shame and a great loss."

Reverend Brother Dharmandanda, leading the memorial service, said of Deuel, "He was a man who loved ... who cared ... perhaps too deeply," and concluded, "He is now free from the body and has risen and rests in the bosom of God."

Readings from the New Testament, the 23rd Psalm, "The Lord Is my Shepherd" and the Hindu Bagahavad-Gita were followed by a request to send love, prayers and wishes of peace to the deceased Deuel. A tearful Dianne Ray recited the poem Duel had written in 1965 entitled "Love."

The following day his body was returned to Penfield, New York.

"My parents paid for a round-trip ticket for eleven people to fly back to Penfield for the funeral," recalled Pamela. "Everyone was so respectful on the plane. I was sitting behind my mother and dad with the fellow I was dating at the time. John Napier was sitting next to Dianne, a couple of seats behind. She was making a list. The Volkswagen convertible — she wanted this, she wanted that. When John gave my parents the list, my mother said, 'Well, she just sealed her fate. We were going to give her the Volkswagen. But now she gets nothing.'"

Lynne Karroll had a different perspective on events: "The Deuel family took everything away from her and told her to go away."

Dianne Ray commented, "Peter had given the Volkswagen to me. They had no right to claim it."

Jack Jobes recalled, "Dianne took Pete's guitar, which was meant to go to me. I didn't attend the Penfield services. David McHugh was the only friend to return to Penfield."

An open casket viewing was held over two evenings at the Nulton Funeral Home, with over 2,000 people paying their last respects. A memorial service took place at the First Baptist Church of Penfield on 5 January. Hundreds of mourners of all ages attended the church funeral rite and listened to Pamela Deuel singing one of her brother's favorite songs, "Free Again," by Robert Colby, from the pulpit. The Reverend Robert Towner recited the poem

"Life," written by Deuel, and "What Is a Child?" written by his mother on the journey back to Penfield from Los Angeles on January 3.

"Dianne stayed at our family home for a few days," said Pamela. "She went upstairs to my bedroom with one of my cousins on my Dad's side. This guy was a little enamored of her because he was a little younger. He brought his guitar, and they would sit up there and play the guitar, and he would sing to her when people were downstairs coming to pay their respects at the house. She would rarely come down. When she would, she would be kind of shrouded.

"I don't recall that she stayed any longer than after the funeral. We never talked to her again."

Following the funeral, Dianne Ray briefly returned to Glen Green to pick up her belongings and stay with her sister before traveling to Europe for a vacation with a friend, visiting Switzerland, France and England.

"Peter's death took Dianne down for decades," declared Lynne. "I was furious at Peter's suicide. That was my overlying attitude. We were kids. It was shocking, but I was so angry at him. Even if he was fooling around, how could he do this? Dianne felt that way as well. But Dianne's anger was mixed with grief."

The Deuel family received thousands of condolence cards.

"Mother, for months and months, was writing people to thank them for their cards," remembered Pamela. "Finally, after about four months, Dad came into the dining room where she was sitting and found her weeping over this lovely letter. She was attempting to answer it and Dad said, 'That's enough. You can't do anymore.' Certainly she wasn't healing at that time, but she would never heal if she continued to reply to all the people who were kind enough to send us these cards. Peter's death affected my mother so much more because of the death of her daughter. She lost two children, not twenty years apart.

"Many people would love you to think they were close to Peter. But close friends would have had more of an impact after Peter's death. They would have made sure they were there with us. The people that were closest to Peter, John Napier and Harold Frizzell, were right there, and they didn't leave our sides. Harold hadn't been afraid to confront Peter. He didn't just tell Peter what he wanted to hear. He got mad as heck with him at times when Peter was being a jerk. Peter loved him, and he probably hated him for his honesty."

The County of Los Angeles Department of Chief Medical Examiner, Office of Coroner, Medical Report, dated 24 January, 1972, stated the cause of death as suicide. The official cause of death was listed as "Cerebral Destruction" due to "Gunshot Wound to Head."

A harsh winter prevented Deuel's immediate burial until the spring weather thawed the grounds of Penfield's Oakwood Cemetery.

"We didn't bury Peter until the end of March or early April because the ground was frozen," declared Pamela. "Geoff and myself weren't there. Mother and Dad attended alone because they didn't want to open those emotions again."

★ 14 ★

LIFE IN THE SHADOW

"Any new actor just reminded the audience that Peter Deuel, who was so good and so likable, was dead. And an imposter was playing the role."
— Frank Price

Deuel's sudden death left many unanswered questions and many loose ends. The producers of *Alias Smith and Jones* were left with a problem. They needed a replacement, and quick. Schedules had to be met. Universal were contracted to ABC to produce a show. The charm of the show had been the chemistry between Deuel and Murphy. It would prove difficult to find the show amusing after Deuel's death.

"As head of Universal Television, my responsibility was to save the show. All of us were under intense pressure, given the shocking and sudden circumstance of Peter's death," recollected Frank Price, "and the fact that we had to act so quickly and immediately to save the show. Peter not only killed himself, but he seemed to have killed a show that all of us had put countless hours of work into making succeed.

"Much talent and dedication went into the show. It was not just a job for the people doing it. And we felt we were close to turning it into a genuine hit. Then this happened. At that time I knew he had killed the show. I was ready to make a valiant effort to save it, to keep it on the air. But such a tragedy cast a terrible blight over the series. We never were able to overcome that. I don't think there's any casting agent that would have saved the show.

"Part of the underlying anger was that Peter gave no hint to us of any problems. Perhaps if we had known, we could have assisted him in getting help. But, of course, no one knew what was in his mind."

The looping of scenes featuring Deuel in "The Men That Corrupted Hadleyburg" (2:18) still remained to be completed for the January 27 ABC broadcast schedule.

"I recall we initially approached Geoffrey Deuel to do the looping on the outstanding scenes," said Frank Price.

Geoffrey Deuel attempted to loop scenes involving his brother but found the process too emotional, and Paul Frees took over looping duties. The possibility of a tribute at the conclusion of Deuel's final episode was never considered by studio executives.

"I don't think the network forbad it," commented Price. "We probably just didn't think of it."

Price and Huggins immediately discussed a replacement for Deuel. "Roy liked Roger

Davis a lot," said Price. "They had worked together before. I had reservations, but I didn't have a better idea for an actor who could be cast immediately. Frankly, my reservations included the fact that Peter was so unique in the role that we couldn't really replace him. But I went to work on the network executives, selling them the idea of Roger Davis as the immediate replacement. No serious consideration was given to anyone else. We had to continue production, and that required casting a replacement *now*. If a debate had started then we might have been forced to shut the show down while awaiting a decision. That could have led to cancellation."

Jo Swerling Jr. recalled the events surrounding the casting of Roger Davis as Deuel's replacement.

"We contacted the production people and cancelled the call for the day," said Swerling, "and went into the studio and had a meeting with Frank Price and other studio executives. Roy's inclination was to just shut the show down. Frank considered that, and then he contacted his counterparts at ABC. The decision that came down was, 'under no circumstances are you going to shut down. You're going to keep shooting. We have a contract to deliver this show. You'll replace the actor and deliver the show or you will be sued.' So we put out the call again and consulted with Ben and asked if he was willing to work, and he said he was. We put together a schedule of scenes that didn't involve Pete, and we were back in production after lunch that day.

"The crew all came back to work, with the exception of the director of photography, who wasn't emotionally up to it and was not happy we were bringing the crew back. We shot around anything that had to do with Pete. We located Roger in Aspen and immediately got him on a plane. I cancelled my weekend trip to San Francisco, which was the minimally professional thing that I could do, and was in Western Costume Company at 6 P.M. with Roger, getting him wardrobe. I was probably there until 10 or 11 P.M. that night. That was that same Friday. This all happened in one day.

"I'm sure Roger had reservations about accepting the role — to step into another actor's shoes, especially someone who was as solid and as good an actor as Pete. But it didn't prevent him from thinking it over and saying yes to it — very quickly. Roger was on the set Monday morning and we were re-shooting the Deuel scenes. Ben's reaction shots were filmed when Pete was still alive."

Frank Price commented, "Roy and Glen had to dig in and figure out how to address the various shows that were in post-production and what to do with the problems Peter's death caused. Each show, of course, represented at least a couple of hundred thousand dollars of production cost, so they couldn't be tossed away. Painful and ghoulish as it may seem, it had to be done. Just like somebody's got to pick up the body parts after a plane crash. I suspect nobody likes the job."

Glen Larson recalled Roy Huggins' decision to cast Roger Davis.

"I had one problem," Larson said. "Roger had just been in one show, *Smiler with a Gun*, playing a bad guy. There wasn't much time given to thinking about who else it could be. So we never got around to even discussing Pete's brother or other things, because this was a chance for Roy to vindicate the fact that the network should have bought *The Young Country*."

Murphy and members of the crew were initially hard on replacement Roger Davis, often comparing him unfavorably to Deuel. Monty Laird described the problems with the working relationship of Davis and Murphy.

"At first Roger and Ben got along good," recalled Laird, "but as it went along they had bad times. Roger was always late or on the phone, and sometimes had trouble with his lines. He would try and re-write or be the director. They did not have the same rapport as Pete and Ben."

Regarding the production of *Alias Smith and Jones* following Deuel's untimely death, and verbal attacks on executive decisions by fellow actors, Price commented, "I think all of us were too busy scrambling to solve the newly created production problems and save the series to pay much attention. I think there was a lot of transference going on. Of course, many people were angry that this event happened and destroyed so much that was important in their lives. Anger at Peter for the senseless act was unseemly, so that anger had to be directed elsewhere. And the executives in the Black Tower were always convenient targets. They didn't attack their writers, producers or directors in that way, probably because they had much closer contact and had to face them the next day."

Despite Murphy's anger at the way Universal handled Deuel's death, the President of Universal Television, Frank Price, viewed him favorably.

"I found Ben to be a good guy," commented Price, "always cooperative and professional. He was not the actor that Peter Deuel was, but he had a similarity in looks to Paul Newman (that's not why he was cast as Kid Curry, however) and an easy way with comedy. He and Peter made a great pair. It took two to tango.

"Peter's death destroyed the career of Ben, who would carry the shadow of Peter Deuel over him the rest of his career. When Ben was light and funny in other series later, it reminded everyone of *Alias Smith and Jones* and Peter Deuel. So his humor was destroyed, and that wasn't his fault."

Pamela Deuel met Ben Murphy again for the first time after her brother's death while filming the *E! Mysteries and Scandals* tribute to her brother in 1999.

"I met Ben Murphy a couple of times," said Pamela, "and he was very pleasant and kind of kidded me: 'Oh, you're Petey's little sister.' When I did the *E! Entertainment* show, and Ben was on there, I wrote him a little note. I hadn't seen him or talked to him since Peter's death. I said it was good to see him and wished him well. But I never received a reply. I guess I didn't necessarily think I would, because Peter's death more or less marked the end of Ben's career.

"There was one thing he said that I didn't agree with. He said that if Pete were here he'd do it all again. I found that offensive. I think if Ben is angry about it I can understand it, but it's a shame if he hasn't been able to get beyond it. But what an awful thing to happen to him, too. He and Peter didn't have a friendship outside of work, but Peter never said a bad thing about him. He said he was a good actor and he really respected him. And Peter was just so glad for the working relationship they had and the fun they had together.

"A couple of times during the show I went up to Frazier Park where they filmed the exteriors. I didn't go up with Petey. On Interstate 5, which takes you up to Frazier Park, up in the mountains, I was passing a car, and I looked to the right and it was Ben Murphy driving a beautiful '57 Chevy. He had a helmet on. I thought, if he looks at me I'm going to laugh. Out on location with Peter I said, 'Petey, Ben Murphy had a helmet on while he was driving.' And Peter said, 'Oh, he always has a helmet on when he's driving a car.' I said, 'Isn't that a little bit paranoid. I don't like to fly but ... wow!!'"

Pamela, commenting on Roger Davis, said, "I think Roger genuinely felt terrible when Peter died, but I don't know that they were friends."

Harold Frizzell commented, "I left the show when Roger Davis came on. I didn't really care for him because of his attitude. Pete didn't care for Roger Davis or particularly like him."

Although Roger Davis would always live in the shadow of Peter Deuel, he survived in the role of Hannibal Heyes for seventeen episodes. Frank Price had some sympathy for Davis' situation.

"Imagine being Roger Davis, thrust into the middle of all of this," began Price. "Irrational people blamed him for stepping in to help save the series because he's not Peter Deuel. Roger was a working professional actor, available for hire."

Monty Laird also expressed sympathy for Davis' situation, but with reservations.

"I liked Roger," Laird said. "We got along. It's a very hard thing to take over where another left off. Pete was a hard act to follow. Roger is a good actor, but he didn't help *Alias Smith and Jones*. I do think that is why the show was cut."

Harold Frizzell declared, "Roger Davis is just a footnote."

Alias Smith and Jones was cancelled in mid-season, with the final scenes being filmed on 2 November, 1972. The final episode would be broadcast two months later on 13 January, 1973. ABC had moved the schedule of the show from Thursday night, opposite NBC's *The Flip Wilson Show*, to Saturday night, opposite *All in the Family*. A reworking of the BBC hit comedy show *Till Death Us Do Part* for the American public, *All in the Family* would dominate the Saturday nighttime slot for the next five years. With *Bonanza* being cancelled three days after *Alias Smith and Jones*, the only Westerns left on TV in 1973 were *Gunsmoke* and *Kung Fu*. Both finally succumbed in 1975.

Letters to the BBC (British Broadcasting Corporation) following Deuel's death confirmed his popularity. They received 7,000 letters a week requesting a rerun of *Alias Smith and Jones*. The BBC acknowledged the requests of the fans and repeated the Deuel segments before showing the new Roger Davis episodes, starting 26 November, 1973, over a year after the show had finished production. A BBC spokesman commented in 1972, "Deuel has inspired a cult here similar to the one started in the U.S. by James Dean's death, but it's not as morbid."

"The show was a much bigger hit in England than it was here," declared Glen Larson. "It would have been nice if Pete could have gotten over there and gotten that sense of appreciation. There was a point where the BBC inquired about picking up the show just for England, without worrying about if it was on the air here or not."

Frank Price, expressing his views on the ultimate failure of *Alias Smith and Jones*, said, "My job as head of the studio was to make sure we produced enough hit television shows. A hit was a show that had ratings success and ran five years, so we had at least 100 episodes. If I failed to get enough of these hits, I would be fired and replaced. So I invested a lot of personal work and ideas in our various series. *Alias Smith and Jones* got more of me than most, because I was in charge of the process of creating and producing the pilot. When I turned it over to Roy, I was turning over something very important to me. I trusted Roy. He was the best television producer I had worked with.

"Shows fail for many reasons. It was hard to see all our work go down the drain because of this bizarre event. I can't label what I felt as anger. Frustration certainly. Dismay. As the old Navy saying went: 'Fucked by the fickle finger of fate.' Had Peter lived I think we would have finally found a time slot that worked for *Alias Smith and Jones*. Since the show was good and the network liked it, and we had terrific demographics, I think we could have secured another renewal. Without Peter, there was no enthusiasm to continue on. A light-hearted series became a gloom-laden series. In *Alias Smith and Jones* the star was Peter Deuel. It couldn't survive his death."

Jo Swerling Jr. commented, "My feeling was that it was working and going along. It lost a certain sparkle, but it didn't seem to matter to the audience because the ratings, as I recall, either were maintained or got better. I always felt the show was unnecessarily can-celled by Barry Diller when it was still getting strong ratings. And our feeling at the time, which is probably true, was that Barry just lost interest in the show after Pete left, and didn't like it as much. Diller was the head of programming for ABC at the time."

Commenting on Peter Deuel's future career, had he lived, Frank Price said, "His career beyond *Alias Smith and Jones* could have taken many paths. His preference for heavy drama was at odds with his international success in a series that highlighted his skills performing light comedy. Perhaps his path would have led him to great acting achievements. Maybe he would have become an American Olivier. Or maybe his talent was more like that of James Garner, who was superb in *Maverick* and *The Rockford Files*, but who respected his work in *The Americanization of Emily* far more. Who are we to say these people are crazy? I think the World War II motion picture *To Be or Not to Be* (1942), starring Jack Benny, handled the question well. Benny was a stage comic who desperately wanted to play *Hamlet*. Unfor-tunately, audiences laughed at him. He put little value on his ability to make an audience laugh. Actors have a self-image we can't really understand.

"The Hannibal Heyes role came easy to Peter," concluded Price. "He did not have to agonize over the emotions of the character. How would you feel if you were stuck being Cary Grant but really wanted to play *King Lear*?"

☆ 15 ☆

RIPPLES THROUGH TIME

"To keep our faces toward change and behave like free spirits in the presence of fate is strength undefeatable."

— Helen Keller

The trauma of Deuel's death continued to affect the family long after the media lost interest and moved on. Of immediate concern was finding a home for the orphaned dogs, Shoshone and Carroll. Initially, Dianne Ray had wanted to care for them, but Geoffrey and Pamela Deuel decided it was preferable to share the dogs.

"Geoff was living in Venice the spring following Peter's death. He took the dogs in for a short period, and we often shared them. We eventually ended up with them permanently. I found Shoshone to be very intuitive. Dogs are profoundly instinctive, and Shoshone proved to be most unique. She had a sense about her. Peter told me that Shoshone would come very close to him before one of his seizures.

"When I moved to Tujunga in 1973 I had this little house. A door led from the kitchen to some steep stairs to the back yard. It was great for the three dogs because they just played and ran. When I opened the back door the dogs would come running up the stairs. Indian, our black Labrador, never got over his puppyish excitement. Shoshone would also run with great excitement, and always won the race to the back door. Then she would step backward and let Indian and Carroll in first. She was such a lady."

Pamela had pursued a singing career throughout the latter half of the 1960s.

"I never consciously followed Peter into show business. I viewed music as completely different than acting. I had no plans or designs to go into acting. I just wanted to be a singer. I started singing in Rochester after Jennifer's father and I were divorced and I had gone back to live with mother and father. I worked at an automobile dealership and the University of Rochester, working for the head of the music department. Even though my music studies were cut short after Jennifer's birth, I still had this great desire to sing.

"I worked at the Channel 13 ABC affiliate in Rochester, WOKR. There was a contest for Miss Rochester. I was 25 and became the coordinator for the beauty pageant. I felt too old to be a contestant. The weatherman at the station had some connections in Rochester and thought I was a great singer. I sang at the Holiday Inn with one of the top dance bands in Rochester. That started my career. I sang around Rochester in various nightclubs. A group called the Entourage came to Rochester, headed by a wonderful jazz musician who played flute and saxophone. He needed another girl singer in the group because

Left to right: Mr. and Mrs. Deuel, Jennifer and Pamela Deuel, John and Sandy Napier, Easter 1972 (courtesy Deuel Family Collection).

one of the two girls had gone back to Kentucky to get married. So I auditioned and was given the job.

"The group was like a mini-revue where you'd go from one person to another to sing. And there was some dancing. We'd practice in my parents' living room during the Christmas of 1969. It was hysterical. I was learning the steps and moves to the little routine we had. Our first engagement on the road was in Jamestown, New York. There was a huge blizzard and very few people turned up at the club. That was just as well because I was still learning and didn't really know what I was doing. The other girl intimidated me because she was very smooth and confident. I still was very shy. Several weeks later I perfected my routine and we ended up in Las Vegas for three separate gigs. We worked at the Sahara and the International. We were singing in the lounge when Elvis Presley was in the main room. Peter knew Elvis, but we never met him. It was phenomenal to see Elvis perform. He was something to behold.

"Peter recommended one his best friends, Don Fanning, to the group as a drummer. We hired him, and then I fired him. It was a foolish decision, influenced by a man I was dating at the time. He was a supposed personal manager to entertainers, and he promised me great things. That was one of the most horrible things I ever did. Don was loyal and loving, and the man I was dating turned out to be a loser. He'd tell me he was seeing people in Beverly Hills to promote me, when in fact he was going down to Venice to hang around with his friends. At the end of the day he'd put his suit back on, pick up his briefcase and return home. A real con man.

"I've always thought that I never became truly successful with my singing career because I was so naive and didn't know how to play the game in a lot of ways. It was so repugnant to me. I knew when I was being a phony around certain people in power in an attempt to ingratiate myself. They act so nice at these parties and say they are going to do things for you, but they never call you. I would wait by the phone and think there was something wrong with the phone. The phoniness was wearing me down and causing me to lose emotional energy.

"After Peter died I had to use everything within me to just get through a day, because the grief was so overwhelming. Months later I would be at a party with my friends and I would just sit over in a corner and cry. I just couldn't function. At the time, in the early 1970s, I should have grabbed hold of myself and gotten help. I needed to have a life and move forward and not be consumed by feelings of 'why did this happen?'"

In 1972 Pamela made her first, and only, venture into acting when she appeared in the movie *The Runaways* (1975) with Steven Oliver, brother of Susan Oliver, and John Russell. The film would take three years to find a release date.

"That movie was terrible," opined Pamela. "I played a lesbian jailbird. My big debut. I was only around for one scene. I didn't get paid. I got dinner. At that time I was concentrating on my singing. I had a couple of potential record deals that never happened. The grief over Peter was so all-encompassing it was hard to concentrate on being a better singer and raising my daughter. It was just enough to get out of bed every day and remember what had happened. Maybe if that part had come along a couple of years later it would have been a different thing, but I was overwhelmed over what had happened."

In 1973 a traumatic event would serve as a call to return to her Christian faith.

"I got locked in and tied up in a guy's apartment that I dated. He got me the part in *The Runaways* and was a Scientologist. He was a good-looking, muscular guy who played 'B' parts where he could be a rough guy. Geoff brought him to hear me sing when I made my Hollywood debut. I went out with him once, and it was a pleasant date. Then a couple of nights later I met him in Westwood. I didn't realize it but he had been drinking quite heavily before. We went to his apartment to pick up something, which ended up being a ruse.

"He locked me in there and tied me up and proceeded to slap me around and tear my clothes off. It was just a hideous experience, and I thought I was going to die. When he started to sober up, about three hours later, he said, 'Get out of here.' So I went home and was so thankful to be alive. I said, 'God, thank you for saving my life.' That was when I had a rebirth of faith. It was a combination of losing Peter and that terrifying situation. It was around August 1973. I'd never really lost my faith, but I was kind of ignoring it. After I made a rededication to God, I utilized the tools that were there to get mental and emotional help.

"John Napier and I had stayed friends. He really loved my daughter Jennifer and took us under his wing. He was a real fine guy. When I started going to this wonderful church in the San Fernando Valley I called John because I knew that he was really hurting. The loss of Peter was horrible for him because he was such a dear friend and cared so deeply for him. So he came and visited my church. He had never been to church as a young boy in West Virginia, but he became a very strong Christian and married a beautiful Christian woman several years later."

Geoffrey Deuel had achieved success in his brother's lifetime playing Billy the Kid opposite John Wayne in *Chisum* (1970). It should have been a platform for gaining regular work in movies, but his personality proved to be a stumbling block.

Jill Andre commented, "Geoffrey was the younger brother who wanted the attention his older brother got. He got wilder and crazier so he would get the attention. Peter was much more in control than Geoff. Geoffrey was always feeling this competition with Peter, so he was also trying to be bigger, louder and more dramatic. Geoffrey never really came to terms with himself after Peter's death. I know he thought for the longest time that Peter had been killed and that it wasn't a suicide."

Lynne Karroll said, "Peter and Geoffrey were pretty different. Peter overpowered Geoffrey, talent-wise. Peter was also stronger as a personality. He was the dominant one. I think some of Geoff's anger has to do with an unfulfilled career and Peter's success."

David McHugh commented, "The firstborn usually has an edge regarding entitlement. Geoff wasn't as tall as Peter. He was actually much better-looking than Peter. Peter had a rugged kind of handsomeness, but Geoff was absolutely perfect-looking in my opinion. He was one of the most extraordinarily handsome men ever. Geoff tried so hard to be big brother. Where Peter had this natural entitlement, Geoff was more of a people pleaser. In a way he was a softer person and didn't have that edge that Peter had. Women would just flock to Geoff. Both brothers had major demons to fight, and Geoff was a bar fighter. He would go in and look around the bar, pick the biggest guy and get into a fight with him. But there was a self-revulsion involved. One night I was sitting with Peter at his parents' house in Penfield, and Geoff came in and showed us the palm of his left hand. He had this burn the size of a quarter in the middle of his palm. I asked him how he got the burn, and he replied, 'I was just sitting out the back burning my hand with a cigarette.'"

Shortly after Deuel's death, a report surfaced that connected Dianne Ray with a magazine article.

"A writer for *The Hollywood Reporter* wrote something about me selling my story of Peter's life with me for $2,000," declared Dianne. "I refuted that, and there was a little retraction on the back page."

Dianne decided to take up Lynne Karroll's offer to move with her to Acapulco in Mexico.

"After Pete died I told Dianne that I was going back to Mexico and invited her to come with me and get out of L.A., because it was a disaster," described Lynne. "It was just a horrible deal. Geoffrey was very nasty to Dianne, and the Deuel family just ignored her. She was being used as a scapegoat. It was devastating for everybody. I've always been of the mind that if things are that hideous, get out. There was no way she could stay in L.A. Dianne accepted my offer and stayed for three years."

Public relations work for the Porto Fino restaurant, and photographic and interview assignments for the society section of the national *El Heraldo* newspaper, couldn't keep Dianne Ray's feelings of isolation and depression at bay. She turned to alcohol and drugs, and became addicted to both.

"When we first got to Mexico there was a brittle, 'let's party' thing," commented Lynne. "Probably the worst thing was that she buried some of it and tried to just party. She had a hell of an alcohol problem. There wasn't a massive period of grief and mourning in Mexico. She was in denial. The grief just about buried her when she came back to L.A. and faced it. I remember her telling me she never really mourned the way she was supposed to. Then she entered into the world of real alcoholism. But she helped herself pull through it eventually."

"It was very hard in Mexico because I was a mess," remarked Dianne. "Whenever anybody would bring a gun out I would just freak. Peter's violent death was what started all that for me. I've suffered from depression since Peter died and wanted to die myself. It was his death that kept me alive through a lot of my alcoholism. I could not leave that legacy with my family, because Peter's death ruined my life and I'm sure that of his family too. I returned to L.A. and worked for the 'Children's Home Society.' This was an agency that educated young women about pregnancies and adopted out babies. I'm older now and I do well. It helped to find someone and fall in love. I eventually got married when I was 47."

Pamela remarked, "Dianne's whole life was inexorably changed that night. I don't blame Dianne for what Peter did, and I never thought that she pulled the trigger. My heart goes out to her even though I found some of the things she did to Peter very harmful. On the other hand, I know Peter was no prince."

Although Pamela found comfort in her Christian faith there was still one question that constantly worried her: Was Peter with God?

"I was concerned and emotionally unsettled because of my faith," said Pamela. "Peter's death brought me back to the Lord and focused my attention. About a year and a half after his death I thought, 'Pamela, you could end up dead too. You know you're being stupid drinking and smoking marijuana.' I remember talking with people from my church and saying to them that the thought of Peter not being with the Lord was awful. I wanted to know that I would be with him again some day. But more importantly, I was concerned about the condition of his soul."

Pamela's first dream about her brother, three years after his death, proved to be a turning point.

"When I finally had this dream about him it was beautiful. In the dream I was in the woods, and there was a beautiful stream tumbling over rocks. The stream had fish swimming in it and it felt cold. It was beautiful countryside, much like you would see in Idaho. I was walking through this wood, and Peter was crouched by the stream with his dogs, whittling a stick. He stood up, and then I saw him and ran to him. I was sobbing as he lifted me up.

"'Petey you're alive, you're alive!'

"He cried and we laughed. I said, 'Why didn't you tell us?'

"He replied, 'I want you to know, I'm okay.'

"I was crying and said, 'That's great. We have to tell Mom and Dad.'

"I started pulling on his arm, but he said, 'Honey, I can't go with you. But I'm fine and we will be together some day.'

"And I thanked him, because in the dream I didn't understand what he was saying.

"I said, 'What do you mean you can't come with me? Come home.'

'No honey. You're fine and you have to know I'm fine.'

"I woke up the next morning and I realized it wasn't true. He wasn't alive. For half a day I was so sad. I just cried and cried. And then I started thinking about him. 'You dummy. This is what you wanted to know.' And since that time I've had peace. That was a very pivotal moment in regard to coming to terms with Peter's death."

The public's reaction to Deuel's death came as a surprise to the Deuel family.

"Our family was incredulous at the number of people who contacted us," related Pamela. "And we were very touched. I know for a time it seemed very strange to me. When I became more visible through my singing career and being on television, I would get letters. The people who wrote personally to me were usually nut cases. In one of the letters I received, a girl went on and on about how she loved Peter and how he was everything to her.

"She said, 'You have no idea how much his death has hurt my life.' This is a girl who has never met him and was so out of touch — not only with reality, but with good taste. It sickened me. My parents got similar letters saying, 'You can't imagine how terrible I feel.' It was all about them. Now it makes me feel close to Peter when I know that people who never met him loved him so much, and that he's still alive to them in some ways."

After the initial shock of Deuel's death lessened, there was time for reflection.

"Several years later my mother and I were talking about what a selfish act suicide is," said Pamela. "At the time, the person is so distraught and so not themselves that they see no way out. But when you think of the ripple effect and of the lives of those affected — if not totally ruined — it is just so damaging.

"I always thought Peter really wanted to be dead. He was depressed and angry with himself because he was failing to defeat his drinking. The way I dealt with the fact was to think, 'He would have done it anyway.' As the years have gone by, not only have I healed and become more mature, I now know he didn't mean to kill himself. He did it in this absolutely foolish moment of drunkenness. Peter didn't really want to die. It was this terrible accident. I now feel that if only he wasn't drunk, and if only he didn't have that gun, he would be alive.

"I always had a desire to move back East, and finally moved to the Philadelphia area in February 1998. Following my divorce, I remarried in October, 2002. I still continue singing gospel music on a part-time basis and speak to women's groups. Since moving back East I changed careers, and I met my husband. I feel very happy and contented with my life today," concluded Pamela.

Jennifer Seymour was only seven years old when her uncle died. It would take many years before the impact of his death affected her.

"Around age 12 and 13 my uncle's death affected me deeply," said Jennifer, "and I would listen obsessively to him reading his poems and talking about the environment on the E.P. he recorded.

"Uncle Peter was the love of my life and very protective of me. He filled in the blanks left by father when he was doing his own thing after my parents' divorce. Before he died, uncle Peter had put a down payment on a horse for me — a Palomino. I only discovered this years after he died.

Pamela Deuel Johnson and husband Richard P. Johnson, 2005 (courtesy Pamela Deuel Johnson).

"As much as I loved my uncle I feel that he did something stupid. The drama with my uncle only happened when he was drunk. The only time I saw him unhappy was when he had been drinking and there were conflicts with Geoffrey or Dianne. I believe the relationship was coming to an end, and he thought, 'Screw you.' I think he was incoherent drunk, and people do really stupid things in those situations. He was only 31 and immature.

"He had lost a certain innocence in becoming an actor and coming out to Hollywood. He was plunged into this dark hole of fans, and he had to be 'on' all the time. When he was with me it was riding horses, going fast in cars, making me laugh and going to the beach. Just being himself. Peter had a very innocent side. My mother would leave me with Peter and say, 'That's precious cargo.' Peter would reply, 'No, it's gold to me.'

Peter would tell my mother, 'She's just a little girl. Let her have some fun.'

"He was my hero. Without my uncle I would never have learnt about horses and made them an important part of my life. I now live and work on a 270,000 acre ranch, and work in conservation as a land planner. It's very rewarding and I love it."

Former girlfriend Beth Griswold, finding her grieving process repressed due to the influence of her mother, decided to contact Geoffrey Deuel.

"I came home to California sometime in April," related Beth. "Later that year, during a visit with my mother, she told me that Geoff had tried to contact me after Peter's death. He had told her that he had some things for me from Peter's belongings. But my mother told Geoff that he shouldn't contact me, that I was a married woman now and my life with Peter should stay in the past.

"I was so angry with her for shutting off that connection. I would have loved to have talked to Geoff, to talk to someone who also loved Peter, to have someone to share my grief with and to somehow share his. I didn't know anyone else who knew Peter as intimately, so there was really no one to talk to about him. I wanted so much to understand why. I visited the local library and looked up on microfiche all the publications that came out right after Peter's death. I was searching for something to help me understand.

"I had been unable to say goodbye to Peter emotionally. With so little information and no tangible experience of a memorial service or conversation with someone who had been there, I sometimes would imagine his death was just a bad dream.

Peter Deuel, September 1968 (courtesy Beth Griswold).

"Sometime in the first few years after his death I was at a nightclub and thought I saw Peter. This man looked so much like Peter it took my breath away. Peter had that kind of effect on people. In my mind I knew it couldn't be him, but in my heart I was hoping it was. I had to tell myself to get a grip. I had to scream inside, 'Peter is dead, it can't he him!' I looked away for a moment, and when I looked back he was gone. At that moment I realized I had never really come to terms with the end of our relationship or his death."

Peter Deuel's two dogs continued to live a contented life with Pamela Deuel and her family until the day Carroll was attacked by a wild animal.

"We believe it was a coyote coming down from the hills," commented Pamela. "Carroll was bitten in the back through her haunches to the point where she had to have steel staples. Sadly she disappeared around 1978. We never knew what happened to her.

"Shoshone died on Peter's birthday in 1980. When we returned from church, Indian was there to greet us as usual but Shoshone was missing. I found her in the small covered area that overlooked the pool where the dogs would sleep. She had died peacefully," concluded Pamela.

✫ 16 ✫

FRACTURED IMAGE

"This is the world; the lying likeness of
Our strips of stuff that tatter as we move"
— Dylan Thomas, *Our Eunuch Dreams* (1934)

Peter Deuel was a proud person with high standards who disliked studio parties and their false camaraderie. Authenticity and a sense of control over his life and career were of prime importance. Both were increasingly difficult to achieve as he became more successful as an actor. The role of Hannibal Heyes made him a recognized face on an international level, but the real Peter Deuel had been conflicted in his personal life and had taken little pleasure in his manufactured image.

"Peter Deuel was an actor. When he acted a role, he 'manufactured' himself," commented Frank Price. "He took on another character. He spoke lines written by someone else. He took direction about his performance — how to do it and how to improve it. His hair was done by a hairdresser. His face and body were done by make-up artists. The cameraman carefully lighted him to achieve the most flattering image. Wardrobe designers were employed to design his costumes, and the wardrobe people outfitted him.

"What else is an actor but 'manufactured?' The actor playing *Hamlet* actually wasn't smart enough or clever enough or endowed with enough depth to think up those marvelous lines that he says. That wretch of a writer is out of sight somewhere while the actor takes the bows before an admiring audience for his brilliant 'manufactured' performance."

Pamela Deuel, commenting on her brother's decline and possible future had he lived, said, "In Hollywood there seemed to be a pervasive sadness. It could have been the epilepsy. It could have been just his drinking. He said to me over and over again that he was so angry with himself that he couldn't beat the drinking. Peter was open and honest about it and admitted he was an alcoholic. It doesn't mean he responded in the right way all the time.

"His drinking and depression went way back. The thought that somehow *Alias Smith and Jones* contributed to his death is so ridiculous. Peter was anxious to go on to other things because he saw he was starting to have a certain power, but he was also very grateful that this was the vehicle that had put him up there. He was getting to that point where I don't think he would have been bothered if the show had been cancelled. But he was still very happy with the opportunity he had been given in the relatively short time he had been in Hollywood."

Dianne Ray expressed a different viewpoint concerning Deuel's attitude toward *Alias Smith and Jones*.

"My memory of him was that he was nearly always in a bad mood," observed Dianne. "It was due to his drinking and the fact he didn't want to do a series because he felt it would ruin his career. Everybody else felt that once the series was over, because it was so good, he could pick and choose whatever he wanted to do. I felt that too. But he didn't. He felt he would get typecast. And he tended towards down. It was his natural temperament."

"Hollywood was full of sleazy and opportunist characters," remarked Pamela. "Peter was so empathetic to so many people and things and causes. I just don't think he was streetwise and tough enough. He wasn't mean enough. He couldn't manage it. We'd go to parties and they would have champagne and hard liquor and the best wines. And over in a little corner people would be snorting cocaine from these trays.

"There's a recklessness to Los Angeles that maybe New York never had. But unless he was able to get his alcoholism under control, I don't think Peter could have ever made any peace. It would be easy to blame other things, but we make choices. Maybe he would have been able to beat it if he'd never gone to Hollywood. He couldn't maintain a successful relationship with the alcohol. And if his partner was also a drunk, they would probably have ended up destroying each other anyway. I don't think any alcoholic can maintain a relationship.

"When Peter had begun to experience celebrity status he was always waiting for people to criticize him. I remember Peter said, 'It's wonderful on the way up. It's a tremendous rush and all that, but I know someday I'm going to come down.' Instead of enjoying it and cultivating it so he wouldn't have to come down, Peter was living in fear of failure.

"He felt he had compromised because he did want to work in New York. But he got smart about it and decided, 'I'll go there for a couple of years, and then I'll be able to pick and choose.' But it never happened for him. Perhaps because he was so hard on himself. He just couldn't put that aside and say, 'I'm doing this now and it's okay.' He was very sensitive and gentle, even though he was so self-destructive. He wasn't psychologically suited for that business. But he definitely had plans for the future because I can remember him saying that one day he wanted to direct."

Deuel also had no trouble obtaining drugs in the liberal atmosphere of Hollywood in the 1960s and early 1970s.

"Drugs were often obtained for the stars by stand-ins or other members of their entourage," explained Frank Price. "Stand-ins served pretty much at the pleasure of the 'star,' so stand-ins went out of their way to accommodate the star's needs."

Cultural influences of the time seemed to include the glorification of a premature death by the media. The tragic death of James Dean in an automobile accident in 1955 had immortalized his image as forever young. The eternal young rebel. The 1960s saw the premature deaths of John F. Kennedy, Marilyn Monroe and rock icons Janis Joplin and Bryan Jones of *The Rolling Stones*. Dying young had a certain perverse glamour attached to it.

"A lot of kids in our town during that time killed themselves," commented Pamela. "There was Peter's best friend, Chris Clarke, who shot himself. In Geoffrey's class there was Luke Carpenter and Bob Filiberti, who was one of Geoff's closest friends, and a great guy named Mike Hagerty, who was a friend of mine. Three guys that Geoff was close to committed suicide."

Was Deuel's death avoidable? The answer has to be in the affirmative, since all suicides are avoidable. The real question is, did Peter Deuel want to avoid death or did he see it as his escape from a world that he no longer wanted to be a part of? We will never know his true motivations. Accidental or self-inflicted, his death can only serve as a reminder that the value of a person rests in their life and not in the manner of their death.

★ 17 ★

TESTIMONY

"Our speech is alive when our words speak!"

— St. Anthony of Padua

Dianne Ray

When Peter was alive I didn't know that much about alcoholism. I knew you got drunk and you acted stupid. I really didn't understand it. After Peter died I became an alcoholic. I became awful when I drank. When I got sober over 27 years ago they had found traces of heredity in alcoholism. Nowadays they've confirmed this. They're trying to separate the gene that might possibly cause one to become an alcoholic. I feel that I was born with that gene. Some people feel they drink their way into alcoholism. When it gets to the acetone stage an average drinker breaks it down into carbohydrates. They get a little tipsy and say that's enough. An alcoholic doesn't metabolize alcohol, and it races through the blood as alcohol. The alcoholic gets a bigger rush and it lasts much longer. They can't have a few drinks. That's where the mental twist comes in.

It's a disease. It's not something you pick and choose. If you have it, you have it. The furthest thing from the truth is the common misconception that alcoholics are weak-willed and self-indulgent. Ninety percent of the world can drink with impunity. Ten percent can't. So alcoholics look weak. I'm anything but a weak person. We are alcoholics not by choice, but by genetics.

It's a physical allergy, coupled with a mental obsession. It affects the brain differently than with other people. You become obsessed with alcohol. If you have one, it usually sets up that obsession. That's what happens when you drink. The mental obsession comes back — to drink more. People in the twelve-step program compare it to someone who's addicted to jaywalking. They get out of the hospital and swear they're never going to do it again, and before they know it they're walking in front of a bus.

It's important to know about alcohol because that was a big part of Peter's life. It isn't a matter of willpower, because you don't know with the first drink that you're going to be allergic to it. You keep trying it, and the more you keep trying it the more the compulsion is there. It's an interesting disease. It's the only one that's arrestable. I'm sorry Peter couldn't get it. As you drink you experience a personality change, and sometimes that sticks with you. I'm sure the Peter I knew was a completely different Peter to what Beth knew.

There are trigger points that will trigger a relapse if you're not maintaining your sobriety with some sort of spiritual program. Had Peter continued to go to AA I think he might not be dead. I tell newcomers in the twelve-step program who don't want to use the word "God" that they can refer to a power greater than themselves. I tell them the only thing you need to know about God, when you're having trouble with the concept, is that you're not it. That's really keeping it simple. I don't think the spiritual part was Peter's problem. I think he just didn't want to go on with it. In my heart I think he believed in God, but that wasn't something we spoke about a lot. You didn't back then.

Look how far down the scale I went. It says in the Bible, "You grew up a child in the way that he should go, and when he is old he will not depart from it." That happened to me. I came back to my spiritual upbringing — after I was able to get sober. After I set it aside and did my thing, I did go back to it.

I truly believe Peter really didn't mean to die. Alcohol and drugs killed Peter. The gun was just the instrument. As I look back on it I think possibly Peter was bipolar. Peter was an actor, and he could put on a good show sometimes on the set. But not always. It took many years to come to terms with Peter's death. I often thought, "Why didn't I throw the gun away?" It never occurred to me I could have thrown the gun away until afterwards.

I went on to drink more and more and more over the next eight years because I couldn't deal with it. And then I was sober seven years before it really hit me. I never dated anyone, and wouldn't for 18 years following Peter's death.

Oddly enough, with little or no information about alcohol, I never thought of Peter as spineless. I thought of him as an actor who stepped from reality into unreality. I always said Peter expected somebody

Dianne Ray, Christmas 1991 (courtesy Dianne Ray).

to say, "Cut. Take. Let's do that again." I just know. I was there and I lived with him. He would never, ever, have used the gun on himself if he hadn't been drunk. He wouldn't have had the guts to do it. He had to be drunk to do it, and I still don't think he thought he was going to die.

We all have personality changes when we drink if we're allergic to it. He could be mean and nasty, he could be stupid, he could be childlike, just like me. I was never afraid of him. But on that final night I was afraid. When I look back on that night I don't understand why he didn't kill me also and take me with him. He was jealous of everything about me, and possessive. If anyone looked at me twice, he didn't like it.

We didn't fight all the time. Peter loved me. Although we were never officially engaged and didn't exchange rings, he was the love of my life. The shock of seeing your boyfriend kill himself is pretty hideous. The visual is what is so hard. Even today. I don't deserve to incur anyone's wrath. I've been through too much to take on any more.

We all have our insecurities, and God knows Peter had plenty, but underneath all that he was a good soul. He might have hurt the people close to him, but he tried to save the world. I think the only reason he hurt the people close to him was that he had a difficulty with closeness. I don't think it was a mean and nasty thing. I think that was the only way he knew how to protect himself from his insecurities. He wasn't comfortable with true intimacy.

Even after I married I still had these very sad feelings about Peter, and a month before my husband died in 2005 I went back into therapy and grieved heavily over Peter's death. I was wrapping up some heavy duty grieving. That's a lot of years later. It was appropriate it happened then. I still have a large piece of Peter in my heart. If Peter had survived I would definitely have married him. We never talked of marriage or getting engaged when he was alive, though. It would have happened. In our minds we had a pretty good life plan together. I knew he was going to be okay if only he could get a handle on it.

I think if Peter had let himself live long enough, between the psychologist and AA I think he could have grasped a sense of a higher power. If he had given himself enough time to explore those things after the series he would have survived. And if the series had been cancelled, there's a possibility he would have been alive today. And if he hadn't been drunk and loaded he'd be alive today. He definitely wouldn't have had the gun, because that came from the set. Some of those closest to him on the *Alias Smith and Jones* set were acting in their own interest.

After Peter died I didn't watch television — and I still don't, to this day. I have nothing to do with the industry, and I seldom go to movies. I guess it was too much. It's just hard for me. I can see the hypocrisy of everything, and it brings back that night. I had PTSS and still do. The visual is the hardest part. I still have occasional vivid dreams of Peter under the Christmas tree. I've been working on that for a couple of years now. I shall survive.

Out of Peter's death the most important thing to impart is the fact that he would not have died if he had not drank and used. That is so important to other people who think they can have a drink and be fine, and then end up dead. This will be a beautiful legacy for Peter. It will be a learning experience that may save someone else's life. That would turn his legacy right around.

Beth Griswold

I still try to figure out *why*. It seemed so quick, his downward spiral. All I know is that he was a different person, completely at odds with himself, when he drank. Without alcohol he could lighten up on himself, see the humor in his experience, and dismiss or release those expectations he had for himself, and others for him.

The expectations he set for himself were exceedingly high, and he would impose time limits on achieving them. He really expected to be at the top of his profession, a "big-screen" star by age 30. He dedicated himself completely to every acting job he got, rehearsing his lines in so many ways. The hall tree mirror was his favorite tool. He'd go over and over the same scene for hours if he thought he could discover a better way to do it. He always appreciated the television work, but he dreamt of doing nothing but serious movies. And he still had several more years on his Universal contract. He must have felt awfully stuck.

Fairly often we would go to those "under contract" parties that he loathed a little stoned (on weed) — just to tolerate the "have-to-do-it" aspect. He would function very nicely — he would laugh and joke easily, quite often becoming the center of attention. He was meticulous about his appearance, even if he was dressed casually.

The few times I saw him drunk in the very beginning of our relationship he was a different person altogether. Meaner than dirt, as they say. Belligerent, destructive, slurring one vulgarity after another after another, and hurtful to everyone around him. He was careless about himself when he was drunk, even about his appearance.

It was night and day! When he quit drinking he seemed so dedicated to staying sober. He would have made a great spokesperson for AA if it had been more acceptable then to be a recovering alcoholic. The fact that he quit cold turkey always impressed me. Having grown up with an alcoholic in my family who never stopped drinking, I was aware of the personal commitment and courage it took to quit with no professional help at all. I'd never take any credit for Pete's sobriety — he did it on his own. And because he was sober, we had a wonderful, exciting, exuberant, tragic (the times), joyful experience together. He was so impressed with how much better he felt and looked without that poison in his system. I thought that fact alone would keep him from ever drinking again.

And that is the reason Peter's death by suicide shocked me so badly. I couldn't imagine how someone who loved his body so much could do that to himself. When he was drinking, even though his appearance suffered, he didn't seem to get down on himself. It was the people around him that he would abuse when he was drunk. That's why I wanted to believe that someone else had shot him — that would have just made more sense to me.

Then again, I think back to the time he got arrested and how he acted. He practically dared those cops to arrest him. As soon as he knew he wasn't going to get away with it, he went about making it 10 times worse — no, 100 times worse. I couldn't believe the stuff he was saying and doing. This was the only indication I ever saw that Peter had any disregard for his own life. He really didn't care at that moment what happened to him, or to his body, anyway. It had to have been a moment like that — of being so out of it that he simply did not care about the results of his actions when he picked up the gun. If he had planned it, wouldn't he have left some kind of note, something written to let us all know what led to his tragic choice? The question of what the combination of events was, and what the biological, psychological, emotional or spiritual conflicts were within him, remains unanswered. Peter left everyone who loved him wondering "why."

I am certain that his death was a foolish choice in an inebriated, depressed state to "take a chance" with death. Peter was impulsive. All he needed was to be stupidly drunk and poisoned by the alcohol. "Let's try this" on an impulse. That daring thing was always there with Peter. Daring fate. I can't imagine that he wouldn't have written something. Had it been planned, thought out, chosen consciously, he would have written something. He would have "set the stage." I can't imagine he would have intentionally ended his life without an exit speech. I could see him picking up the gun, in a drunken and depressed state, and with careless abandon test fate like he did with the cops the night he was arrested in Foster City. There must have been within him the rage that, coupled with depression, can turn inward to self-abuse. My first thought was, "He is opening the presents from the parents"—that the parents somehow triggered the whole depression aspect of his success.

Geoff looked up to Peter in so many ways. Their love for each other was palpable when they were in the same room. Peter definitely felt responsible for his brother. I remember Geoff having a similar intensity to Peter's, but just slightly less.

Today I imagine Peter's spirit getting a big chuckle out of this review of his life. He's back in my mind almost daily. He always loved being the center of attention. Years ago, I would think of my time with Peter and I would be overcome with such sorrow and loss. But lately I find myself envisioning his little jigs, hearing his exuberant laugh, feeling his enthusiasm, seeing his smile. I'm finding joy there and feeling grateful that he was in my life, however briefly. The memory of him now lives peacefully within me.

David McHugh

Peter had read John Steinbeck's *Travels with Charly* and bought a pickup truck with a little pop-up cabin on the back in the summer of '69. We drove way up past San Francisco and spent five or six days on the road. And he told me how his erections weren't as stiff as when he was 16. Here's a guy who's 29 years old, and he's saying he's done everything and made all this money. He's famous and life is just going to be repetitious from now on. He had done it all, and there was no convincing him it was going to get any better. He was constantly letting his intimate circle know he was thinking of ending his life.

If someone commits suicide it's the ultimate inability to process the events of one's life. He was so overwhelmed by his early psychology it finally caught up with him. Nothing he accomplished was fulfilling. People were making a fuss over him for things he didn't value. When people achieve success that they don't feel they deserve, it has no lasting substance and value. It just created greater contempt in Peter.

I think if he had had a child that would have been a step in the right direction. The magic of having children is that you finally think about somebody else. Peter was totally self-absorbed and immature in many ways. It takes many years to take a career to the level you want. You work on so many pieces of crap before you achieve success. Peter was impatient. In the meantime, the guy was rich. So there wasn't too much to complain about. He couldn't view his success as a step in his progression. At the end of the day he was a TV actor making a lot of money and getting famous.

Peter was very disturbed emotionally, and he finally killed himself. I wouldn't attribute Peter's depression to *Alias Smith and Jones*. That's really superficial. Generally, he had great contempt for all of his work. He had wanted to progress from television, but his movie work, such as *Generation*, was a disaster.

Dianne was used as a scapegoat. The Deuel family looked on her as a dark woman who led Peter down the wrong path. Peter always talked of suicide. Everybody knew he was flirting with his own death. They were in denial to think he didn't kill himself, and they had to place the blame on somebody. He definitely had some manic depressive qualities. You just never knew who you were going to get with Peter. He could be in a great mood or a nasty, bitter mood. He just went back and forth. You always felt like there was a grenade ready to go off when Peter had those extremes.

Ultimately, what keeps us alive is a combination of our genetics and our emotional experiences. If you're overwhelmed by them, you may end up taking your life. He didn't have what it takes to continue. His death was something we all feared.

I cannot emphasize what an incredible person he was. Peter had a quality far and away above anyone I have ever known. My mother and younger brother moved out to Pasadena after her divorce, and I discovered Peter was visiting her and acting as older brother to my brother, and helping my mother financially. He was a generous guy. But he didn't like you to take his generosity for granted. One time he left me standing on my own outside a theater because he decided I had to pay for my own ticket, even though I was down to my last three dollars.

When Peter was on the *Dick Cavett Show* he took over. He just wouldn't take shit from anyone. If you said something stupid or annoying he would let you have it. But at the same time he was the most instantly charming and insightful guy, and he could be the most attentive listener. When he died, for years I felt like I had reached a peak of intensity with this person and his perception and intelligence. It was like I was diminished by his loss. He had that kind of effect on people.

C. Davey Utter

Peter was a mad creative genius. We're not talking about a regular person. He was an extraordinary individual. Peter was always demonstrative with his affection. We did everything to make each other feel good. I'm still not over his death. I miss him so intensely that I just want to cry. I think about what it would have been like if he'd been there all these years. He missed so much fun and caused his friends so much pain when he killed himself.

The suicide was planned out and thought about months in advance. After Peter died I put together a memorial tape that expressed how I felt. Geoff read a memorial poem he wrote. "The Man with the Stage Fright" by the Band was featured. I always thought the lyrics of this song applied to Peter.

Peter was the definition of charisma. He could walk into a room crowded with people, and the room would just go silent. It was amazing, but also a curse because he was always expected to perform. He was born to be an actor, but he did have trouble dealing with fame. The adoring fans bothered him, and he got tired of it.

My theory is that Peter was obsessed with not dying poor. He was also in a lot of physical pain with a hip problem. That depressed him. Peter's epilepsy was not a big factor. It wasn't a constant worry. He would have seizures in his sleep. In all the time I knew him he only had two seizures.

Peter was never a danger to anyone else, but he was a danger to himself. His death was a loss to humanity.

Donald Fanning

All the girls want to be with young, exciting and handsome men. Peter was a man for himself. Peter was dynamic, charismatic, intense and annoying. When Peter stopped, everybody stopped. His attitude was, "Well, this party's over. We better leave." He was an outstanding actor. You could watch Peter perform, and you suddenly realized you weren't watching Peter but the character he was doing. Peter went beyond the line and was in the same caliber of acting as Montgomery Clift, Marlon Brando, James Dean and Sean Penn. He was that good. Peter was in the same category as all these actors who explode from the screen. Peter shared that kind of intensity. Colin Farrell and Edward Norton always remind me of Peter.

There is still the conjecture it was an accidental death. The only medication Peter was on was for his epilepsy. He wasn't diagnosed as bipolar, although he did have extremes of mood.

Connie Meng

Peter was very much an instinctive actor and was always more interested in film than theater. I recall he said he always wanted to do a scene where he got shot and died dramatically on film. He got his wish in *The Hell with Heroes*.

Peter had a terrific personality, and was very funny and bright, but was a troubled person. Even back when I knew him, with all the fun and the silliness there was a dark streak underneath. He would all of a sudden go morose and then come out of it. The gregariousness and the joking and the fun was sometimes almost manic.

In 1967 I was working as an actress and appearing in Palm Springs. I saw Pete and the gang in L.A. and found the changes in him disturbing. He had begun drinking heavily, and there was a lot of marijuana around.

On the night Pete died Davey Utter phoned me when I was visiting my sister in Denver. My reaction to Peter's death was one of total shock.

I suffered from survivor's guilt. I didn't visit his friends in L.A. for many years because I always felt I could have done more to help Peter. I thought if I didn't go to L.A. I wouldn't have to cope with it. It was a form of denial. I didn't want to be in that city. I wouldn't go there because I would have to accept he was gone. It was years before I finally went back to L.A. I still have trouble watching Peter's work today.

Peter was such a strong personality, if you ever met him you didn't forget him.

Jack Jobes

I'm sure everyone had an extreme warm spot in their heart for Peter. He would do things that were so off the wall, and even if it was done just to attract attention, it was always a lot of fun. He was an outrageous individual for his time, and he was not going to conform. Peter was a much warmer person than people might imagine. He was always very warm to his friends. Even when we were unhappy with him there was still a warmth that came through.

I was sad and angry at the same time when Peter took his own life. His death breaks my heart to this day because of the personal hours I spent with him shortly before his death. Peter was a dear, dear friend. Everything was a blur after he died. It forever leaves a hole that I don't want to have. I felt he was finally getting rid of his own demons, and it was onward and upward. The alcohol threw him off. I see Peter fooling around with the revolver and depressed with alcohol. He pointed the gun to his head, and when it went off he was surprised.

Jill Andre

Peter's death was horrifying and unbearably sad to me, but not totally unexpected. Peter would say, "You know, I'm not going to be around much past 30." He would kid around about that from time to time, and not only for me to hear. It seemed to me that this feeling came from a deep sense of being undeserving and not knowing how to change it.

During the 1960s the world was in such upheaval, including the drugs and sex and rock 'n' roll scene. And though Peter partook in all the excesses, his true nature never seemed to match, and it often seemed like a role he was playing. The stardom trip wasn't the be-all and end-all for him. But he couldn't make the adjustment and put the pieces together and say, "Okay, now I'm making money and getting attention, so I can do a lot of the personal things I've wanted to do." He felt there wasn't anybody out there he could trust and feel comfortable with. I'm sure he felt isolated in Hollywood. And of course I was in my own little cave of confusion, trying to be a good mother, knowing I was in a marriage that wasn't working, so I wasn't much help. He was fun and sweet and extremely frustrating. He was either putting blue food dye in the milk (with our friend Dom DeLuise) for my kids to discover the next morning, or I was anxiously calling his agent to help me bail him out at the Van Nuys police station after being picked up for drunk driving.

Sadly, the 60's eventually led to the "Me Generation." There was little sense of community, of giving, of social responsibility, and really being conscious of other human beings in the world. Yet somehow Peter was very conscious of other human beings, in his own secret way, at a time when everyone was focused on how much money they made, on the drugs they took, and the number of people they slept with. But Peter couldn't justify this awareness, or make it work for him, or even find the value in his own humanity.

Peter felt so out of step with the social climate of the times. I remember when I started to investigate the possibility of therapy, he was terrified to even entertain the idea. He wanted so may good things, and he was so impatient. All the studies about suicide that I have read, and the discussions I've had with people who are knowledgeable about this, indicate that there is a point in time when a person makes an internal pact with himself— and from that point everything seems fine. It is hard for an outsider to detect any problems. And this could be made two weeks before, or two years before, or two days before the final act is committed.

Kim Darby

I have a strong feeling that if Peter could just have made it through I knew he would be sober today. You have everything here to help you, and there's nothing shaming because it seems everyone in Hollywood has gone through it. I personally started taking amphetamines after I married James Westmoreland. Producer Hal Wallis wanted me to appear in a movie as a romantic lead. It was a different kind of role for me. Unfortunately, I was never thin enough for my career or my agents. They should have left me alone and let me be a character actress. The amphetamines did make me lose weight and also helped in treating a chemical imbalance. But I became addicted to the amphetamines. It was so easy to get them. And of course you have to take downers to counteract them. When you're on drugs you don't deal with grief and you just bury it. The amphetamines changed my life. As the tolerance builds it does not become your friend, but it becomes a living hell. It reaches a level where it doesn't work anymore, so you have to keep taking more and more and more. That's when it just finally kicks you in the ass. You have just lost so much sleep and have not eaten for so long that the side effects of coming off of it send you into a deep depression.

I was making movies and in episodic TV, so I would use my periods between jobs to try and get off the amphetamines. Peter also had this luxury before he got caught up in a weekly TV show. Working on the show meant he didn't have the rest periods necessary, and he found himself totally stressed out. Peter also had many other problems that added to his stress.

Peter was a wonderful person. He never had an agenda and was fighting so hard. But I think Peter embraced a fascination with suicide — that he was going to do it one day. Peter had a tremendous anger in him. He was enraged. It's the angriest act you can commit. I think he was telling all of us, "Fuck you!" He felt trapped because the studio dictated what he did and what he didn't do. He thought it was politically unjust that he couldn't get out of the contract. He hated the institution and being caught there, and didn't like the idea of a corporation dictating his life.

Peter could be outrageous. He did things to make people go, "Oh, my God, he's off his rocker." This could have been one of those times when he was looking for a reaction. Someone once told me people who kill themselves are often very politically inclined and see themselves as martyrs. I believe he was acting out with intent.

Psychologists or doctors can lead you towards recovery, but going to a self-help group is the only answer. I've been sober for 26 years. Pete was very disciplined. If he saw more people doing it in his own age range it might have helped. I think he felt so terribly alone in it. Maybe he couldn't grasp the idea of a higher power. I don't think he was that spiritual a person. The family needs to recover as much as the alcoholic. There are self-help groups for the friends and families of an alcoholic or a drug addict.

I believe it was a psychotic break with reality on that final night. I don't think it was him at the end. You have to get to a state like that to carry out that act. I'm sure the amphetamines just made him crazy, on top of the alcohol. Amphetamines can make you fidgety and restless.

I've never met anybody since Peter that loved me the way he loved me. He had empathy, and was solicitous, caring and protective of me. In our happy times Peter was verbal, expressive and vulnerable. He never talked with me about suicide. We lived in our own world and had our own way of talking to each other. It was a special intimacy.

Peter was the only man to see inside of me. He would have completed my life at that time.

APPENDIX A:
EPISODE GUIDES

Gidget

Cast (featured on title sequence): Frances Elizabeth "Gidget" Lawrence, Sally Field; Professor Russell Lawrence, Don Porter.

First prime-time broadcast— September 15, 1965

Final prime-time broadcast— April 21, 1966 (first run)

Network— ABC: Wednesday 8:30–9:00 p.m.

Running time— 30 min.

Production— Columbia–Screen Gems

Format— 35 mm

Ratio—1.33: 1

Film— Pathecolor

Executive Producer: Harry Ackerman

Music: Howie Greenfield, Jack Keller

Theme Song: Howie Greenfield; vocals — Johnny Tillotson

* = Peter Deuel appearances

Season One

32 × 30 min.

"Dear Diary — Et Al." (1:01)*
Air date: September 15, 1965; Guest Stars: Stephen Mines, Pamela Colbert; Teleplay: Ruth Brooks Flippen; Director: William Asher.

Anne reads Gidget's diary and jumps to the wrong conclusion.

"In God, and Nobody Else, We Trust" (1:02)*
Air date: September 22, 1965; Guest Stars: Beverly Adams, Heather North; Teleplay: Ruth Brooks Flippen; Director: William Asher.

John uses a luau as an exercise in interpersonal behavior.

"The Great Kahuna" (1:03)*
Air date: September 29, 1965; Guest Stars:

Martin Milner, Julie Parrish; Teleplay: Albert Mannheimer; Story: Frederick Kohner; Director: William Asher.

A famous Hawaiian surfer pretends to fall for Gidget to make his girlfriend jealous.

"Daddy Come Home" (1:04)*
Air date: October 6, 1965; Guest Stars: Marian Collier, Joseph Perry, Harvey Korman; Teleplay: Ruth Brooks Flippen; Director: William Asher.

Gidget worries when her father starts to date an attractive woman.

"Gidget Gadget" (1:05)*
Air date: October 13, 1965; Guest Stars: Dick Gautier, Janis Hansen; Teleplay: Stephen Kandel; Director: E.W. Swackhamer.

Following an argument, Gidget schemes to bring Anne and John back together again but ends up making matters worse.

"A Hearse, a Hearse, My Kingdom for a Hearse" (1:06)
Air date: October 20, 1965; Guest Stars: James Davidson, Richard Sinatra, Herb Ellis; Teleplay: John McGreevey; Story: Louella McFarlane; Director: William Asher.

Gidget makes a bid for independence and buys a hearse, but her attempts to be "one of the boys" at the auto shop backfires.

"Gidget is a Proper Noun" (1:07)*
Air date: October 27, 1965; Guest Stars: Noam Pitlik, George Winters, Astrid Warner; Teleplay: Austin and Irma Kalish; Director: E.W. Swackhamer.

Gidget believes her English teacher, a former student of her father's, is prejudiced against her.

"Image Scrimmage" (1:08)*

Air date: November 3, 1965; Guest Stars: James M. Crawford, Melissa Murphy; Teleplay: Barbara Avedon; Director: E.W. Swackhamer.

Gidget tries to adopt a mature image for Larue's cousin Roger, and Gidget's father is the object of a student crush.

"Is It Love or Symbiosis?" (1:09)*

Air date: November 10, 1965; Guest Stars: Judy Carne, Roy Stuart, Kevin O'Neal; Teleplay: A.J. Mady and Frederick Kohner; Director: E.W. Swackhamer.

Anne and John arrange for Gidget to attend school in Paris, but Gidget and her father soon realize it's a bad idea.

"All the Best Diseases Are Taken" (1:10)*

Air date: November 17, 1965; Guest Stars: Henry Jaglom, Dick Wilson, Noah Keen, Dick Balduzzi; Teleplay: Tony Wilson; Director: E.W. Swackhamer.

Gidget decides that theater prices are becoming too expensive and stages a demonstration with a popular protest singer.

"My Ever Faithful Friend" (1:11)*

Air date: November 24, 1965; Guest Stars: Stephanie Hill, Russ Bender, Mike Nader; Teleplay: Ruth Brooks Flippen; Director: Gene Reynolds.

Gidget does a make-over on her friend Larue and is shocked to find her father and Larue forming a relationship.

"Chivalry Isn't Dead" (1:12)

Air date: December 1, 1965; Guest Stars: Barbara Hershey, Bob Random, Bonnie Franklin, Bob Beach, Rick Cooper, Pam McMyler, Beverly Washburn; Teleplay: John McGreevey; Story: Mark Ragaway; Director: E.W. Swackhamer.

The boys are taking Gidget and her friends for granted, and Gidget schemes to rectify the situation with a slumber party.

"The War Between Men, Women and Gidget" (1:13)

Air date: December 8, 1966; Guest Stars: Mako, Linda Gaye Scott, Randy Kirby, Charla Doherty, Caroline Kido, John Fain, Skip Torgerson, Karen Lawrence; Teleplay: Pauline and Leo Townsend; Director: E.W. Swackhamer.

Possession of an isolated cove at the beach becomes cause for a battle between Gidget and her friends and the boys.

"Gidget's Foreign Policy" (1:14)

Air date: December 15, 1966; Guest Stars: Walter Koenig, Brooke Bundy, Bob Random; Teleplay: Stephen Kandel; Director: Jerry Bernstein.

Gidget's attempts to bring a Swedish bride-to-be up to date almost wrecks a marriage.

"Now There's a Face" (1:15)*

Air date: December 22, 1966; Guest Stars: Daniel J. Travanti, Sabrina Scharf, Lillian Adams; Teleplay: Dorothy Cooper Foote; Director: E.W. Swackhamer.

Gidget has a teenage crush on a photographer who also happens to be engaged.

"Too Many Crooks" (1:16)

Air date: December 29, 1966; Guest Stars: Peter Brooks, Larry Merrill, Bonnie Franklin, Don Washbrook; Teleplay: Albert Mannheimer; Director: Oscar Rudolph.

Gidget, to her consternation, unwittingly makes a date with both the Cook brothers on the same evening.

"I Love You, I Love You, I Love You, I Think" (1:17)

Air date: January 5, 1966; Guest Stars: Tom Gilleran, Maida Severn, Leonard Bremen; Teleplay: Ruth Brooks Flippen; Director: William Asher.

Gidget's latest crush is a surfer. Unfortunately, he's also her new math teacher.

"Like Voodoo" (1:18)*

Air date: January 13, 1966; Guest Stars: Jeanne Gerson, Peggy Rea, Arthur Adams; Teleplay: Albert Mannheimer; Director: E.W. Swackhamer.

A gypsy's curse on Gidget appears to be coming true when accidents start to occur, and soon superstitions are ruining her life.

"Gidget's Career" (1:19)*

Air date: January 20, 1966; Guest Stars: Sandy Kenyon, Jimmy Hawkins, Dennis Joel, Steve Rinaldi; Teleplay: Joanna Lee; Director: E.W. Swackhamer.

Gidget and Larue appear on TV as part of a new singing group.

"Ego-a-Go-Go" (1:20)

Air date: January 27, 1966; Guest Stars: Richard Dreyfuss, Ed Griffith, Susan Yardley, Leslie Touner; Teleplay: Barbara Avedon; Director: Jerry Bernstein.

Gidget tries to instill confidence into a nerdy teenager.

"In and Out with the In-Laws" (1:21)

Air date: February 3, 1966; Guest Stars: Hal March, Hazel Court, Janis Hansen, Ray Hastings; Teleplay: Ruth Brooks Flippen; Director: Bruce Bilson.

Misunderstandings abound when Gidget visits with Jeff's parents.

"We Got Each Other" (1:22)*

Air date: February 10, 1966; Guest Stars: Michael York, Anne Bellamy, Pat McCaffrie, Ila Britton; Teleplay: John McGreevey; Director: Bruce Bilson.

Gidget tries her best not to ruin her father's dates, but just makes matters worse.

"Operation Shaggy Dog" (1:23)*

Air date: February 17, 1966; Guest Stars: Lew Parker, Tim Rooney, Burt Douglas, Don Edmonds; Teleplay: Dorothy Cooper Foote; Director: Hal Cooper.

Gidget tries to save a hamburger shack from demolition.

"Ringa-Ding-Dingbat" (1:24)*

Air date: February 24, 1966; Guest Stars: Jimmy Murphy, Irwin Charone, Gregory Mullavy, Lindsay Workman, Dorothy Konrad; Teleplay: Barbara Avedon; Director: Hal Cooper.

Gidget and Larue pose as members of a popular singing duo.

"Love and the Single Gidget" (1:25)*

Air date: March 3, 1966; Guest Stars: Barbara Hershey, David Macklin, Bridget Hanley, Ron Rifkin, Carl Reindel, Tim Rooney; Teleplay: John McGreevey and Stephen Kandel; Director: Hal Cooper.

Gidget stays with Anne and John while her father is away, causing them to hire a chaperone for her.

"Take a Lesson" (1:26)

Air date: March 10, 1966; Guest Stars: Paul Lynde, Jeff Donnell, Mark Sturges, Beverly Washburn; Teleplay: Ruth Brooks Flippen; Director: Jerry Bernstein.

When Shirley's parents take Gidget, in her pajamas, to find a new car, Russ mistakes it for a kidnapping.

"Independence — Gidget Style" (1:27)*

Air date: March 17, 1966; Guest Stars: Viola Harris, Carol Williams, Celeste Yarnall; Teleplay: Joanna Lee; Director: Bruce Bilson.

Gidget decides to find herself a job to pay for her father's birthday present but ends up being spied on by her father, who mistakenly thinks she's working as a hostess at a risqué nightclub.

"One More for the Road" (1:28)*

Air date: March 24, 1966; Guest Stars: John McGiver, Doug Lambert, Jimmy Cross, Murray Alper; Teleplay: Austin and Irma Kalish; Director: Jerry Bernstein.

Gidget's enlists Larue's help in driving the delivery truck at her new job at the florist shop.

"Ask Helpful Hannah" (1:29)*

Air date: March 31, 1966; Guest Stars: Barbara Hershey, Jim Connell, Candace Howard, Norman Connolly, Sari Price, Jewel Jaffe; Teleplay: Don Richman; Director: Lee Philips.

Gidget is the new writer on the school advice column, but a case of mistaken identity causes her advice to create more problems.

"A Hard Day's Night" (1:30)

Air date: April 7, 1966; Guest Stars: Frank DeVol, Bill Zuckert, Vince Howard, Joseph Mell, Holly Irving; Teleplay: Barbara Avedon; Director: Don Porter.

Gidget thinks the Lawrence home is haunted when, unknown to her, Russ's friend moves in. Cameo by Victor Jory.

"I Have This Friend Who" (1:31)*

Air date: April 14, 1966; Guest Stars: Bob Beach, Herb Voland, Joel Fluellen; Teleplay: Gary Flavin; Director: Chris Cary.

The father of Gidget's boyfriend insists on joining them on their dates.

"Don't Defrost the Alligator" (1:32)*

Air date: April 21, 1966; Guest Stars: Marvin Kaplan, Jack Fletcher, Richard Jury, Frankie Abbott; Teleplay: Ruth Brooks Flippen; Director: E.W. Swackhamer.

Gidget attempts to comfort young Davey Seldon over the death and impending burial of his pet alligator by preserving him in her refrigerator.

Love on a Rooftop

Cast (on title sequence) — David Willis, Peter Deuel; Julie Willis (Hammond), Judy Carne.

First prime-time broadcast — September 6, 1966

Final prime-time broadcast — April 6, 1967 (first run)

Network — ABC: Tuesday 9:30–10:00 p.m.

Running time — 30 min.

Production— Columbia Pictures TV-Screen Gems, Inc.
Format— 35 mm
Ratio—1.33: 1
Film— Pathecolor
Creators— Bernard Slade and Harry Acker-man
Executive Producer— Harry Ackerman
Associate Producer— Stan Schwimmer
Producer— E.W. Swackhamer
Music— Warren Barker; Mundell Lowe

Season One
30 × 30 min. (1966–67)

"Pilot" (1:01)
Air date: September 6, 1966; Teleplay: Albert Mannheimer; Director: E.W. Swackhamer.
David and Julie try to hide their windowless apartment from their parents.

"117 Ways to Cook a Hamburger" (1:02)
Air date: September 13, 1966; Guest Stars: Noam Pitlik, Norm Burton, Majel Barrett, Vince Howard; Teleplay: Bernard Slade; Direc-tor: E.W. Swackhamer.
Julie spends all of their food money on fifty pounds of chopped meat.

"My Husband, the Knight" (1:03)
Air date: September 20, 1966; Guest Stars: Charles Lane, Hope Summers, Joseph Perry; Teleplay: Bernard Slade; Director: E.W. Swack-hamer.
In order to pay for a new chair, Dave takes a job that requires him to wear a suit of armor.

"The Big Brass Bed" (1:04)
Air date: September 27, 1966; Guest Stars: Vic Tayback, Milton Frome, Howard Morton; Tele-play: Bernard Slade; Director: E.W. Swack-hamer.
While hunting for a bed, Julie buys an old brass one, which breaks loose on top of a hill and crashes into a cop.
"I just had a visual image, and it worked very well, of a bed being pushed through the streets of San Francisco. It was shot on the crookedest street in the world."— Bernard Slade

"The Six Dollar Surprise" (1:05)
Air date: October 4, 1966; Guest Stars: Digby Wolfe, Paul Micale; Teleplay: Bernard Slade; Director: E.W. Swackhamer.
Dave agrees to let Julie give a birthday party, despite hating them, as long as she doesn't spend more than six dollars.

"The Chocolate Hen" (1:06)
Air date: October 11, 1966; Guest Star: Peter Robbins; Teleplay: Bernard Slade; Director: E.W. Swackhamer.
Dave loses his temper after Julie gives his chocolate hen to a six-year-old kid.
"This is exactly as it happened in Canada. My son got up and ate my chocolate hen. A lot of the stuff you see, especially in situation comedy, with kids, is because it was based on something that hap-pened."— Bernard Slade

"Homecoming" (1:07)
Air date: October 18, 1966; Guest Stars: Frank Wilcox, Bridget Hanley, Dick Anders, Rollin Moriyama; Teleplay: Bernard Slade; Director: E.W. Swackhamer.
Dave learns how well Julie lived before they were married when they visit her parents' estate.

"One Picture Is Worth..." (1:08)
Air date: October 25, 1966; Guest Star: Daniel J. Travanti; Teleplay: Bernard Slade; Director: E.W. Swackhamer.
Dave becomes jealous when Julie's former artist boyfriend turns up.

"Chinchilla Rag" (1:09)
Air date: November 1, 1966; Guest Star: Harold Gould; Teleplay: James Henerson; Director: Robert Rosenbaum.
Stan convinces Julie to keep his chinchillas, even though they could face eviction.
Preempted — Air date: November 8, 1966

"Who Is Sylvia?" (1:10)
Air date: November 15, 1966; Guest Star: Bridget Hanley; Teleplay: Richard Baer; Direc-tor: Claudio Guzman.
After they both dream about a girl called Sylvia, the "real" Sylvia calls on Dave and Julie and causes confusion.

"War on a Rooftop" (1:11)
Air date: November 22, 1966; Guest Stars: Julie Foster, Milton Frome; Teleplay: Bernard Slade; Director: E.W. Swackhamer.
Stan's new pigeon, Homer, causes trouble between David, Julie, Stan and Carol.

"Dave's Night Out" (1:12)
Air date: November 29, 1966; Guest Stars: Reta Shaw, Virginia Sale; Teleplay: John McGreevey; Director: Claudio Guzman.
Dave plays poker one night a week but ends up helping two old ladies with their wash at a laundromat.

"There's Got to Be Something Wrong with Her" (1:13)

Air date: December 6, 1966; Guest Stars: Gayle Hunnicutt, Arlene Charles; Teleplay: John McGreevey; Director: Jerry Bernstein.

After Julie meets Dave's old girlfriend, she can't understand why he didn't marry her instead.

"But Is It Really You?" (1:14)

Air date: December 13, 1966; Guest Stars: Anne Seymour, Benny Baker, Corinne Conley; Teleplay: Bernard Slade; Director: E.W. Swackhamer.

Sheila has to redecorate David and Julie's apartment after they receive an expensive Chinese vase as a gift.

"The Fifty Dollar Misunderstanding" (1:15)

Air date: December 20, 1966; Guest Stars: Paul Mazursky, Larry Tucker; Teleplay: James Henerson; Director: Alex Grasshoff.

Stan spends Dave's $50 bonus on art materials for Julie's one-woman show.

"Frocks of Trouble" (1:16)

Air date: December 27, 1966; Guest Star: Ron Masak; Teleplay: Barbara Avedon; Director: Claudio Guzman.

David and Mr. Hammond buy dresses for Julie to wear at a banquet.

"Going Home to Daughter" (1:17)

Air date: January 3, 1967; Guest Star: David Brian; Teleplay: James Henerson; Director: Robert Ellenstein.

Julie's mother leaves her father on their 25th wedding anniversary.

"Let It Rain" (1:18)

Air date: January 12, 1967; Guest Star: Sidney Clute; Teleplay: Dorothy Cooper Foote; Director: E.W. Swackhamer.

Julie and her parents decide to see how the other half lives by switching apartments.

"King of the Castle" (1:19)

Air date: January 19, 1967; Guest Stars: Oliver McGowan, Owen Bush; Teleplay: Bernard Slade; Director: Jerry Bernstein.

When Dave learns that Julie is earning more than he is, he decides to take on extra jobs to make up the difference.

"My Father, the TV Star" (1:20)

Air date: January 26, 1967; Guest Stars: Don Keefer, Yau Shan Tung; Teleplay: Bernard Slade; Director: Richard Kinon.

Julie's father becomes a comic smash after starring in a TV commercial.

"Who Was That Husband I Saw You With?" (1:21)

Air date: February 2, 1967; Guest Stars: Richard Gautier, David Lewis; Teleplay: Marty Roth; Director: Gene Reynolds.

Stan sends Julie's relatives a shocking photograph after they request copies of their wedding photos.

"Shotgun Honeymoon" (1:22)

Air date: February 9, 1967; Guest Stars: Howard Morton, Byron Foulger, Hoke Howell; Teleplay: Dorothy Cooper Foote; Director: Mack Bing.

Mr. Hammond thinks that David and Julie have just gotten married after living together for eight months.

"Musical Apartments" (1:23)

Air date: February 16, 1967; Guest Stars: Robert Ellenstein, Connie Sawyer; Teleplay: James Henerson; Director: Jerry Bernstein.

David and Julie are forced to move into a shabby hotel after Stan's ant colony takes over their apartment.

"Low Calorie Love" (1:24)

Air date: February 23, 1967; Guest Stars: Charles Lane, Hal Baylor, Jan Arvan; Teleplay: Tom and Helen August; Director: Russell Mayberry.

Julie tries to gain weight, while Dave tries to lose weight.

"The Sell Out" (1:25)

Air date: March 2, 1967; Guest Stars: Ned Glass, Maxine Stuart; Teleplay: Ron Friedman; Director: Lee Phillips.

In order to put Julie through art school, Dave must redesign a house against his better judgment.

"The Letter Bug" (1:26)

Air date: March 9, 1967; Guest Star: John S. Ragin; Teleplay: James Henerson; Director: Russell Mayberry.

A computer dating questionnaire, a tape recording and an opened letter lead to marital strife between Dave and Julie.

"Stork on a Rooftop" (1:27)

Air date: March 16, 1967; Guest Stars: Marjorie Bennett, Ivan Booker; Teleplay: Bernard Slade; Director: E.W. Swackhamer.

Everyone thinks Julie is pregnant after she embarks on a strange diet.

"One Too Many Crooks" (1:28)

Air date: March 23, 1967; Guest Stars: Chick Chandler, Jill Foster, Vince Howard; Teleplay: James Henerson; Director: Mack Bing.

Dave dreads telling Julie that he is an expert cook, for fear of upsetting her.

"Debt of Gratitude" (1:29)

Air date: March 30, 1967; Guest Stars: David Winters, Ivor Barry; Teleplay: John McGreevey; Director: Russell Mayberry.

Dave's old army buddy and his weird friends move into a tent on the roof.

"Murder in Apartment D" (1:30)

Air date: April 6, 1967; Guest Stars: Ian Wolfe, Wesley Addy; Teleplay: Bernard Slade; Director: Jerry Bernstein.

Everyone believes the new tenants murdered a rich old man.

Alias Smith and Jones

Cast (featured on title sequence)— Hannibal Heyes (alias Joshua Smith), Pete Duel (1971–72); Hannibal Heyes (alias Joshua Smith), Roger Davis (1972–73); Jedediah "Kid" Curry (alias Thaddeus Jones), Ben Murphy (1971–73)

First prime-time broadcast— January 21, 1971

Final prime-time broadcast— January 13, 1973 (first run)

Network— ABC, Season One: Thursday 7:30– 8:30 p.m.; Season Two: Thursday 8:00–9:00 p.m.; Season Three: Saturday 8:00–9:00 p.m.

Running time— 50 min.

Production— Universal TV, in association with Public Arts Inc.

Format— 35 mm

Ratio—1.33:1

Film— Technicolor

Executive in Charge of Production: Frank Price

Executive Producer: Roy Huggins

Creator-Producer: Glen A. Larson

Associate Executive Producer: Joe Swerling Jr.

Associate Producers: Steve Heilpern, Nicholas E. Baehr

Theme: Billy Goldenberg

Season One

14 × 50 min.

"The McCreedy Bust" (1:01)

Air date: January 21, 1971; Guest Stars: Burl Ives, Cesar Romero; Teleplay: Sy Salkowitz;

Story: John Thomas James; Director: Gene Levitt.

A feud between a wealthy rancher (Burl Ives) and a Mexican neighbor (Cesar Romero) escalates when Heyes and Curry retrieve a stolen Roman bust.

"Exit from Wickenburg" (1:02)

Air date: January 28, 1971; Guest Stars: Pernell Roberts, Susan Strasberg, Slim Pickens, Mark Lenard; Teleplay: Robert Hamner; Story: John Thomas James; Director: Jeannot Szwarc.

Physically thrown out of Wickenburg while helping a widow (Susan Strasberg) keep order in the local saloon, Heyes and Curry return to the town to uncover the reasons behind their forced eviction.

"The Wrong Train to Brimstone" (1:03)

Air date: February 4, 1971; Guest Stars: William Windom, J. Pat O'Malley, J.D. Cannon, Beth Brickell; Teleplay: Stephen Kandel; Director: Jeffrey Hayden.

Heyes and Curry, posing as Bannerman detectives, unwittingly find themselves on a train full of Bannerman detectives setting a trap to capture Heyes and Curry.

"The Girl in Boxcar # 3" (1:04)

Air date: February 11, 1971; Guest Stars: Alan Hale Jr., Heather Menzies, Jack Garner; Teleplay: Howard Browne; Story: Gene Roddenberry; Director: Leslie H. Martinson.

Kid Curry's attempt to transport $50,000 in cash are complicated by a 17-year-old girl (Heather Menzies) he encounters on his travels.

"The Great Shell Game" (1:05)

Air date: February 18, 1971; Guest Stars: Diana Muldaur, Sam Jaffe, Peter Breck; Teleplay: Glen A. Larson; Story: John Thomas James; Director: Richard Benedict.

Heyes becomes involved with an attractive widow (Diana Muldaur) and a gambling sting.

"Return to Devil's Hole" (1:06)

Air date: February 25, 1971; Guest Stars: Fernando Lamas, Diana Hyland; Teleplay: Knut Swenson; Story: John Thomas James; Director: Bruce Kessler.

Outlaw leader Jim Santana (Fernando Lamas) must decide who is telling the truth — Heyes' lady friend, Clara Phillips (Diana Hyland), or the gang member she's trying to kill.

"A Fistful of Diamonds" (1:07)

Air date: March 4, 1971; Guest Stars: John

McGiver, Sam Jaffe, Michele Carey; Teleplay: Robert Hamner; Story: John Thomas James; Director: Jeffrey Hayden.

Heyes and Curry attempt to clear their name, with the help of "Soapy" Saunders (Sam Jaffe), after a crooked banker (John McGiver) implicates them in a bank robbery and murder.

"Stagecoach Seven" (1:08)

Air date: March 11, 1971; Guest Stars: Keenan Wynn, Steve Ihnat, L.Q. Jones; Teleplay: Dick Nelson; Story: John Thomas James; Director: Richard Benedict.

Way-station master Charlie Utley (Keenan Wynn) puts the lives of himself and a group of stagecoach passengers at risk seeking the reward for the capture of Heyes and Curry.

"The Man Who Murdered Himself" (1:09)

Air date: March 18, 1971; Guest Stars: Patrick MacNee, Juliet Mills, Slim Pickens; Teleplay: Robert Hamner and John Thomas James; Story: John Thomas James; Director: Jeffrey Hayden.

Heyes becomes suspicious of an archaeologist (Patrick McNee) who hires him to track down a tribe of giant red-haired Indians thought to have lived in the area surrounding Devil's Hole.

"The Root of It All" (1:10)

Air date: March 25, 1971; Guest Stars: Judy Carne, Tom Ewell; Writer: Howard Browne; Director: Barry Shear.

Heyes and Curry find themselves in serious trouble when they decide to help a lady from Philadelphia (Judy Carne) find buried Confederate money.

"The Fifth Victim" (1:11)

Air date: April 1, 1971; Guest Stars: Joseph Campanella, Sharon Acker, Ramon Bieri; Teleplay: Glen A. Larson; Story: John Thomas James; Director: Fernando Lamas.

Kid Curry attempts to uncover the killer behind a series of deaths following a game of poker, while Hannibal Heyes recuperates from a bullet wound to the head.

"Journey from San Juan" (1:12)

Air date: April 8, 1971; Guest Stars: Claudine Longet, Susan Oliver, Nico Minardos; Teleplay: Dick Nelson; Story: John Thomas James; Director: Jeffrey Hayden.

Heyes and Curry become involved in a case of deception when they cross the border into San Juan in an attempt to bring Blanche Graham (Susan Oliver) to justice.

"Never Trust an Honest Man" (1:13)

Air date: April 15, 1971; Guest Stars: Severn Darden, Marj Dusay, Richard Anderson; Teleplay: Phil DeGuere; Story: John Thomas James; Director: Douglas Heyes.

Finding a fortune in jewels hidden inside a Bible, Heyes and Curry return them to railroad owner Oscar Harlingen (Severn Darden), who thanks Heyes and Curry by sending a posse after them after discovering the jewels are quartz.

"The Legacy of Charlie O'Rourke" (1:14)

Air date: April 22, 1971; Guest Stars: Joan Hackett, J.D. Cannon; Teleplay: Dick Nelson; Story: Robert Guy Barrows; Director: Jeffrey Hayden.

Bannerman detective Harry Briscoe (J.D. Cannon) and saloon entertainer Alice Banion (Joan Hackett) believe condemned robber Charlie O'Rourke (Billy "Green" Bush) has told Heyes and Curry where he buried $100,000 in stolen gold bars.

Season Two

22 × 50 min.; 1 × 75 min.

"The Day They Hanged Kid Curry" (2:01)

Air date: September 16, 1971; Guest Stars: Walter Brennan, Robert Morse, Belinda Montgomery, Slim Pickens, Earl Holliman; Teleplay: Glen A. Larson; Story: John Thomas James; Director: Barry Shear.

Fred Philpotts (Robert Morse), posing as Kid Curry, earns a reprieve from the gallows when Silky O'Sullivan (Walter Brennan) arrives in town claiming to be Kid Curry's grandma.

"How to Rob a Bank in One Hard Lesson" (2:02)

Air date: September 23, 1971; Guest Stars: Jack Cassidy, Joanna Barnes, Karen Machon; Teleplay: David Moessinger; Story: John Thomas James; Director: Alexander Singer.

Kid Curry is held hostage by two attractive women while Hannibal Heyes is forced to blow open the latest Pierce & Hamilton bank safe, with the "help" of Harry Wagoner (Jack Cassidy).

"Jailbreak at Junction City" (2:03)

Air date: September 30, 1971; Guest Stars: George Montgomery, James Wainwright, Jack Albertson; Teleplay: John Thomas James; Director: Jeffrey Hayden.

Accepting temporary jobs as deputies, Heyes and Curry find themselves in jail when Sheriff

Clitterhouse (George Montgomery) double-crosses them.

"Smiler with a Gun" (2:04)

Air date: October 7, 1971; Guest Stars: Roger Davis, Will Geer; Teleplay: Max Hodge; Story: John Thomas James; Director: Fernando Lamas.

Heyes and Curry join Danny Bilson (Roger Davis) and an old miner (Will Geer) in a dig for gold, unaware that the ever-smiling Bilson is planning a double-cross.

"The Posse That Wouldn't Quit" (2:05)

Air date: October 14, 1971; Guest Star: Vera Miles; Teleplay: Pat Fielder; Story: John Thomas James; Director: Harry Falk.

Heyes and Curry find refuge from a pursuing posse at the home of Belle and Jesse Jordan (Vera Miles and Charles H. Gray), and their two daughters (Cindy and Lisa Eilbacher).

"Something to Get Hung About" (2:06)

Air date: October 21, 1971; Guest Stars: Monte Markham, Meredith MacRae, Roger Perry, Noah Beery; Teleplay: Nicholas E. Baehr and John Thomas James; Story: John Thomas James; Director: Jack Arnold.

An attempt to find a runaway wife (Meredith MacRae) results in a love triangle involving murder.

"Six Strangers at Apache Springs" (2:07)

Air date: October 28, 1971; Guest Stars: Sian Barbara Allen, Patricia Harty, Carmen Mathews; Teleplay: Arnold Somkin and John Thomas James; Story: John Thomas James; Director: Nicholas Colasanto.

Heyes and Curry find themselves in dangerous Indian territory when they decide to help a widower (Carmen Mathews) find hidden gold.

"Night of the Red Dog" (2:08)

Air date: November 4, 1971; Guest Stars: Jack Kelly, Rory Calhoun, Joe Flynn, Robert Pratt; Teleplay: Dick Nelson and John Thomas James; Story: John Thomas James; Director: Russ Mayberry.

Finding their gold dust stolen and themselves trapped for the winter in a snow-bound cabin with their fellow gold prospectors, Heyes and Curry attempt to recover their losses and discover the thief.

"The Reformation of Harry Briscoe" (2:09)

Air date: November 11, 1971; Guest Stars: J.D. Cannon, Jane Wyatt; Teleplay: B.W. Sandefur and John Thomas James; Story: John Thomas James; Director: Barry Shear.

Heyes and Curry are shocked to discover Harry Briscoe (J.D. Cannon) and a fake nun (Jane Merrow) to be "partners" in crime.

"Dreadful Sorry Clementine" (2:10)

Air date: November 18, 1971; Guest Stars: Sally Field, Don Ameche, Rudy Vallee, Keenan Wynn; Teleplay: Glen A. Larson; Story: John Thomas James; Director: Barry Shear.

Heyes and Curry become involved in a series of confidence tricks when Clementine Hale (Sally Field) resorts to blackmail to steal $50,000.

Preempted: November 25, 1971

"Shootout at Diablo Station" (2:11)

Air date: December 2, 1971; Guest Stars: Neville Brand, Howard Duff, Pat O'Brien, Anne Archer; Teleplay: William D. Gordon; Story: John Thomas James; Director: Jeffrey Hayden.

Seven stagecoach passengers, including Heyes and Curry, are held by outlaws in an attempt to ambush and kill sheriff Lom Trevors.

"The Bounty Hunter" (2:12)

Air date: December 9, 1971; Guest Stars: Lou Gossett Jr., R.G. Armstrong, Robert Middleton; Teleplay: Nicholas E. Baehr; Story: John Thomas James; Director: Barry Shear.

Black bounty hunter Joe Sims (Lou Gossett Jr.) shows his gratitude to Heyes and Curry for twice saving his life by displaying a grim determination to collect his reward for their capture.

"Everything Else You Can Steal" (2:13)

Air date: December 16, 1971; Guest Stars: Patrick O'Neal, Jessica Walter, Ann Sothern, David Canary; Teleplay: John Thomas James; Director: Alexander Singer.

Heyes and Curry are back in trouble with the law when they become involved with con man Kenneth Blake and his girlfriend.

"Miracle at Santa Marta" (2:14)

Air date: December 30, 1971; Guest Stars: Ina Balin, Patricia Crowley, Nico Minardos, Joanna Barnes, Craig Stevens; Teleplay: Dick Nelson and John Thomas James; Story: John Thomas James; Director: Vincent Sherman.

Hannibal Heyes has to clear Kid Curry of a false murder charge.

"Twenty One Days to Tenstrike" (2:15)

Air date: January 6, 1972; Guest Stars: Walter Brennan, Steve Forrest, Pernell Roberts, Linda Marsh, Glenn Corbett, Dick Cavett, Robert Colbert; Teleplay: Irving Pearlberg and

John Thomas James; Story: John Thomas James; Director: Mel Ferber.

Kid Curry finds himself the chief suspect when cowboys on a cattle drive are murdered.

"The McCreedy Bust—Going, Going, Gone" (2:16)

Air date: January 13, 1972; Guest Stars: Burl Ives, Caesar Romero, Lee Majors, Bradford Dillman; Teleplay: Nicholas E. Baehr; Story: John Thomas James; Director: Alexander Singer.

Kid Curry is forced to humble himself before the local bully, Joe Briggs (Lee Majors), while waiting for Big Mac McCreedy's Roman bust to be deposited in a well.

"The Man Who Broke the Bank at Red Gap" (2:17)

Air date: January 20, 1972; Guest Stars: Broderick Crawford, Rudy Vallee, Ford Rainey; Teleplay: Ronson Howitzer and John Thomas James; Story: John Thomas James; Director: Richard Benedict.

A banker (Broderick Crawford) frames Heyes and Curry for a bank robbery in an effort to embezzle money, forcing them to undertake a bank robbery to clear their names.

"The Men That Corrupted Hadleyburg" (2:18)*

Air date: January 27, 1972; Guest Stars: J.D. Cannon, Sheree North, Wally Cox, Andy Devine, Adam West; Teleplay: Dick Nelson and John Thomas James; Story: John Thomas James; Director: Jeff Corey.

Heyes and Curry find themselves victims of a family seeking reward money for their capture. But a change of heart, resulting in Heyes' and Curry's escape from jail, is rewarded when they attempt to clear the family of any wrongdoing.

ROGER DAVIS—BEN MURPHY EPISODES

"The Biggest Game in the West" (2:19)

Air date: February 3, 1972; Guest Stars: Jim Backus, Chill Wills, Rod Cameron, Ford Rainey; Story: John Thomas James; Director: Alexander Singer.

Hannibal Heyes uses a bag of counterfeit money as a stake to get into a poker game.

"Which Way to the OK Corall?" (2:20)

Air date: February 10, 1972; Guest Stars: Michele Lee, Cameron Mitchell, Neville Brand, Jackie Coogan, Burl Ives; Teleplay: Glen A. Larson; Story: John Thomas James; Director: Jack Arnold.

Heyes and Curry encounter Sheriff Wyatt Earp in Tombstone while trying to clear Big Mac McCreedy of a murder charge.

"Don't Get Mad, Get Even" (2:21)

Air date: February 17, 1971; Guest Stars: Michele Lee, John Banner, Robert Middleton, Walter Brennan; Teleplay: John Thomas James; Director: Bruce Bilson.

After Heyes is cheated in a poker game, he arranges for the saloon owner to purchase a false pearl necklace to get his money back. But his plan backfires.

"What's in It for Mia?" (2:22)

Air date: February 24, 1971; Guest Stars: Ida Lupino, Buddy Ebsen, Sallie Shockley; Teleplay: William D. Gordon; Story: John Thomas James; Director: John Dumas.

In return for being rescued from a beating, Heyes and Curry help George Austin (Buddy Ebsen) get his revenge on the saloon owner (Ida Lupino) who put him out of work by arranging a counterfeit money scheme.

"Bad Night in Big Butte" (2:23)

Air date: March 2, 1971; Guest Stars: Michele Lee, Arthur O'Connell, Jack Elam, Sam Jaffe, Pat Buttram; Teleplay: Glen A. Larson; Director: Richard Bare.

Heyes and Curry attempt to locate a hidden diamond.

Season Three
12 × 50 min. (1972–73)

"The Long Chase" (3:01)

Air date: September 16, 1972; Guest Stars: James Drury, Frank Sinatra Jr., J.D. Cannon; Teleplay: John Thomas James; Director: Alexander Singer.

A determined sheriff pursues Heyes and Curry.

"High Lonesome Country" (3:02)

Air date: September 23, 1972; Guest Stars: Buddy Ebsen, Rod Cameron, Marie Windsor; Teleplay: Dick Nelson; Story: John Thomas James; Director: Alexander Singer.

An elderly couple hire a bounty hunter to capture Heyes and Curry.

"The McCreedy Feud" (3:03)

Air date: September 30, 1972; Guest Stars: Burl Ives, Cesar Romero, Katy Jurado, Dennis Fimple, Claudio Miranda; Teleplay: Jaunita Bartlett; Story: John Thomas James; Director: Alexander Singer.

*This was the last episode to be filmed with Pete Deuel in the starring role.

Heyes and Curry decide to play matchmaker for Big Mac and Armendiraz's sister, Carlotta.

"The Clementine Ingredient" (3:04)

Air date: October 7, 1972; Guest Stars: Sally Field, Alejandro Ray, Mills Watson, Ramon Bieri, Cody Bearpaw; Teleplay: Gloryette Clark; Story: John Thomas James; Director: Jack Arnold.

Clementine Hale upsets Heyes' and Curry's plans for a peaceful retirement in Mexico when she blackmails them into helping her with one of her schemes.

"Bushwack!" (3:05)

Air date: October 23, 1972; Guest Stars: Glenn Corbett, Christine Belford, Michael Conrad, Frank Converse, Ford Rainey; Teleplay: David Moesinger and John Thomas James; Story: John Thomas James; Director: Jack Arnold.

A man sets up Heyes and Curry as witnesses to his murder of two bushwhackers.

"What Happened at the XST?" (3:06)

Air date: October 28, 1972; Guest Stars: Keenan Wynn, Ed Nelson, William Smith, Geoffrey Lewis; Teleplay: John Thomas James; Director: Jack Arnold.

Heyes and Curry visit old friend Art Gorman and promise to keep out of trouble until Gorman asks for their help in digging up money from an old robbery.

"The Ten Days That Shook Kid Curry" (3:07)

Air date: November 4, 1972; Guest Stars: Shirley Knight, Edd Byrnes; Teleplay: Gloryette Clark; Story: John Thomas James; Director: Edward M. Abrams.

Kid Curry is bailed out of jail by an attractive schoolteacher who has her own reasons for freeing him.

"The Day the Amnesty Came Through" (3:08)

Air date: November 25, 1972; Guest Stars: Lane Bradbury, John Russell, Brett Halsey, Robert Donner, Charles Dierkop, Jeff Corey; Teleplay: Dick Nelson and John Thomas James;

Story: John Thomas James; Director: Jeff Corey. Heyes and Curry attempt to rescue a fair lady from her outlaw lover.

"The Strange Fate of Conrad Meyer Zulick" (3:09)

Air date: December 2, 1972; Guest Stars: Sorrell Brooke, Slim Pickens, David Canary, John Kellogg; Teleplay: Nicholas E. Baehr; Story: John Thomas James; Director: Richard Bennett.

An illegal sortie into Mexico endangers Heyes' and Curry's amnesty.

"McGuffin" (3:10)

Air date: December 9, 1972; Guest Stars: Darleen Carr, Clarke Gordon, Jack Manning, Walter Brooke, Jackie Coogan, L.Q. Jones; Teleplay: Nicholas E. Baehr; Story: John Thomas James; Director: Alexander Singer.

Heyes' and Curry's offer of help to a wounded man called McGuffin takes a strange twist when he asks them to deliver a package of counterfeit $20 plates for him.

"Witness to a Lynching" (3:11)

Air date: December 16, 1972; Guest Stars: John McGiver, Brenda Scott, G.D. Spradlin, Ann Doran, Barry Cahill, Kenneth Tobey; Teleplay: Nicholas E. Baehr; Story: John Thomas James; Director: Richard Bennett.

Heyes and Curry find themselves guarding a key witness against a murdering rancher who has escaped conviction because of the disappearance of previous witnesses.

Preempted: December 23, 1972
Preempted: December 30, 1972
Preempted: January 6, 1973

"Only Three to a Bed" (3:12)

Air date: January 13, 1973; Guest Stars: Laurette Sprang, Dean Jagger, John Kerr, Jo Ann Pflug, Dana Elcar, Paul Fix; Teleplay: Richard Morris; Story: John Thomas James; Director: Jeffrey Hayden.

Deciding they need a vacation, Heyes and Curry end up helping a man round up wild horses from a herd that runs on land claimed by a cantankerous old man.

APPENDIX B:
THEATER CAREER
AND FILMOGRAPHY

Plays

Freshman year—1958: *Caesar and Cleopatra*; Playwright: George Bernard Shaw; Drama department, St. Lawrence University, Canton, NY.

Sophomore year—1958: *Teahouse of the August Moon*; Playwright: John Patrick; Drama department, St. Lawrence University, Canton, NY.

1959: *A View from the Bridge*; Playwright: Arthur Miller; Drama department, St. Lawrence University, Canton, NY.

1959: *The Rose Tattoo*; Playwright: Tennessee Williams; Drama department, St. Lawrence University, Canton, NY.

1960: *Twelfth Night*; Playwright: William Shakespeare; Stock theater, PA.

1961: *Born Yesterday*; Playwright: Garson Kanin; Drama department — Student Union, St. Lawrence University, Canton, NY.

1961: *Electre*; Playwright: Jean Giraudoux; Shakespeare Wrights Repertory Theatre; Performed at the Players Theatre, Greenwich Village, New York.

1961: *A Visit to a Small Planet*; Playwright: Gore Vidal; Mateer Playhouse; Pennsylvania State University, PA.

1962–1963: *Take Her, She's Mine*; Playwrights: Phoebe Ephron and Henry Ephron; National Road Company; Walnut Theatre, Philadelphia, PA.

1963: *The Case of the Crushed Petunias*; Playwright: Tennessee Williams; Columbia College, California.

TV Guest Spots

1961: *Armstrong Circle Theatre*

1961/62: *Target: The Corrupters*

1963: *Channing*, a.k.a. *The Young and the Bold*

"The Last Testament of Buddy Crown" (1:12)
Air date: December 18, 1963.
A young college professor finds he has much to learn from the Dean.

1964: *Combat*

"Vendetta" (3.02)
Air date: September 22, 1964; Peter Deuel as Szigeti; Teleplay: Ron Bishop and Wells Root; Producer: Gene Levitt; Director: John Peyser.

Lt. Hanley runs into fanatical Corporal Kapalis (Telly Savalas) and his dancing Greeks.

Twelve O'Clock High

"Appointment at Liege" (1:09)
Air date: November 20, 1964; Guest Stars: Gary Lockwood, Nancy Kovack; Peter E. Deuel as Lt. Jake Benning.

"The Hero" (1:32)
Air date: May 7, 1965; Guest Star: James Whitmore; Teleplay: Albert Aley;
Peter E. Deuel as Lt. Ditchik; Producer: Frank Glicksman; Director: Ralph Senensky.

Mickey

"Crazy Hips McNish," a.k.a. "One More Kiss" (1:13)
Air date: December 16, 1964; Guest Stars:

Peter E. Deuel as Crazy Hips McNish, Sandra Descher.

Star athlete Crazy Hips McNish wants to star in the school play, and he isn't the least bit happy when Timmy wins the leading role.

Gomer Pyle U.S.M.C.

"Gomer and the Dragon Lady" (1:08)
Air date: November 13, 1964; Alan Dexter, Peter Deuel as First Man, Mark Slade, Richard Sinatra, Barbara Stuart.

"Dance Marine, Dance" (1:16)
Air date: January 8, 1965; Gavin McCleod, Sylvia Lewis, Frank Maxwell, Peter Deuel.

1965: The Fugitive

"Fun and Games and Party Favors" (2:19)
Air date: January 26, 1965; Guest Stars: Katherine Crawford, Mark Goddard, Dan Holt, Peter E. Deuel as Buzzy.

Dr. Richard Kimble (David Janssen) falls victim to adolescent blackmail.

The F.B.I.

"Slow March Up a Steep Hill" (1:04)
Air date: October 10, 1965; Guest Stars: Graham Denton, Harold Gould,

Dabney Coleman, Lee Meriwether, Pete Deuel as Wayne Everett Powell; Teleplay: Charles Larson; Producer: Charles Larson; Director: William A. Graham.

Baffled by a series of bank robberies by a man dressed in 1930's clothing, the F.B.I. finally trace the robberies to his abandoned son who has been trying to emulate his absent father.

1967: The F.B.I.

"False Witness" (3:11)
Air date: December 10, 1967; Guest Stars: Carol Lynley, Peter Deuel, Victor French, Parley Baer; Teleplay: E. Arthur Kean; Producer: Charles Larson; Director: Jesse Hibbs.

1968: The Virginian

"The Good-Hearted Badman" (6:20)
Air date: February 7, 1968; Guest Stars: Peter Deuel as Jim Dewey (a.k.a. Thomas Baker), Anthony Zerbe, John Larch.

Pursued by a bounty hunter, wounded outlaw Jim Dewey takes refuge at Shiloh Ranch and becomes the focus of Elizabeth's (Sara Lane) affections.

Ironside

"The Perfect Crime" (1:24)
Air date: March 7, 1968; Guest Stars: Peter Deuel as Jonathan Dix, Shelly Novack as Roger Simmons, Bill Baldwin as George, Paul Hough as Byron Shelley Crawford III, and Brenda Scott; Producer: Paul Mason; Director: Charles S. Dubin.

A sniper, attempting to prove the perfect crime exists, wreaks terror on a college campus.

The Name of the Game

"The White Birch" (1:11)
Air date: November 29, 1968; Guest Stars: Peter Deuel as Chernin, Susan Oliver, Roddy McDowell, Jean-Pierre Aumont, Boris Karloff; Teleplay: Dean Hargrove and Luther Davis; Story: Robert Soderberg; Producer: Richard Irving; Director: Lamont Johnson.

Publisher Glenn Howard (Gene Barry) travels to Soviet-occupied Czechoslovakia in an attempt to recover a government suppressed manuscript by noted writer Mikhail Orlov (Boris Karloff).

1969: The Virginian

"The Price of Love" (7:18)
Air date: February 12, 1969; Guest Stars: Peter Deuel as Denny Todd, James Gregory; Teleplay: Dick Carr; Producer: David Levinson; Director: Michael Caffey.

Denny Todd is reunited with Clay and Holly Grainger, who took him in as a child. But a dispute over water rights sees Todd accused of murder.

1970: Insight

"A Woman of Principle"
Air date: January 1, 1970; Guest Stars: Audrey Totten as Mrs. Goddard, Nehemiah Persoff, Ed Asner as Mr. Watkins; Pete Duel as Edward [uncredited].

Threatened with eviction by landlord Mr. Watkins, Mrs. Goddard attempts to obtain money by tutoring the untalented Edward with music lessons.

Matt Lincoln

"Nick" (1:06)
Air date: October 29, 1970; Guest Stars: Jackie Coogan, Joan Van Ark, Marc Hannibal, Pete Duel as Father Nicholas Burrell; Teleplay:

Preston Wood and Don Ingalls; Story: Don Ingalls; Director: Akkeb Reisner.

A psychiatric social worker starts a clinic to help the poor.

The Interns

"The Price of Life"
Air date: October 30, 1970; Guest Stars: Pete Duel, Gene Raymond, Susan O'Connell, Paul Hampton, Bill Hayes; Teleplay: Jack Miller; Producer: Charles Larson; Director: Michael O'Herlihy.

The Young Lawyers

"The Glass Prison" (1:07)
Air date: November 2, 1970; Guest Stars: Pete Duel as Dom Acosta, Barbara Luna; Teleplay: John W. Bloch; Producer: Matthew Rapf; Director: Jud Taylor.

Forbidden from associating with anyone connected with drugs while on parole, Aaron Silverman attempts to lift the curtailment of Dom Acosta's civil rights as a parolee. (Note: This episode was nominated for an Eddie Award for Best Edited Television Program—Joseph Dervin—by the American Cinema Editors.)

The Bold Ones: The Lawyers

"Trial of a PFC" (2:03) [33]
Air date: November 8, 1970; Guest Stars: Pete Duel as Jerry Perdue, Jane Elliot; Teleplay: Frank Fenton; Story: Gloryette Clark; Producer: Joe Swerling Jr.; Director: Alexander Singer.

Vietnam veteran and bronze star recipient Jerry Purdue is charged with the murder of fellow vet and best friend Peter Calender (Jared Martin).

1971: Marcus Welby M.D., a.k.a. Robert Young, Family Doctor

"A Passing of Torches" (2:16)
Air date: January 26, 1971; Guest Stars: Pete Duel as Roger Nastili, Walter Pidgeon.

A young Chiricahua Apache (Pete Duel) suffers from bad migraines following his tribe's decision to send him to medical school.

The Psychiatrist

"In Death's Other Kingdom"
Air date: February 3, 1971; Guest Stars: Pete Duel as Casey T. Poe, Ketty Lester, Melendy Britt, James McEachin, Peter Brocco, Regis J.

Cordic; Executive Producer: Norman Felton; Director: Jerrold Freedman.

Dr. Whitman (Roy Thinnes) fights to get Casey T. Poe, a parolee wanting to kick his drug habit, admitted into his methadone maintenance program, with the help of his parole board.

The Name of the Game

"The Savage Eye" (3:20)
Air date: February 19, 1971; Guest Stars: Pete Duel as Ted Sands, Geoffrey Deuel, Jim Hutton, Marianne Hill, John Randolph; Producer: George Eckstein; Director: Leo Penn.

Talk and Variety Shows

1966: Baron and His Buddies
Air date: August 1966.

Charly's Place
Air date: August 1966.

1968: The Woody Woodbury Show
Air date: March 25, 1968; with Judy Carne.

Happening '68, a.k.a. Happening
Air date: September 7, 1968.

1971: A.M. Los Angeles
Filmed: August 2, 1971; Ralph Story, with Ben Murphy.

The Dick Cavett Show
Air date: 1971; with Ben Murphy.

The Merve Griffin Show
Air date: December 3, 1971; with Ben Murphy.

Game Shows

1966: Hollywood Squares
Air dates: December 12–16, December 26–30, 1966.

1967: The Dating Game
Air date: December 1967.

1970: Name Droppers
Air dates: March 2–6, 1970.

Documentaries

E! Mysteries and Scandals (1999)

Pete Duel (2:36)
Air date: November 1, 1999
Profile of the life of Peter Deuel.

Target Espionage — You!

U.S. Department of Defence Training Film.

1963: The Man Nobody Liked

Service film.

1970: Ah Man ...
See What You've Done

Ecology documentary; Narration.

Movie Credits

W.I.A. Wounded in Action (1966)

U.S. Premiere: March 1966; Main Cast: Steve
Marlo, Maura McGiveney, Leopold Salcedo,
Mary Humphrey, Albert Quinton, Victor Izay,
Bella Flores, John Horn, Peter E. Deuel as Private Myers; Screenplay: Irving Sunasky; Producers: Irving Sunasky and Samuel Zerinsky;
Director: Irving Sunasky; 80 min. for U.S.
release; Uncut length: 130 min.; Myriad Productions; B/W.

The Hell with Heroes (1968)

Premiere: August 28, 1968; Main Cast: Rod
Taylor, Claudia Cardinale, Kevin McCarthy,
Harry Guardino, Peter Deuel as Mike Brewer;
Screenplay: Halsted Welles and Harold Liv-
ingston; Story: Harold Livingston; Producer:
Stanley Chase; Director: Joseph Sargent; 102
min.; 95 min. edited version; Universal Pictures;
Technicolor.

Generation (1969), a.k.a. A Time for
Giving and a Time for Caring

Premiere: December 15, 1969; Main Cast:
David Janssen, Kim Darby, Pete Duel as Walter
Owen, Carl Reiner, Andrew Prine, James Coco,
Sam Waterston, Lincoln Kilpatrick; Screenplay:
William Goodhart; Producer: Frederick Brisson;
Director: George Schaeffer; 109 min.; AVCO
Embassy Pictures; Technicolor.

Cannon for Cordoba (1970), a.k.a.
The Condor and Dragon Master

Premiere: October 1970; Main Cast: George
Peppard, Nico Minardos, Pete Duel as Andy
Rice, Giovanna Ralli, Raf Vallone, Don Gordon;
Screenplay: Stephen Kandel; Story: Eva Del
Castillo; Producer: Vincent M. Fenelli; Direc-
tor: Paul Wendkos; 104 min.; United Artists–
Mirisch Production Company; Panavision
Eastmancolor.

TV Movies — Pilots

Diamond Jim:
Skullduggery in Samantha (1965)

Unsold pilot; Main Cast: Dale Robertson,
Walter Burke, Jeff York, Robert Emhardt, Karl
Swenson, Paulie Clark, Patsy Garrett, Peter
Deuel; Writer: Harry Brown; Producer: Andy
White; Director: John Peyser.

Diamond Jim ventures out West in an attempt
to save the railroad.

Marcus Welby M.D. (1969), a.k.a.
A Matter of Humanities

Air date: March 26, 1969; Main Cast: Robert
Young, James Brolin, Anne Baxter, Peter Deuel
as Lew Sawyer, Susan Strasberg, Lew Ayres, Tom
Bosley; Teleplay: Don M. Mankiewicz; Story:
David Victor; Producer: David J. O'Connell;
Director: David Lowell Rich.

Following a car accident, Lew Sawyer suffers
from a condition which severely limits his speech
patterns. His wife (Susan Strasberg) faces the
dilemma of committing him to an asylum for
treatment.

The Young Country (1970)

Air date: March 17, 1970; Main Cast: Roger
Davis, Pete Duel as Honest John Smith (a.k.a.
Deputy Sheriff John Closkey), Joan Hackett,
Walter Brennan, Wally Cox; Teleplay-Producer-
Director: Roy Huggins.

Finding $38,000 on the body of a dead man,
Stephen Foster Moody (Roger Davis) attempts
to track down the heirs to the money.

The Psychiatrist: God Bless
the Children (1970), a.k.a.
Children of the Lotus Eater

Air date: December 14, 1970; Main Cast: Roy
Thinnes, Luther Adler, Pete Duel as Casey T.

Poe, John Rubinstein, Joy Bang; Executive Producer: Norman Felton; Teleplay: Jerrold Freedman; Story: Richard Levinson and William Link; Producer: Edgar Small; Director: Daryl Duke.

A psychiatrist (Roy Thinnes) and ex-addict Casey T. Poe join forces to fight drug addiction in a teenage community.

Alias Smith and Jones (1971)

Air date: January 5, 1971; Main Cast: Pete Duel as Hannibal Heyes (a.k.a. Joshua Smith), Ben Murphy, James Drury, Earl Holliman, Dennis Fimple, Forrest Tucker, Susan Saint James, Jeanette Nolan, John Russell; Executive Producer: Frank Price; Teleplay: Matthew Howard and Glen A. Larson; Story: Glen A. Larson; Producer: Glen A. Larson; Director: Gene Levitt.

The governor offers amnesty to two outlaws if they agree to bring to justice a desperado and his gang — and stay out of trouble with the law for one year.

How to Steal an Airplane (1971)

Original title: *Only One Day Left Before Tomorrow*, a.k.a. *The Scavengers*; Filmed November 1968; Air date: December 10, 1971; Main Cast: Peter Deuel as Sam Rollins, Sal Mineo, Clinton Greyn, Claudine Longet, Katherine Crawford, Julie Sommars, Don Diamond; Executive Producer: Roy Huggins; Teleplay: Robert Foster and Philip de Guere Jr.; Producer: Jo Swerling Jr.; Director: Leslie H. Martinson.

Two adventurers attempt to repossess a Lear jet from the playboy son of a banana republic dictator.

The Scarecrow (1972) — Hollywood Television Theatre

Air date: January 10, 1972; Main Cast: Gene Wilder, Peter Duel as Richard Talbot, Will Geer, Nina Foch, Blythe Danner, Norman Lloyd, Joan Tompkins, Sian Barbara Allen, Elisha Cook Jr.; Original Story: Nathaniel Hawthorne; Play: Percy MacKaye; Director: Boris Sagal.

This production of the 1910 play by Percy MacKaye is a tale of witchcraft and romance set in 17th century Massachusetts in which a scarecrow is transformed into a gentleman to win the heart of Squire Talbot's fiancée. (Note: Jan Scott won an Emmy for Outstanding Achievement in Art Direction or Scenic Design for a Dramatic Programme or Feature Length Film made for Television.)

Compilation Feature

The Gun and the Nun (1970s)

Air date: 1970s; Main Cast: Pete Duel as Hannibal Heyes (a.k.a. Joshua Smith), Ben Murphy, J.D. Cannon, Jane Wyatt, Jane Merrow; Teleplay: Stephen Kandel, B.W. Sandefur and John Thomas James; Director: Jeffrey Hayden and Barry Shear.

Compilation of "The Wrong Train to Brimstone" (1:03) and "The Reformation of Harry Briscoe" (2:09) from *Alias Smith and Jones* TV series.

BIBLIOGRAPHY

Published Sources — Books

Bradbury, Malcolm, ed. *The Atlas of Literature*. London: De Agostini, 1996.

Brogan, Hugh. *The Pelican History of the United States of America*. Harmondsworth: Pelican, 1986.

Carne, Judy. *Laughing on the Outside: Crying on the Inside*. New York: Rawson, 1985.

Chester, Lewis; Godfrey Hodgson and Bruce Paige. *An American Melodrama: The Presidential Campaign of 1968*. New York: Viking, 1969.

Clapham, Walter C. *Western Movies*. London: Octopus, 1974.

Crane, Stephen. *The Red Badge of Courage*. Ware: Wordsworth, 1994.

Daley, Dennis C. *Kicking Addictive Habits Once and for All: A Relapse-Prevention Guide*. San Francisco: Jossey-Bass, 1991.

Fitzgerald, Michael C. *Universal Pictures*. Rochelle: Arlington House, 1980.

Hayden, Tom. *Reunion: A Memoir*. London: Hamish Hamilton, 1989.

Henke, James, and Puterbaugh Parke, eds. *I Want to Take You Higher: The Psychedelic Era 1965–1969*. San Francisco: Chronicle, 1997.

Horowitz, Carroll, and Lee Horowitz. *On the Edge: A New History of 20th Century America*. St. Paul: West, 1990.

Jackson, Ronald. *Classic TV Westerns*. New York: Citadel, 1994.

Jamison, Kay Redfield. *Night Falls Fast: Understanding Suicide*. New York: Alfred A. Knopf, 1999.

Kenna, Rudolph, and William Grandison. *Somethin' Else: 50s Life and Style*. Glasgow: Richard Drew, 1989.

Kerouac, Jack. *On the Road*. London: Penguin, 1991.

Marwick, Arthur. *The Sixties*. Oxford University Press, 1998.

Neville, Richard. *Playpower*. St. Albans: Paladin, 1973.

Newcomb, Horace, ed. *Museum of Broadcast Communications Encyclopedia of Television*. (3 vols.) Chicago: Fitzroy Dearborn, 1997.

O'Donnell, Monica M., ed. *Contemporary Theatre, Film and Television*. (12 vols.) Detroit: Gale Research, 1986.

O'Sullivan, Tim; Dutton Brian and Rayner Philip. *Studying the Media*. London: Arnold, 1998.

Peer, Kurt. *A Bibliography of TV Tie-In Paperbacks*. Tucson: Neptune, 1997.

Pilato, Herbie J. *Bewitched Forever*. Arlington: Summit, 1996.

Richard, Adrienne, and Joel Reiter, M.D. *Epilepsy: A New Approach*. New York: Prentice-Hall, 1990.

Sagala, Sandra K., and JoAnne M. Bagwell. *Alias Smith & Jones: The Story of Two Pretty Good Bad Men*. Boalsburg: BearManor Media, 2005.

Sann, Paul. *The Angry Decade: The Sixties*. New York: Crown, 1979.

Stewart, Robert. *Ideas That Shaped Our World*. London: Marshall, 1997.

Terrace, Vincent. *The Complete Encyclopedia of Television Programs 1947–1976*. (2 vols.) Cranbury, N.J.: A.S. Barnes, 1976.

_____. *Television 1970–1980*. La Jolla: A.S. Barnes, 1981.

Thomas, Evan. *Robert Kennedy: His Life*. New York: Touchstone, 2000.

Thoreau, Henry David. *Walden and Civil Disobedience*. New York: Penguin, 1986.

8

Turner, Steve. *Angelheaded Hipster: A Life of Jack Kerouac.* London: Bloomsbury, 1996.
Williams, Mark. *Cry of Pain: Understanding Suicide and Self-Harm.* London: Penguin, 1997.

Published Sources — Periodicals, Newspapers, Archives

Amory, Cleveland. "Love on a Rooftop Review." *TV Guide,* Jan. 7, 1967: 14.
Du Brow, Rick. "Stick with 'The Scarecrow'." *St. Paul Pioneer Press,* Jan. 9, 1972.
Felchner, William J., and Reed, Bob. "Gidget." *TV Search,* n.d.: 40–52, 55.
Gillilan, Cinda. *Duel Memories.* 1–29. Nov.-Dec. 1987–1999.
Helm. "Love on a Rooftop" Review. *Daily Variety,* Sept. 7, 1966.
"Love on a Rooftop." *ABC News.* Promotional Package 1966–1967.
"Peter Duel Killed by Gunshot." *Rochester Times Union,* Dec. 31, 1971.
"Play Debuts Festive Week End. Peter Deuel to Star in 'Born Yesterday'." *St. Lawrence Plaindealer,* May 1961.
"Who's Who in the Cast." *Playbill,* June 3, 1963: 27.
Stone, Judy. "He's Alias Smith or Alias Jones." *TV Guide,* May 15, 1971.
A Time for Giving. Avco Embassy Exhibitor's Showmanship Manual. 1969.
Warga, Wayne. "Kim Darby's True Grit." *Los Angeles Times West* magazine, Oct. 5, 1969: 24–25.

Official Reports

Ellis Island List of United States Citizens (For the Immigration Authorities). U.S. Department of Labor Immigration Service.
Municipal Court of Beverly Hills Judicial District County of Los Angeles. The People of the State of California vs. Peter E. Deuel. Bail Bond Oct. 24, 1971
Municipal Court of Beverly Hills Judicial District County of Los Angeles. Case No. A061791. The People of the State of California vs. Peter E. Deuel. Reporter's Transcript Preliminary Hearing, Friday, April 23, 1971.
Superior Court of California for the County of Los Angeles. The People of the State of California vs. Peter E. Deuel. Superior Court No. A061791. May 7, 1971, June 22, 1971.
Combined Superior Court of California for the County of Los Angeles. Disposition Report. June 25, 1971
County of Los Angeles Department of Chief Medical Examiner. Office of Coroner. Case Report 71–13812. Peter Deuel aka Duel December 31 1971. Final Jan. 24, 1972.
Office of the Chief Medical Examiner-Coroner. Report of Toxicological Analysis. Case Report 71–13812. Peter Deuel aka Duel Jan. 3, 4, 1972
Office of the Chief Medical Examiner-Coroner. Pathology Laboratory Report. Jan. 5, 1972

Internet Sources

Alias Smith and Jones Collection. <www.asjcollection.com>
Classic TV Archive. <www.geocities.com/TelevisionCity/Stage/2950>
Ecology Hall of Fame. <www.ecotopia.org/ehof/index.html>
Henry David Thoreau. <http://www.transcendentalists.com/1thorea.html>
Internet Broadway Database. <http://ibdb.com>
Internet Movie Pro Database. <http://pro.imdb.com>
Köping, Sweden. <http://www.koping.se>
Mark Lindsay: Happening. <http://marklindsay.com/happening.htm>
Massawepie Staff Alumni Association. <www.massstaffalumni.org>
Pete Duel Forum. <www.peteduelforumwebsite.com>
Pete Duel Site. <www.peteduelsite.com>
Synanon. <http://religiousmovements.lib.virginia.edu/nrms/synanon.html>
Syracuse New Times Net. "The Monster in Me." <http://newtimes.rway.com/1999/102799/cover.shtml>
Town of Penfield, New York. <http://www.penfield.org>

U.C.L.A Library Catalog Film and Television Archive <http://cinema.library.ucla.edu>
Wikipedia. <http://en.wikipedia.org>

Interviews

Anderson, Bill. E-mail interview. January 1, 2006.
Andre, Jill. Telephone interviews. June 14, July 10, 2006.
Darby, Kim. Telephone interviews. June 8, 15, 20, 22, 28, July 22, August 1, 6, 10, September 2, 12, 23, 2006.
Drury, James. Telephone interview. October 24, 2001.
Fanning, Donald. Telephone interview. September 13, 2006.
Farrell, Mike. E-mail interview. December 8, 2005.
Fassett, Matthew. E-mail interview. March 12, 2006.
Freedman, Jerrold. Telephone interview. February 12, 2006.
Frizzell, Harold. Telephone interviews. April 23, September 20, 2006.
Griswold, Beth. Telephone interviews. May 14, June 11, 15, 18, July 9, August 13, 28, September 30, 2006.
Hanley, Bridget. Telephone interview. April 4, 2006.
Jobes, Jack. Telephone interviews. September 17, 18, 2006.
Johnson, Pamela Deuel. Telephone interviews. April 4, 5, 7, 12, 19, 25, 26, 27, May 1, 3, 10, 18, 25, June 6, 11, 12, 18, 21, July, 9, 14, 25, August 10, 24, October 1, 4, 2006.
Johnson, Richard P. Telephone interviews. May 1, August 10, 2006.
Konstanturos, John. Telephone interviews. March 8, 31, 2006.
Karroll, Lynne. Telephone interviews. June 30, August 6, 2006.
Koster, Robert. Telephone interview. December 9, 2005.
Lane, Sara. Telephone interviews. April 8, September 6, 2006.
Larson, Glen A. Telephone interviews. January 17, 20, 2006.
Luna, BarBara. E-mail interview. September 28, 2006.
Martin, Jared. Telephone interview. December 20, 2005.
McHugh, David. Telephone interview. August 31, 2006.
Meng, Connie. Telephone interview. September 26, 2006.
Mills, Juliet. Telephone interview. September 12, 2006.
Price, Frank. E-mail interviews. October 21, 2005 to September 8, 2006.
Parrish, Leslie. Telephone interview. February 6, 2006.
Ray, Dianne. Telephone interviews. May 17, 20, 26, 27, 28, June 2, 10, 15, 22, 26, 29, July 1, 22, August 6, 19, September 22, 2006.
Seymour, Jennifer. Telephone interview. September 6, 2006.
Slade, Bernard. Telephone interview. March 31, 2006.
Swerling,. Jo, Jr. Telephone interview. April 24, 2006.
Utter, C. Davey. Telephone interview. September 12, 2006.
Van Ark, Joan. E-mail interviews. January 9, 10, 2006.
Van Husen, Dan. E-mail interview. December 18, 2005.
Watson, Phil. E-mail interviews. May 24, 26, 2001.
Yarnall, Celeste. E-mail interview. March 15, 2005.

INDEX

Numbers in *bold italics* indicate pages with photographs.